TOEFL WRITING
MASTER
COURSE

Right Before the Test!

**Written by
an ETS TOEFL Rater & a TOEFL Master**

Why TOEFL Writing Master Course

Have you heard that in August 2019, ETS redesigned and shortened the TOEFL? How does this affect students around the world? What is the new format? What are the new trends in 2019-2020?

If you are planning on taking the TOEFL test and want to improve your writing score quickly, then this book is for you. "TOEFL Writing Master Course" is a complete guide to help you master TOEFL writing skills created by a TOEFL master and an official ETS TOEFL rater. It will help you not only prepare for the test but also for your academic success.

Aaron Hahn has helped thousands of international students achieve TOEFL success and get accepted to some of the top universities around the world. He is one of the best test prep instructors in Seoul, Korea. Over the years, he has taught at numerous institutes such as, PSU, YBM, LStudy, Global English Institute, Concordia International University, and Manhattan Institute.

Jamie Ortolano, MAT, MS.Ed, is a current ETS TOEFL rater and has taught English for Academic Purposes for many years. She has taught at several universities and colleges including UMass Amherst, Yonsei University, CCSU, UConn, Hudson County Community College, Middlesex County College, and ELS (an English language school).

For more information, please contact us at mastercoursebooks@gmail.com.

You can also visit our website to download the audio files and video tutorials for this book:

http://masterpreps.weebly.com/

Special Thanks

Coleen Dwyer for her proofreading

CONTENTS

Basic Templates & Mini Lesson

Let's skip the chitchat and get down to the nitty-gritty. Check out our TOEFL Writing templates to quickly boost your TOEFL score and learn how you can use them in Jamie's mini lesson.

Part 1: Question 1 (Integrated Task)

1. Dirty & Simple Tips

Check the most critical TOEFL tips and strategies including the TOEFL format, a scoring criteria and our test proven method to write a perfect essay.

2. Practice Tests (5 practices)

Master TOEFL Integrated Writing in just five days! You will see all types of questions and perfect sample essays as benchmarks.

3. Trending Questions & Sample Answers (20 questions)

We all know that the official practice material from ETS is the best practice material. However, ETS has only released a few sample test materials, and they don't reflect on the most trending questions. In this section, we will see 20 practice questions that were developed based on the most recent real TOEFL tests.

Part 2: Question 2 (Independent Task)

1. Dirty & Simple Tips

Check the most critical TOEFL tips and strategies including the TOEFL format, a scoring criteria and our test proven method to write a perfect essay.

2. Practice Tests (15 Practices)

Master TOEFL Independent Writing in fifteen days! You will see all types of questions and perfect sample essays as benchmarks.

3. Trending Questions & Sample Answers (20 questions)

We all know that the official practice material from ETS is the best practice material. However, ETS has only released a few sample test materials, and they don't reflect on the most trending questions. In this section, we will see 20 practice questions that were developed based on the most recent real TOEFL tests.

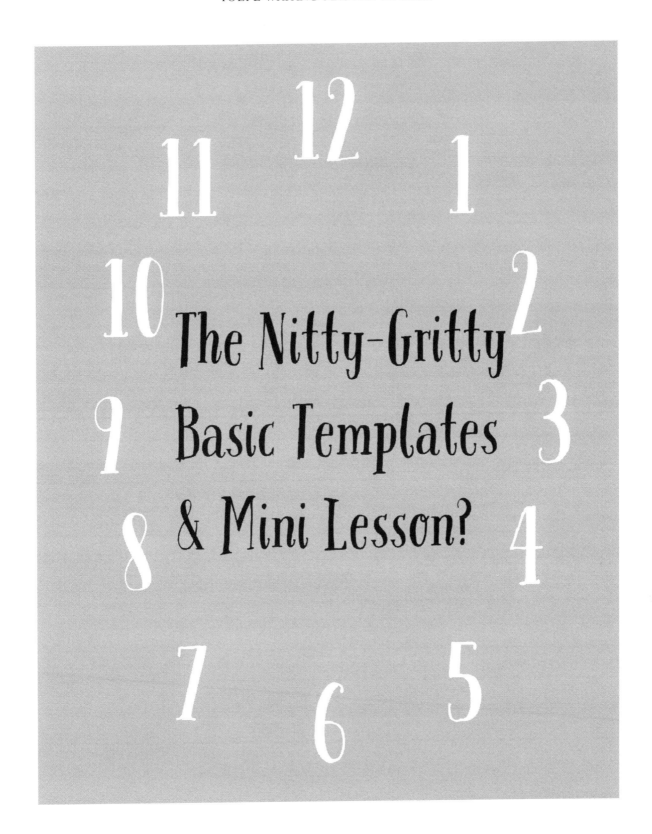

The Nitty-Gritty Basic Templates & Mini Lesson?

Basic Templates for both Integrated and Independent Tasks

Paragraphs	Integrated Task	Independent Task
Introduction	1. **Both** the reading and the lecture discuss (write the topic here) 2. The reading **states** that (write the readings' theory here) 3. However, the lecturer **refutes** the belief presented in the reading by stating that (explain the other side of the topic theory)	1. It is **undeniable** that (the relevant fact to the topic) 2. **After all**, (give a clear and ultimate reason for that) 3. Yet, there could be a **debate** over(the specific topic) 4. **Some** might argue that (the opposite side) 5. However, **I believe** that (your side) for two/three reasons.
Body 1	1. To begin with, the passage **claims** that (provide the first point mentioned in the reading) 2. This is **because** (offer the supporting details) 3. Nevertheless, the lecturer **contrasts** this idea by pointing out that (put the lecturer's first point here) 4. Furthermore, she **says** that (offer the supporting details)	1. To begin with, it is **important** that (the argument and reasons) 2. From my **personal experience**, I learned that (cause and effect) 3. This clearly **depicts** that (make a point)
Body 2	1. Secondly, the reading **mentions** that (put the second point here – summarized) 2. **As** (offer the supporting details) 3. Yet, the lecturer **challenges** this argument by revealing that (put the lecturer's second point here) 4. She **states** that (offer the supporting details)	1. **Another major consideration** is that (the argument and reasons) 2. **For example**, (cause and effect) 3. This **indicates** that (make a point)
Body 3	1. Lastly, the reading **argues** that (summarize the reading's third point) 2. **Since** (offer the supporting details) 3. On the other hand, the lecturer **rebuts** this theory by explaining that (put the lecturer's last point here) 4. She **asserts** that(offer the supporting details)	1. Lastly, **one should think about** (the argument and reasons) 2. **For instance**, (make a point) 3. This **points** to the fact (there is a clear causality.)
Conclusion	1. Thus, there is **a stark difference** between the reading and the lecturer.	1. In summary, there are **numerous reasons to believe** that (your point) 2. **This will allow** us to (reasons)

Reading

As cities expand rapidly with no room for nature to be conserved, more animals are losing their habitats and suffering from serious damages caused by reckless human activities. A recent alarming such event involved illegal professional-grade fireworks. Scientists believe that fireworks may have caused thousands of blackbirds to fall from the sky over an Arkansas town on New Year's Eve.

First, the time of the fireworks corresponds to the time of the birds' massive deaths. At 10 p.m., residents heard several extremely loud, "window-shaking" noises that were believed to have come from professional-grade fireworks, which no one had permission to set off. About 15 minutes later several people went outside and looked up; instead of the birds being above treetop level, like they usually are, they were crashing into houses, cars, trees, mailboxes, shrubbery, and everything around. This indicates that there was a correlation between the two events.

Second, after examining the birds' bodies, scientists found out that the "fireworks theory" made sense because the cause of the deaths was physical trauma. The Game and Fish Department took hundreds of bodies of the birds for testing to try to determine what happened. Initial laboratory reports said the birds had died from trauma primarily to the chest, hemorrhaging in the body cavity, bruised skulls, and blood clots in brain. It's consistent with crashing into something as the birds were shocked by the loud noises of fireworks and were flying into one another or fatally hitting buildings.

Finally, most of the dead birds were blackbirds which are well known for their poor eyesight. Blackbirds don't usually fly at night, but the big booms apparently flushed the birds from their roost, and then poor eyesight and disorientation stymied them from making it back safely. This would have caused the collisions as they were flying at rooftop level to avoid the fireworks.

Listening

Fireworks and loud noises have been used to scare off unwanted birds without killing them for decades. So, it's highly unlikely that they caused the deaths of thousands of blackbirds in Arkansas and the three arguments made in the reading are not convincing.

First of all, it's true that the two events took place on the same day, but this doesn't necessarily mean that one caused another considering the great distance between the locations. Remember the blackbirds died in the suburbs, which are far away from the city where the fireworks used? And there were a large number of birds spreading across an extensive area. So, when the fireworks went off during the evening, only a small portion of the birds would have been affected by the noises.

Second point, the birds' deaths and internal injuries may have been caused by strong winds. In fact, some witnesses reported that they saw the birds getting blown away and smashed to bits by the wind. Tornadoes swept through Arkansas on 31 December and they even killed seven people in the same region. The violent storms might have disoriented the flock, or one bird could have led other birds into a fatal plunge to the ground.

And third, many blackbirds die at the beginning of the year because they have poor eyesight. Blackbirds don't have those special eyes that nocturnal birds usually have but still have to fly in the dark because of the shorter daytime around the New Year's Day. The blackbirds were grouped together in one location which is typical behavior for the winter season. And while flying in the nighttime, they naturally fell to death due to their poor vision.

Student's Response (scored 5 out of 5)

Both the reading and the lecture discuss the thousands of blackbirds that died on New Year's Eve in Arkansas. The reading states that fireworks may have been the cause of the blackbirds' death. However, the lecturer refutes the belief presented in the reading by stating that the fireworks are not likely to be the cause of their deaths.

To begin with, the passage claims that the fireworks probably caused the blackbirds to fall from the sky and crash into houses, cars, trees, mailboxes, and everything considering the time the event took place. This was because the residence heard a loud noise that sounded like it came from professional grade fireworks at 10p.m., and soon after that the birds fell. Nevertheless, the lecturer contrasts this idea by pointing out that the blackbirds died in the suburbs, which was at a great distance from the city where the fireworks were used. Furthermore, she says that the birds were spread out in a large area so only a few of them would have been affected by the fireworks.

Secondly, the reading mentions that the fireworks theory made sense because when examining the bodies, scientists found out that the birds died from physical trauma.
As the birds were shocked by the loud noises of the fireworks, they would have been crashing into something, which was consistent with their cause of death. Yet, the lecturer challenges this argument by revealing that the injuries may have been caused by strong winds. She states that some witnesses saw the birds getting blown away and smashed by the winds because there were tornados in Arkansas on December 31st.

Lastly, the reading argues that the blackbirds might have been startled by the loud boom and left their places at night. Since they are known for their poor eyesight and do not usually fly at night, they may have gotten disorientated and crashed into each other or other things as they try to avoid the fireworks above rooftop level. On the other hand, the lecturer rebuts this theory by explaining that many blackbirds die at the beginning of the year because of their poor eyesight, and they do not have the special eyes that nocturnal birds may have. She asserts that the birds naturally fly to their death this time of year because around New Year's Day the daytime is shorter causing them to fly in the dark.

Thus, there is a stark difference between the reading and the lecture.

Independent Task

Do you agree or disagree with the following statement?

In many places, students aged 12-18 are typically taught different subjects by different teachers while younger students are usually taught by only one teacher all day long. However, it would also benefit younger students to be taught by several different teachers every day.

Student's Response (scored 5 out of 5)

It is undeniable that teachers play a vital role in children's academic and intellectual development. After all, young students rely on their teachers to gain knowledge for success and pursue their interests. Yet, there could be a debate over whether or not younger students need different teachers for different subjects. Some might argue that one teacher should suffice in order for them to learn all core subjects. However, I believe that they can benefit from having several different teachers every day for three reasons.

To begin with, it is important that a teacher has the expertise and experience needed in order to give his students a high quality education. In other words, they need to possess profound knowledge of the subjects they teach. Otherwise, there is no point in going to school and learning from teachers because children could also gain general education from their parents. Nonetheless, most primary school teachers teach every core subject to their students but may only be highly skilled in one or two of those. As a result, it is not easy for a teacher to effectively conduct lessons on each and every one of them. From my personal experience, I learned that I was lacking in math and science skills in the fourth grade because I was not properly prepared by my third grade teacher who taught every single subject all by herself. To be honest, the teacher was terrible at teaching science and math although she was good at language arts and social studies. Because of this, I fell behind and was not able to build a good foundation in those subjects in order to do well in other grade levels. This clearly depicts that even young learners need a quality education offered by many specialized educators in school rather than learning from one teacher with general knowledge.

Another major consideration is that young students should be able to have the chance to be taught by multiple teachers to build their interests and get a balanced and multifaceted education needed to pursue them. Primary school teachers all have their own interests and biases about certain subjects. Therefore, the teachers' lessons may reflect on their unbalanced personal views regardless of the students' passion. For example, if a student is into art and wants to get feedback from his teacher, his teacher may ignore his request and try to sway him towards a different subject preferred by the teacher. This would not happen if the student had a separate teacher for art. The art teacher could give the student encouragement or show different art skills for improvement or creativity. This indicates that having different teachers will likely give students the motivation to pursue diverse interests and develop as individuals.

Lastly, one should think about the physical and mental limitations of an individual teacher and the number of students a teacher has to accommodate. Teaching can be extremely demanding with long hours and a heavy workload, and it's easy for them to fall prey to burnout, which will affect the quality of education greatly. That is why different teachers have to work as a team. For instance, team teaching, especially for subjects like science and math, can be advantageous to both teachers and students. Teachers don't always have to singularly meet the needs of all of their students when they work as a team. From the student's perspective, the good thing about having several teachers is that even if one of them is not very good, the student only has him or her for part of the day. Also, shuffling from class to class breaks up the monotony. This points to the fact that children would learn better from multiple teachers.

In summary, there are many reasons why young learners should be taught by a variety of teachers in school. This will allow students to have access to a more qualified, diverse, and robust education, giving students the chance to develop and pursue their own interests with the specialized support they deserve.

Integrated Task Mini Lesson

Reading

Step 1: Find the general topic in the beginning of the first paragraph. Identify the opinion or thesis of the writer at the end of the first paragraph.

As cities expand rapidly with no room for nature to be conserved, more animals are losing their habitats and suffering from serious damages caused by reckless human activities. A recent alarming such event involved illegal professional-grade fireworks. Scientists believe that fireworks may have caused thousands of blackbirds to fall from the sky over an Arkansas town on New Year's Eve

Notes on Topic: damage humans animal

Notes on Thesis: fireworks birds die

Step 2: Read the topic sentences and find the three key arguments. The topic sentences are in the beginning of each body paragraph. Keep in mind when you take notes, you will write down only the key words (1-4 words) because the reading passage will reappear after the listening.

First, the time of the fireworks corresponds to the time of the birds' massive deaths. At 10 p.m., residents heard several extremely loud, "window-shaking" noises that were believed to have come from professional-grade fireworks, which no one had permission to set off. About 15 minutes later several people went outside and looked up; instead of the birds being above treetop level, like they usually are, they were crashing into houses, cars, trees, mailboxes, shrubbery, and everything around. This indicates that there was a correlation between the two events.

Topic Sentence: fire death time

Second, after examining the birds' bodies, scientists found out that the "fireworks theory" made sense because the cause of the deaths was physical trauma. The Game and Fish Department took hundreds of bodies of the birds for testing to try to determine what happened. Initial laboratory reports said the birds had died from trauma primarily to the chest, hemorrhaging in the body cavity, bruised skulls, and blood clots in brain. It's consistent with crashing into something as the birds were shocked by the loud noises of fireworks and were flying into one another or fatally hitting buildings.

Notes on Topic Sentence: trauma cause

Finally, most of the dead birds were blackbirds which are well known for their poor eyesight. Blackbirds don't usually fly at night, but the big booms apparently flushed the birds from their roost, and then poor eyesight and disorientation stymied them from making it back safely. This would have caused the collisions as they were flying at rooftop level to avoid the fireworks.

Notes on Topic Sentence: eyesight poor

Step 3: Catch at least three words from the supporting details. Write down the key words in your notes.

First, the time of the fireworks corresponds to the time of the birds' massive deaths. At 10 p.m., residents heard several extremely loud, "window-shaking" noises that were believed to have come from professional-grade fireworks, which no one had permission to set off. About 15 minutes later several people went outside and looked up; instead of the birds being above treetop level, like they usually are, they were crashing into houses, cars, trees, mailboxes, shrubbery, and everything around. This indicates that there was a correlation between the two events.

Notes on Details: noises min later crash correlation

Second, after examining the birds' bodies, scientists found out that the "fireworks theory" made sense because the cause of the deaths was physical trauma. The Game and Fish Department took hundreds of bodies of the birds for testing to try to determine what happened. Initial laboratory reports said the birds had died from trauma primarily to the chest, hemorrhaging in the body cavity, bruised skulls, and blood clots in brain. It's consistent with crashing into something as the birds were shocked by the loud noises of fireworks and were flying into one another or fatally hitting buildings.

Notes on Details: lab trauma crash injuries

> Finally, most of the dead birds were blackbirds which are well known for their poor eyesight. Blackbirds don't usually fly at night, but the big booms apparently flushed the birds from their roost, and then poor eyesight and disorientation stymied them from making it back safely. This would have caused the collisions as they were flying at rooftop level to avoid the fireworks.

Notes on Details: poor eyesight disoriented and collide

Listening

Step 1: Expect what will be discussed and write down the possible three key points even before you listen to the lecture. Remember the listening will go against the reading or offer counter arguments about the three points.

Notes on possible 3 key points: time trauma eyesight

Rejecting the Argument	Accepting with Counterargument
Time wrong	Time is no point
Trauma no cause	Trauma caused by something else
Eyesight no problem	Eyesight but not fireworks

Step 2: Listen for the key words in each argument. Remember the beginning of each argument is signified by the following signposts: pause, question, negation, etc.

> Fireworks and loud noises have been used to scare off unwanted birds without killing them for decades. So, it's highly unlikely that they caused the deaths of thousands of blackbirds in Arkansas and the three arguments made in the reading are not convincing.

Notes on Argument: fireworks, scare off birds without killing, unlikely caused, not convincing

First of all, it's true that the two events took place on the same day, but this doesn't necessarily mean that one caused another considering the great distance between the locations. Remember the blackbirds died in the suburbs, which are far away from the city where the fireworks used? And there were a large number of birds spreading across an extensive area. So, when the fireworks went off during the evening, only a small portion of the birds would have been affected by the noises.

Notes on Argument: same day, great distance location

Second point, the birds' deaths and internal injuries may have been caused by strong winds. In fact, some witnesses reported that they saw the birds getting blown away and smashed to bits by the wind. Tornadoes swept through Arkansas on 31 December and they even killed seven people in the same region. The violent storms might have disoriented the flock, or one bird could have led other birds into a fatal plunge to the ground.

Notes on Argument: strong wind

And third, many blackbirds die at the beginning of the year because they have poor eyesight. Blackbirds don't have those special eyes that nocturnal birds usually have but still have to fly in the dark because of the shorter daytime around the New Year's Day. The blackbirds were grouped together in one location which is typical behavior for the winter season. And while flying in the nighttime, they naturally fell to death due to their poor vision.

Notes on Argument: begin year die, poor eyes

Step3: Write down as many key words as possible (at least two words from every sentence the speaker utters). Keep in mind that you have to write the detailed reasons.

First of all, it's true that the two events took place on the same day, but this doesn't necessarily mean that one caused another considering the great distance between the locations. Remember the blackbirds died in the suburbs, which are far away from the city where the fireworks used? And there were a large number of birds spreading across an extensive area. So, when the fireworks went off during the evening, only a small portion of the birds would have been affected by the noises.

Notes on Details: die suburbs fire in city far small affected

Second point, the birds' deaths and internal injuries may have been caused by strong winds. In fact, some witnesses reported that they saw the birds getting blown away and smashed to bits by the wind. Tornadoes swept through Arkansas on 31 December and they even killed seven people in the same region. The violent storms might have disoriented the flock, or one bird could have led other birds into a fatal plunge to the ground.

Notes on Details: witnesses wind blown tornadoes kill people

And third, many blackbirds die at the beginning of the year because they have poor eyesight. Blackbirds don't have those special eyes that nocturnal birds usually have but still have to fly in the dark because of the shorter daytime around the New Year's Day. The blackbirds were grouped together in one location which is typical behavior for the winter season. And while flying in the nighttime, they naturally fell to death due to their poor vision.

Notes of Details: new year, short day, night fly, no special eyes, death natural

Writing

Step 1: Template

Both the reading and the lecture discuss the thousands of blackbirds that died on New Year's Eve in Arkansas. The reading states that fireworks may have been the cause of the blackbirds' death. However, the lecturer refutes the belief presented in the reading by stating that the fireworks are not likely to be the cause of their deaths.

To begin with, the passage claims that the fireworks probably caused the blackbirds to fall from the sky and crash into houses, cars, trees, mailboxes, and everything considering the time. This is because the residence heard a loud noise that sounded like it came from professional grade fireworks at 10p.m., and soon after that the birds fell. Nevertheless, the lecturer contrasts this idea by pointing out that the blackbirds died in the suburbs, which was at a great distance from the city where the fireworks were used. Furthermore, she says that the birds were spread out in a large area so only a few of them would have been affected by the fireworks.

Secondly, the reading mentions that the fireworks theory made sense because when examining the bodies, scientists found out that the birds died from physical trauma. As the birds were shocked by the loud noises of the fireworks, they would have been crashing into something, which was consistent with their cause of death. Yet, the lecturer challenges this argument by revealing that the injuries may have been caused by strong winds. She states that some witnesses saw the birds getting blown away and smashed by the winds because there were tornados in Arkansas on December 31st.

Lastly, the reading argues that the blackbirds might have been startled by the loud boom and left their places at night. Since they are known for their poor eyesight and do not usually fly at night, they may have gotten disorientated and crashed into each other or other things as they try to avoid the fireworks above rooftop level. On the other hand, the lecturer rebuts this theory by explaining that many blackbirds die at the beginning of the year because of their poor eyesight, and they do not have the special eyes that nocturnal birds may have. She asserts that the birds naturally fly to their death this time of year because around New Year's Day the daytime is shorter causing them to fly in the dark.

Thus, there is a stark difference between the reading and the lecture.

Step 2: Turning key words into sentences.

Introduction

Reading Key Words	damage humans animal
Details	fireworks birds die
Listening Key Words	fireworks unlikely caused, not convincing
Details	scare off birds without killing

The first sentence has to show the common topic between the reading and listening.

Both the reading and the lecture discuss the thousands of blackbirds that died on New Year's Eve in Arkansas.

The second sentence presents the main idea of the reading on the topic.

The reading states that fireworks may have been the cause of the blackbirds' death.

The third sentence simply refutes the reading's point of view.

However, the lecturer refutes the belief presented in the reading by stating that the fireworks are not likely to be the cause of their deaths.

Body 1:

Reading Key Words	fire, death, time
Details	noises min later crash correlation
Listening Key Words	same day, great distance
Details	die suburbs, fire in city, far, small affected

The first sentence has to offer the writer's clear opinion or argument by using opinion words including such as, "probably, might have been, may have been, could have been, likely to be, must be." Remember that you can add more details by utilizing the reading passage because it is on the screen.

To begin with, the passage claims that the fireworks probably caused the blackbirds to fall from the sky and crash into houses, cars, trees, mailboxes, and everything considering the time.

The second sentence has to provide the reason to believe the argument. You must include why the writer believes that.

This is because the residence heard a loud noise that sounded like it came from professional grade fireworks at 10p.m., and soon after that the birds fell.

The third sentence has to offer the lecturer's counterargument. For that reason, you should include a negative transition in the beginning of the sentence.

Nevertheless, the lecturer contrasts this idea by pointing out that the blackbirds died in the suburbs, which was at a great distance from the city where the fireworks were used.

Finally, you might want to add more details to support the lecturer's counterargument. This will prove that you understood the listening thoroughly, which will allow you to score higher.

Furthermore, she says that the birds were spread out in a large area so only a few of them would have been affected by the fireworks.

Step 3: Proofreading.

Review your essay to ensure consistency and accuracy in grammar, spelling, punctuation, and formatting.

Independent Task Mini Lesson

Step 1: Introduction

Identify the **topic of the question**.

In many places, students aged 12-18 are typically taught different subjects by different teachers while younger students are usually taught by only one teacher all day long. However, it would also benefit younger students to be taught by several different teachers every day.

Type the key words: teachers, children

Using the key words and the template, **develop your introduction.** The introduction paragraph will have the following elements: **a general fact about the topic, the reason to believe the fact, the point of contention, what others might say about this issue, and your opinion about the topic.**

It is undeniable that teachers play a vital role in children's academic and intellectual development. After all, young students rely on their teachers to gain knowledge for success and pursue their interests. Yet, there could be a debate over whether or not younger students need different teachers for different subjects. Some might argue that one teacher should suffice in order for them to learn all core subjects. However, I believe that they can benefit from having several different teachers every day for three reasons.

Step 2: Body

Come up with two or three specific reasons to support your thesis or main idea. Each body paragraph will have the following elements: **point, explanation, example, and connecting the example to the point.**

To begin with, it is important that a teacher has the expertise and experience needed in order to give his students a high quality education. In other words, they need to possess profound knowledge of the subjects they teach. Otherwise, there is no point in going to school and learning from teachers because children could also gain general education from their parents. Nonetheless, most primary school teachers teach every core subject to their students but may only be highly skilled in one or two of those. As a result, it is not easy for a teacher to effectively conduct lessons on each and every one of them. From my personal experience, I learned that I was lacking in math and science skills in the fourth grade because I was not properly prepared by my third grade teacher who taught every single subject all by herself. To be honest, the teacher was terrible at teaching science and math although she was good at language arts and social studies. Because of this, I fell behind and was not able to build a good foundation in those subjects in order to do well in other grade levels. This clearly depicts that even young learners need a quality education offered by many specialized educators in school rather than learning from one teacher with general knowledge.

Another major consideration is that young students should be able to have the chance to be taught by multiple teachers to build their interests and get a balanced and multifaceted education needed to pursue them. Primary school teachers all have their own interests and biases about certain subjects. Therefore, the teachers' lessons may reflect on their unbalanced personal views regardless of the students' passion. For example, if a student is into art and wants to get feedback from his teacher, his teacher may ignore his request and try to sway him towards a different subject preferred by the teacher. This would not happen if the student had a separate teacher for art. The art teacher could give the student encouragement or show different art skills for improvement or creativity. This indicates that having different teachers will likely give students the motivation to pursue diverse interests and develop as individuals.

Lastly, one should think about the physical and mental limitations of an individual teacher and the number of students a teacher has to accommodate. Teaching can be extremely demanding with long hours and a heavy workload, and it's easy for them to fall prey to burnout, which will affect the quality of education greatly. That is why different teachers have to work as a team. For instance, team teaching, especially for subjects like science and math, can be advantageous to both teachers and students. Teachers don't always have to singularly meet the needs of all of their students when they work as a team. From the student's perspective, the good thing about having several teachers is that even if one of them is not very good, the student only has him or her for part of the day. Also, shuffling from class to class breaks up the monotony. This points to the fact that children would learn better from multiple teachers.

Step 3: Conclusion

The conclusion paragraph will have the following elements: **the main idea and the summary of the two or three points in the body paragraphs.**

In summary, there are many reasons why young learners should be taught by a variety of teachers in school. This will allow students to have access to a more qualified, diverse, and robust education, giving students the chance to develop and pursue their own interests with the specialized support they deserve.

PART 1

The Integrated Task

Dirty & Simple Tips

1. The format of the question

(1) For the integrated task of the TOEFL writing section, you will be given the reading passage first, which will be about a particular topic. The topic and an argument about it will be followed by three main points or theories. Those are important to know since the lecturer in the listening portion will refute those same points.

(2) **The reading passage** will be about 300 words, and you will have about 3 minutes to read it. You want to look for the main idea of the passage and find the three theories or points that are related to the topic. It is recommended that you take notes on the three key points. Each body paragraph will have a key point or an idea.

(3) Next, you will have 2 minutes to **listen to the lecture**. Notes should also be taken, and as mentioned previously, you should listen for the main points and counterarguments made by the lecturer using the same note-taking points. However, this time you have to pay more attention to the details and jot down as much as possible to score higher.

(4) Finally, you are required to type your **response** on the computer by summarizing the provided reading passage and listening and explaining how the lecture responds to the arguments made in the reading passage within 20 minutes.

(5) The minimum number of words you can use for this essay is 200 words (150-225 words) while there is no maximum word limit.

(6) There are many types of topics that you can see in this question.

A) A new policy (for/against)

(e.g.) A new policy that requires companies to offer their employees the option of a four day workweek (the reading is for it while the listening is against it.)

B) Approaches, methods, theories (for/against)

(e.g.) The best way to approach new projects is to work as a team (the reading is for it while the listening is against it.)

C) **An assumption (true/false)**

(e.g.) A long assumption was that dinosaurs were not endotherms, but recent research shows the possibility that they were actually endotherms. (The reading is for it while the listening is against it.)

D) **A thing with problems/benefits**

(e.g.) Are the communal online encyclopedias more beneficial than traditional printed encyclopedias? (The reading is for it while the listening is against it.)

E) **A problematic phenomenon/trend (why/why not)**

(e.g.) A certain international organization began issuing certifications to show what companies are eco-friendly, but American companies might not join this movement. (The reading says American companies will not pay attention to it while the listening will say the opposite is true.)

2. Skill Development

(1) What the raters want to see in your essay is the following:

A) You should mention all of the important information not only in the lecture but also in the reading. There will be three main points in each of the two provided materials and you should also include specific supporting details for those points. You may notice that often the three main points are the effects of the supporting details (causes). For example, the reading might argue that **"the number of Monarch butterflies is declining (effect=a key point) because of the impact of GM-related herbicide use on the monarch's food plants, milkweeds."** (cause=supporting details) Then, the lecturer might say that **"milkweed losses may not fully explain monarch butterfly declines."** (effect) The lecturer will further elaborate the argument by offering supporting details. **"Now we have more milkweeds in natural areas than previous studies suggested. I would say the milkweeds in natural areas are buffering the loss of milkweeds in the agricultural areas. Also, the overall drop in the number of milkweeds in the United States is not as large as the huge decline in monarch butterflies making it back to Mexico."** (causes or reasons for the contradiction= supporting details) You need to include as much details as possible to receive a high score.

B) You need to use proper and effective transitions to show the relationship between the reading passage and the lecture.

C) The information you write about should be directly from the reading passage and the lecture, and they have to be always accurate. In other words, you are not allowed to present your own opinion.

D) The language (vocabulary and expressions) you use has to be as clear as possible and should not be confusing.

E) Write in paragraphs.

F) Avoid redundancy.

G) Use good grammar with complex sentences.

(2) How to approach the **reading passage and the lecture**

A) The reading passage

This is how the reading passage is structured. Make sure you understand where to find the key information.

■ **The structure of the reading passage**

Introduction

1. Topic: a well-known fact about a certain topic
2. Details: the point of contention (the subject of a disagreement or argument)
3. Thesis: the writer's opinion about the topic (this is the key point to write down.)

Body 1

1. Claim: an opinion and the reason to believe this opinion (notes)
2. Supporting details: 1-2 sentences (notes)
3. Confirming the claim

Body 2

1. Claim: an opinion and the reason to believe this opinion

2. Supporting details: 1-2 sentences
3. Confirming the claim

Body 3

1. Claim: an opinion and the reason to believe this opinion
2. Supporting details: 1-2 sentences
3. Confirming the claim

■   **Note-taking points (reading)**

The topic and the author's opinion are found in the introductory paragraph. In the body paragraphs of the reading passage, you have to identify three main arguments and three supporting details. Write down the key words as you read quickly. The beginning of each body paragraph has the key point. Your notes should look like this:

Topic & opinion (positive/negative)
Argument 1
Detail 1
Argument 2
Detail 2
Argument 3
Detail 3

B) The listening passage

You should listen for the main points and counterarguments made by the lecturer using the same note-taking points. However, this time you have to pay more attention to the details and jot down as much as possible to score higher.

Your notes should look like this:

Topic & opinion (positive/negative)
Argument 1 (the opposite of the argument in the reading or a counter argument)
Detail 1 (two or three supporting details)
Argument 2
Detail 2 (two or three supporting details)
Argument 3
Detail 3 (two or three supporting details)

C) The strategies to understand listening passage

The most difficult part of responding to this task is that you have to incorporate the reading with the lecture. This means that you have to identify the points made in the reading and listening as quickly and accurately as possible. This can be challenging for test takers who are not familiar with the structure and language used in the reading and listening. In addition, the listening will be a fast and content driven lecture. For this reason, it is recommended that students know when and how to take notes during the listening as well as the common expressions ETS uses in the listening passage.

■ **Know the structure of the listening passage**

Introduction (It's usually a simple disagreement with the main idea in the reading)

> (e.g.) *The evidence that/ the claim that/ the hypothesis that... is unconvincing.*
> *... won't affect ... in the ways the reading suggests.*
> *Now I want to tell you about what one company found when it decided that...*

Body 1 (4-6 sentences to disagree with a specific argument in the reading)

Claim: the topic + opinion (You can predict this part, right? The opposite of the argument in the reading passage or the counter argument with a more important point will be stated. You should write this part even before you actually listen to the lecture, so you can focus on the details.)

Supporting details: 2-3 supporting points (You have to write down this part! Don't write this in complete sentences. Write down the key words only. Remember you won't have enough time to jot down everything you hear.)
Confirming the claim (Not important)
Body 2

Claim: the topic + opinion
Supporting details: 2-3 supporting points
Confirming the claim
Body 3

Claim: the topic + opinion
Supporting details: 2-3 supporting points
Confirming the claim

■ **Predict what claims will be made in the listening**

The claims in the listening part will be either the opposite of the claims in the reading passage or justification of the claims (partial agreement with a stronger counter argument). By effectively predicting the lecturer's arguments, you will be able to focus more on the key words in the lecturer's supporting details.

1. The opposite of the corresponding claim in the reading (disagreement & reasons)

(e.g.) The reading passage might claim that "the mysterious Sea Peoples were actually the Trojans who had been displaced following the mythic Trojan War with the Greeks because the two events happened in the same period." Then, you can predict that the listening might argue that "it is unlikely that the Sea Peoples were the Trojans because the only description about the Sea Peoples by Egyptians indicates that they were from the North. This rules out the possibility of the Trojans being the Sea Peoples since the Trojans would have come from the South."

2. Justification (partial agreement and partial disagreement with more reasons)

(e.g.) The reading might claim that "genetically modified strawberries are designed to be more resilient than natural strawberries and are more likely to survive than their unmodified counterparts." Then, you can predict the listening might argue that "genetically modified strawberries may be resistant in general, but it doesn't necessarily guarantee their survival."

■ **When to take notes**

1. After the speaker uses any transition: first, second, finally, another point, so, thus, now, OK, For example,
2. After the speaker questions: what about...? why? And guess what?
3. After the speaker uses negatives: but, not, and yet, however, although
4. After a pause: a pause is followed by the beginning of a new argument.

■ **The general structure of the listening:**

1. First (second, finally), X might look good. (responding to the argument in the reading)
2. But it is wrong because of Y. (listening point 1: the argument)
3. Let me explain.
4. Here is the detail. (listening point 2: supporting details)

5. So, X is wrong (Y is right).

■ **The following expressions can be utilized for you to identify the listening points more effectively.**

Positive expressions

1. benefit from this system
2. increase our knowledge
3. would be accomplished
4. reduce unemployment rates
5. would be better for
6. could improve the quality of their lives
7. perhaps the best way to approach certain new projects is
8. has a wider range of knowledge, expertise, and skills than
9. can work more quickly
10. can come up with highly creative solutions to problems and issues
11. can be very rewarding
12. it's indeed work of Da Vinci
13. strongly supports the idea that
14. would have been effective
15. there are good reasons to believe

Negative expressions

1. won't affect the company's profits
2. force companies to spend more
3. requires more office space
4. additional costs would quickly cut company profits
5. Hiring new workers is costly
6. it also presents some risks that could end up reducing their quality of life
7. didn't contribute much at all
8. just the opposite of what the reading predicts
9. there are problems with the painting
10. there is something inconsistent about the way
11. these elements do not fit together
12. would have been unconvincing.
13. critics have opposed the idea
14. critics argue that
15. A third objection is based on the fact
16. This suggests that the lines do not represent
17. The arguments of the critics are unconvincing.
18. several reasons to suspect that

19. did not exist
20. would have taken a long time
21. is unsupported by evidence
22. would therefore have been very impractical and ineffective.
23. does not seem like an improvement
24. isn't well supported either.
25. The idea might sound attractive, but
26. that doesn't mean that

Transitions

1. First
2. Second
3. Third
4. Finally
5. Moreover
6. Ok, so how about bone structure?
7. Now
8. Yet
9. But
10. However
11. Although

Point

1. So (at the end of an argument)
2. Most important,
3. A third theory proposes that
4. A second theory contends that
5. One theory holds that
6. This suggests that
7. **The real point is that**
8. Let me explain
9. That means that
10. In fact

Cause and effect

1. Since
2. As a result
3. That is because
4. Thus
5. That is why

Hypothetical situations

1. If the great houses were used for storage, why isn't there more spilled

maize on the floor? Why aren't there more remains of big containers?

2. The pots in the pile could be regular trash too, left over from the meals of the construction workers.
3. If...were...it would

Examples and evidence

1. Take the polar dinosaur argument.
2. These growth rings are evidence that
3. For example
4. It is a prime example
5. is characteristic of nocturnal animals
6. Excavations of the mound revealed deposits containing
7. This finding has been interpreted as evidence that
8. And another example

3. The advanced template

Introduction (b-s-r)	**Both** the reading and lecture discuss (write the topic here).
	The reading **states** that (write the readings' theory here).
	However, the lecture **refutes** the belief presented in the reading by stating that (explain the other side of the topic theory).
Body 1 (c-s-c-s)	**To begin with**, the passage **claims** that (provide the first point mentioned in the reading).
	This argument is supported by the fact that (offer the supporting details).
	Nevertheless, the lecturer contradicts this idea by pointing out (Put the lecturer's second point here).
	Furthermore, the lecturer(she/he) **states that** (offer the supporting details).
Body 2 (m-s-c-e)	Secondly, the reading **mentions** that (put the second point here – summarized).
	This notion is **substantiated** by the fact that (offer the supporting details).
	Yet, the lecturer **challenges** the argument found in the reading by **revealing that** (put the claim made by the lecturer).
	Moreover, the lecturer **elaborates this by mentioning that** (add more details to the lecturer's claim).
Body 3 (p-v-r-a)	The third and last **point** found in the reading is that (summarize the readings third point).
	According to the reading passage, this opinion is **validated** by the fact that (offer the supporting details)
	On the other hand, the lecturer **rebuts** this theory by explaining that (place the lecturer's third argument here).
	Moreover, in contrast to the article, the lecturer **asserts that** (add more details that contrasts with the article.)
Conclusion	Thus, there is **a stark difference between** the reading and the lecturer.

By diversifying the range of vocabulary and expressions that you use, you can make essays richer and improve your grades. **Remember the following key expressions:**
    A) **State**: mention, argue, assert, maintain, suggest, point out, claim, etc.
    B) **Support**: substantiate, validate, confirm, corroborate, etc.
    C) **Refute**: challenge, reject, disagree, disprove, contradict, take issue with, dispute, differ on/about, rebut, cast doubt on, etc.
    D) **Explain**: this means that, that is, in other words, to put it another way, specifically, clarify, expound, illustrate, etc.

PART 1

The Integrated Task

Practice Tests

Practice 1: A new policy

The Reading

In the United States, employees typically go to the regular office and work five days a week. However, many employees are willing to telecommute, or work from home or another place other than the conventional office these days. A mandatory policy necessitating companies to provide their employees the option of working from home at least two weeks a month would benefit both employers and employees who decided to take the option.

One of the major benefits of telecommuting is the option to save money on travel to and from work, and as a result, not only employees but also companies would increase their profits by saving on real estate, office supplies, and other overhead costs. Implementing this policy at individual companies would not result in excessive additional investments because the recent progress of technology has already helped accommodate the telework option. Free web applications and collaboration tools, such as an online meeting software, make it easier to interact with managers and colleagues when employees are not in the office.

The option of telecommuting would be better for individual employees as they can save their time, aggravation, and stress. In fact, studies have found that telecommuting creates happier and less stressed employees. Employees who could avoid a high-traffic area and gridlock on a regular basis and enjoy more free time could improve the quality of their lives by spending the extra time with their families, pursuing private interests, and enjoying leisure activities.

Finally, telecommuting would also encourage productivity. If many full-time employees started working from home, they would not waste time on the road, and that's additional hours employees can dedicate to tackling projects and meeting deadlines. Furthermore, they can better focus on their tasks with fewer disruptions, which will minimize possible errors. And that, in turn, can help companies produce more and better products.

The Listening

Offering employees the option of telecommuting won't affect the profits of the company and employees, the lives of employees, or productivity in the ways the reading suggests.

First, offering telecommuting will probably force companies to spend more money. Adopting telecommuting means putting much more money into providing employees with equipment and training. Think about the costs of buying computer programs for telecommuting and training of new employees. Even if it works, nobody knows how much financial loss can be caused if serious technical problems happen to telecommuters. What can they do if the project the employees are working on is time-sensitive? These additional costs and financial risks would quickly cut into company profits.

Second, with respect to the better lives of individual employees, working from home doesn't guarantee happiness. In fact, telecommuters can easily be depressed as they lack social interaction. Since these employees are confined to their houses, they don't get to take a break with their fellow co-workers and relieve their stress. They might actually use their time to do more work. In fact, studies show that the capacity to work from home mostly extends the workday and encroaches into what was formerly home and family time. If this happens, employees will have more stressful lives than now.

Finally, it's not clear whether telecommuting really helps companies increase their productivity. In reality, the opposite is true. Employers can't observe or control how employees use their time. This leads to worries about the lost productivity. And when workers are on hourly contracts, there's no guarantee that paid time is spent on work-related activities. For example, a big company recently banned telecommuting because of the possible abuse of the remote work system.

	Reading	Listening
Thesis		
Point 1		
Details		
Point 2		
Details		
Point 3		
Details		

Write your response here.

Student's response (5/5)

Both the reading and lecture discuss telecommuting. The reading states that telecommuting offers many advantages for the company and employee. However, the lecturer refutes this belief presented in the reading by stating that the option of telecommuting will not bring great benefits to both the company and employee.

To begin with, the passage claims that there are significant cost benefits to telecommuting. This argument is supported by the fact that employees do not have to travel to and from work and companies do not have to worry about real estate, office supplies, and other overhead costs, which leads to greater profits. Nonetheless, the lecturer contradicts this idea by pointing out that the investment in equipment and training would increase costs since all employees would need laptops and proper training in order to use the technology. Furthermore, the lecturer states that there could be a financial loss and the employee is not going to be able to complete the project on time if a serious technical problem happens.

Secondly, the reading mentions that telecommuting could enhance the employees' wellbeing because they would have less stress. This notion is substantiated by the fact that telecommuting would allow employees to avoid high-traffic areas, to be able to pursue private interests, and to enjoy leisure activities. Yet, the lecturer challenges the argument found in the reading by revealing that telecommuters lack social interaction and could easily be depressed. Moreover, the lecturer elaborates this by mentioning that working hours can blend into home hours since the workers are confined to their homes and are not able to take breaks with their fellow co-workers to destress.

The third and last point in the reading says that workers would be more productive since they don't need to spend time traveling and it enables them to meet deadlines and finish projects easily. According to the reading passage, this opinion is validated by the fact that without the disruptions that happens in the office, employees can focus better in order to complete their projects and tasks. On the other hand, the lecturer rebuts this theory by explaining that productivity doesn't increase because employers cannot physically monitor the employees. Moreover, in contrast to the article, the lecturer asserts that it isn't guaranteed that an hourly employee would be using their paid time for work.

Thus, there is a stark difference between the reading and the lecture.

Practice 2: Approaches, methods, and theories

Moon landing?

The Reading

A conspiracy theory offers an explanation of an event or situation with a surprising, sinister, and political motivation even though there are other more plausible explanations. One of the most long-lasting conspiracy theories is about the moon landing in 1969. While there is a huge amount of evidence that shows the whole scientific process of the great feat, recent polls show almost 6% of Americans still believe the Apollo 11 astronauts never landed on the moon. Conspiracy theorists claim the entire mission was an elaborate hoax by NASA to fake beating the Russians in the space race during the cold war era.

Conspiracy theorists hold that the moon landing is fake because you can't see the stars. The photographs and video footage that Armstrong and Aldrin took on the moon don't show any stars in the sky even though the photos were taken from different locations including the International Space Station, the space shuttle, and from lunar satellites. If the pictures and footage were true, there wouldn't be any stars in the lunar sky. However, scientists have proven that it is possible to see the brightest stars and planets in daylight from the space station. For example, Mars is so bright that even when astronauts are on the lit side of the Earth, it is clearly visible against the black background of space.

Another thing they point out as evidence is the American flag's movement that clearly shows the presence of wind. If you look at the American flag in NASA's still pictures from the Apollo 11 mission, it appears to be flapping in the wind. However, this is impossible on the real moon because it is supposed to be in a vacuum. Therefore, a more reasonable explanation can be that a film director created the moon landing footages and pictures from a special set in Alabama.

The third argument proposes that the moon landing was staged because the shadows aren't right. In particular, conspiracy theorists point to an iconic color photo where Aldrin is descending the ladder of the lunar module Eagle. As the sun was hidden behind the other side of the spacecraft, they claim that Aldrin appears too brightly illuminated in the shadows for the picture to be real and that this is clear evidence of using the aid of artificial studio spotlights.

The Listening

Unfortunately none of the conspiracy theorists' arguments about the moon landing is convincing.

First, the idea about the absence of stars in the photos is not clear evidence to prove that it was a hoax. If you've ever used a camera before, it's easy to understand why. A limited exposure range is the reason why we can't see stars in any of the Apollo photos. All of the exposures of the astronauts on the moon are daylight exposures. The surface was brightly illuminated from the sun, and the astronauts are wearing bright white space suits that are highly reflective. So, the exposure on the astronauts' cameras was not enough to capture the relatively dimmer stars. The same thing happens if you go onto someone's back porch at night and turn on the lights. Even though you can see the stars with your naked eyes, a quick-exposure camera won't be able to capture them.

Second, sure, from the footage and pictures, the American flag looks like a normal flag flapping in the wind. But it is a specially designed flag with a little rod. This casts serious doubt on the idea that it was a hoax. I'll explain. NASA knew that image was everything, and if it wanted to secure more government funding, the public needed to be impressed. A flag standing on the surface of the Moon, which is limp isn't nearly as good a photo-op. So, they made it look like it was waving in the wind by installing a horizontal rod on top of the flag. However, the astronauts were unable to extend it all the way, giving it that waving effect. In other words, it was just an illusion.

Third, the idea that the shadows in the pictures are wrong isn't well supported either. Conspiracy theorists point out that since the Sun is the only light source on the moon, shadow angles should be consistent. However, when sunlight hits the surface of the Moon, some of it bounces off and the moon itself becomes a reflective light source. In the Apollo 11 pictures, the sunlight is being scattered or reflected off the ground. This is why, in some images, you can make out a plaque that Armstrong and Aldrin left on the moon even though it's lying in the shadow.

	Reading	Listening
Thesis		
Point 1		
Details		
Point 2		
Details		
Point 3		
Details		

Write your response here.

Student's response (5/5)

Both the reading and the lecture discuss whether or not conspiracy theories surrounding the moon landing are convincing. The reading states that there are still some Americans that consider the moon landing a hoax by NASA. However, the lecture refutes the belief presented in the reading by stating that none of the conspiracy theorist's arguments are believable.

To begin with, the reading passage claims that the moon landing was a hoax because there is no star in the photos taken on the moon. This argument is supported by the fact that it would still be possible to see the brightest stars and planets from the space station. Nevertheless, the lecturer contradicts this idea by pointing out that since the astronauts were wearing bright, reflective suits, the exposure from the sun made it difficult to capture any stars. Furthermore, the lecturer states that it wouldn't be possible to take a picture of the stars in a lit area outside in the dark due to the exposure from the astronauts' camera by comparing this to taking pictures on a back porch at night and turn on the lights.

Secondly, the reading mentions that the moon landing didn't take place because the American flag seems to be waving in the wind in the pictures taken by the astronauts. This notion is substantiated by the fact that this would be impossible as space is a vacuum. Yet, the lecturer challenges the argument found in the reading by revealing that a metal rod was actually inserted onto the flag to keep it standing up for a photo opportunity as NASA did not want to show a limp flag. Moreover, the lecturer elaborates this by mentioning that the flag appears to be waving because the astronauts were not able to extend the flag all the way.

The third and last point found in the reading says that the moon landing was a fraud because the shadows are not correct and studio lighting was used. According to the passage, this opinion is validated by the fact that even though the sun was behind the spacecraft, Aldrin is too brightly illuminated. On the other hand, the lecturer rebuts this theory by explaining that the moon becomes reflective whenever sunlight hits it, so sunlight is scattered all around. Moreover, in contrast to the article, the lecturer asserts that this is true since we are able to see a plaque left by the astronauts that was placed in the shadows in some of the pictures.

Thus, there is a stark difference between the reading and the lecturer.

Practice 3: Assumptions

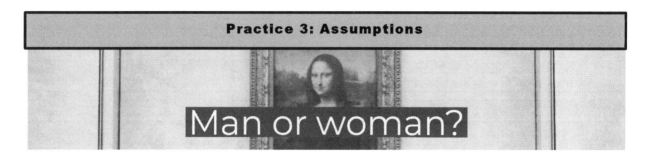

The Reading

The Mona Lisa is perhaps one of the most famous portraits of a woman in the world. However, there are some doubts over the real model of the masterpiece. Most recently, Art historian Silvano Vinceti used infrared technology to discover that the Mona Lisa was based not just on a Florentine merchant's wife but also on Leonardo da Vinci's male apprentice, Gian Giacomo Caprotti otherwise known as Salai. Indeed, there is some evidence that shows that the Mona Lisa may be actually androgynous, a blend of a male and female.

One reason for believing that the Mona Lisa was based on two models is that there are uncanny similarities between the facial features of the Mona Lisa and those of other works by Leonardo that used Salai as a model. This can be seen in the paintings of St. John the Baptist and the Incarnate Angel, for which Salai modeled. Vinceti examined these three paintings and saw that there were striking similarities in the forehead, smile and nose.

There are mysterious initials L and S in Mona Lisa's pupils. According to Vinceti, the L represents Leonardo and the S for Salai. Although it isn't easily seen with the naked eye, Vinceti used infrared technology and found the initials in the first layer of the painting. This could not have been a mistake or a random coincidence as other versions of the Mona Lisa also have the same initials. This strongly suggests that the painting was connected not only to Mona Lisa but also to Salai.

Also, the examination of the first layer of the painting shows that Mona Lisa was not smiling, but looking rather sad and somber. It is known that Mona Lisa's husband had to hire clowns to make his depressed wife smile for the painting. So, it is highly likely that Da Vinci painted another layer of the smile based on Salai's smile. In fact, the smile closely resembles the smile of Salai in the second layer of the painting. This is a strong indicator that the Mona Lisa is a blend of the two people.

The Listening

Everything you read about the Mona Lisa is not entirely true. After thorough examination, the model for the Mona Lisa was found to be, in fact, a woman, the wife of a rich Italian merchant. Here is why.

First, the infrared technology does nothing to support the theory that the forehead, eyes and nose were those of Salai. In fact, no one knows what Salai looked like exactly. As it turns out, the only knowledge of Salai's appearance was that he was a pretty boy with curly hair, which was pretty common during that time period. And, in fact, many of Leonardo's paintings before Salai entered into Leonardo's household had those similar characteristics.

Second, the Louvre museum carried out every possible test and did not find any inscriptions or initials in Mona Lisa's pupils. Well, it turns out that there were a lot of cracks due to the aging of the painting, a lot of cracks have developed, and these cracks could resemble inscriptions or numbers. So, there isn't any concrete evidence that shows the first layer of the painting to have the initials L and S inscribed in the pupils.

Finally, Mona Lisa's smile. It may, indeed, be true that the model's husband hired clowns to help make her smile for the painting. However, art historians have noticed that Leonardo actually used a blending technique using two layers of the painting of the same model to make her smile seem more mysterious and aesthetically satisfying. In fact, studies show that Leonardo has used this technique for his other paintings. Moreover, it depends on the viewer's disposition at the time when looking at the painting.

	Reading	Listening
Thesis		
Point 1		
Details		
Point 2		
Details		
Point 3		
Details		

Write your response here.

Student's response (5/5)

Both the reading and lecture discuss the model for the Mona Lisa. The reading states that the model for the Mona Lisa was a blend of a man and a woman. However, the lecturer refutes the belief presented in the reading by stating that the Mona Lisa is indeed a portrait of a woman, an Italian merchant's wife.

To begin with, the passage claims that there are similarities between the facial features of the Mona Lisa and those of other paintings of Leonardo because the same male model, named Salai, was used for those paintings. This argument is supported by the fact that when comparing the paintings using infrared technology, the remarkable similarities in the forehead, smile, and nose were clearly observable. Nevertheless, the lecturer contradicts this idea by pointing out that Salai's appearance is unknown, and the only known details were that he was a pretty boy with curly hair, which was quite common during Leonardo's time. Furthermore, the lecturer states that Leonardo's paintings before he met Salai had similar features as well.

Secondly, the reading mentions that there are the initials L for Leonardo and S for Salai in Mona Lisa's pupils to signify who the real model and painter were. This notion is substantiated by the fact that even in other paintings of the Mona Lisa, the inscription is presented. Yet, the lecturer challenges the argument found in the reading by revealing that there is no evidence of those initials in her pupils after going through a series of tests. Moreover, the lecturer elaborates this by mentioning that what appeared to be initials could be mere cracks due to the painting's age.

The third and last point found in the reading says that Mona Lisa's smile was actually a frown, and Leonardo painted another layer using Salai's smile. According to the reading passage, this opinion is validated by the fact that Mona Lisa's husband had to hire clowns to make his depressed wife smile. On the other hand, the lecturer rebuts this theory by explaining that Leonardo used a blending technique on the smile to make it more mysterious and pleasing. Moreover, in contrast to the article, the lecturer asserts that Leonardo used this technique for his other paintings and whether it was a smile or frown depends on the viewer's mood.

Thus, there is a stark difference between the reading and the lecturer.

Practice 4: A thing with problems/benefits

Homework?

The Reading

Homework has been around for more than a century, and it is one way of assessing students' learning. It is, in many respects, a part of the learning process: a way to reinforce what was learned during the day. The idea might sound attractive, but homework has several important problems that make it much less valuable than other types of school activities. In fact, over the last several years, there has been a lot of debate over whether homework should continue to be set by schools, and a number of schools have now taken the step of removing homework (especially from primary years) in the United States.

First, homework can lead to the loss of interest in academics among students. Often times, too much homework is given, thereby putting a lot of pressure on students' minds. This could cause them to lose their interest in learning and become less enthusiastic in completing their tasks. Students need time to switch focus and engage in other activities, if not, they will not be able to focus and learn in school. This is why repetitive homework assignments can be actually harmful to students.

Second, even if homework promotes a good study routine and habit, it also leads many students to start cheating and plagiarizing because they either cannot or will not strive to complete the work. Students suffer from a large number of home assignments at school. As students get tired, they can hardly do their home assignments on time, and this increases the desire for cheating while there is no one monitoring them. What's worse is that the cheaters get higher marks and learn nothing substantial in doing so.

Third, homework creates pressure to both the students and parents because some of the assignments may be too complicated. A student doing an assignment with which he or she may need help would turn to the parents since he or she would want to perform well in school. For some homework assignments, parents may feel as though they are incapable of helping their son or daughter, thus creating pressure on the parents as well.

The Listening

Homework will probably always be a controversial topic. but that's a small price to pay for what it does offer. The criticisms in the reading are rooted in the frustration over the complexity of the issue. However, there are plenty of good reasons as to why students should do additional work at home or outside school.

First, potential loss of interest in academics. It's hardly a fair criticism that homework can be challenging. If you are looking for an easy academic task with profound academic benefits, you are not going to find it. The real point is that homework actually increases students' understanding. Studies show that homework improves student achievement in terms of grades, test results, and the likelihood to attend college. In fact, students who did homework scored about 40 points higher on the SAT-Math subtest than their peers, who didn't do homework.

Second, increased opportunities for cheating. Although it is easier now to spread answers and plagiarize other's work found on the internet, teachers try to catch students cheating on an essay or copying something. The consequences of cheating while doing homework are pretty serious, too. Not only does cheating affect a student's reputation, it also means that the student can be expelled from the school in the worst case. So students actually have to improve their critical thinking skills to do their homework independently. Without having a teacher to guide them, students will have to find effective ways of completing work.

Finally, increased pressure on both parents and students. Well, the truth is that homework allows parents to be involved with their child's learning in a positive way. Thanks to homework assignments, parents are able to track their children's learning process at school as well as their academic strengths and weaknesses. A recent research found that interactive homework enhances student achievement and also helps parents detect any learning disabilities their children may have. So, there is no pressure involved in homework.

	Reading	Listening
Thesis		
Point 1		
Details		
Point 2		
Details		
Point 3		
Details		

Write your response here.

Student's response (5/5)

Both the reading passage and the lecture talk about homework. The reading states that homework is more harmful than helpful to students. However, the lecturer refutes the belief presented in the reading by stating that it is still beneficial for students to do work outside of school.

To begin with, the reading passage claims that homework could lead to a loss of interest in academics among students. This argument is supported by the fact that it puts pressure on students because they need time to switch focus and engage in other activities to learn in school. Also, repetitive homework assignments are harmful to the students. Nevertheless, the lecturer contradicts this idea by pointing out that it is not a fair criticism that homework can be challenging. Furthermore, the lecturer states that one cannot find profound academic benefits in easy tasks, and the students who did homework improved grades, test results, and were more likely to attend college. These students actually scored about 40 points higher on the SAT mathematics subtest than their peers who didn't do homework.

Secondly, the reading mentions that homework can lead to many students to start cheating and plagiarizing because they either cannot or will not strive to complete the work. This notion is substantiated by the fact that students receive too much homework and are not able to finish the assignments since they get tired, resulting in cheating. Yet, the lecturer challenges the argument found in the reading by revealing that teachers try to catch students cheating on an essay or copying other's work. Moreover, the lecturer elaborates this by mentioning that there are serious consequences to cheating and this could lead to expulsion. In fact, in order for students to do their homework independently, they need to improve their critical thinking skills.

The third and last point found in the reading says that it can put pressure on both students and parents since the assignments can be too complicated. According to the reading passage, this opinion is validated by the fact that students would turn to their parents for help, but the parents may not be able to help them, causing pressure on the parents as well. On the other hand, the lecturer rebuts this theory by explaining that homework allows parents to be involved with their child's learning in a positive way. Moreover, in contrast to the article, the lecturer asserts that parents are able to track their children's academic progress as well as their strengths and weaknesses. Interactive homework also enhances student achievement and helps parents detect any learning disabilities their children may have.

Thus, there are stark differences between the reading and the lecturer.

Practice 5: A problematic trend/phenomenon

Drones?

The Reading

In an effort to benefit from new technology, many industries consider taking advantage of one of the latest trends: drones, also known as unmanned aerial vehicles (UAVs). Commercial drone use applies to any use of a drone from which companies hope to profit, and it can cover a wide variety of activities. Although the drone industry in the U.S. is somewhat limited by the Federal Aviation Administration's regulations, commercial growth of that industry is quickly changing the market for the better environment, robust economy, and easier physical access to hard-to-reach places.

First, reducing the need for trucks by delivering packages and other goods with electric drones could save fuel and significant amount of carbon emissions. On average in America, truck delivery of a package results in approximately 1 kg of greenhouse gas emissions while drone delivery of a small package would result in about 0.42 kg of greenhouse gas emissions. This clearly shows that drones are better for the environment than other types of vehicles.

Second, commercial drones will have a positive economic impact because the increased use of drones will employ hundreds of thousands of people and lift overall GDP. Over a 5-year span, the economic benefits of commercial drone use will consist of the vigorous job creation in the manufacturing sector and improved productivity in the agricultural industry. Similarly, states will benefit from tax hike stemming from increased economic activity. Accordingly, America will add $82.1 billion in job creation and economic growth by 2025 thanks to drones.

Third, commercial drones will have physical access to hard-to-reach places. This means that drones can assist police officers, fire fighters, and property owners to maintain areas that are difficult to reach manually. As a result, commercial drones will improve the safety of households and companies while decreasing the criminal activity risks and accident hazards.

The Listening

Well, it is unlikely that drones will have any profoundly positive impact on the American economy although you just read three reasons why it is a good economic trend. Not one of these three reasons is convincing.

First of all, commercial drones are not always better for the environment. Although in some cases, using electric-powered drones could reduce energy consumption and greenhouse gas emissions, in other cases, using electric-powered trucks would be more efficient and cleaner. And manufacturing batteries still produces large quantities of carbon dioxide. Think about the ever increasing number of drones in the sky. They will cause more air pollution, not the other way around.

Second point. Of course, it's true that drone manufacturing companies will create some new jobs in America. But many recent reports find that drones could replace $127 billion worth of human labor and services across multiple industries. For example, drones will replace commercial pilots and truck drivers. People have already turned to drones as replacements for soldiers and lifeguards. In fact, most jobs that are related to human vision and judgment will likely have to rely on drones in the future.

And third, companies that use commercial drones should definitely pay attention to privacy concerns. Drone's ability to reach any location at any time can be dangerous as it poses a serious security threat and could result in cyberattacks, terrorism, and crimes against privacy. Commercial drones will use GPS to find your house and will have a camera in order to safely land and navigate its surroundings. With this incredible ability, drones are becoming major tools for criminals. For instance, last year Mexican smugglers used drones to drop drugs into prisons. This is a security nightmare.

	Reading	Listening
Thesis		
Point 1		
Details		
Point 2		
Details		
Point 3		
Details		

Write your response here.

Student's response (5/5)

Both the reading passage and lecture discuss the possibility of using drones and its impact on the economy. The reading states that using these unmanned aerial vehicles could positively impact the economy. However, the lecture refutes the belief presented in the reading by stating that the usage of drones is not necessarily a good economic trend.

To begin with, the passage claims that drones can save fuel and help reduce carbon emissions. The argument is supported by the fact that truck delivery produces 1kg of greenhouse gas versus 0.42kg from a drone. Nevertheless, the lecturer contradicts this idea by pointing out it would be cleaner and more efficient to use electric powered trucks in some cases. Furthermore, the lecturer states that manufacturing batteries still produces large quantities of carbon dioxide.

Secondly, the reading mentions that using drones can have a positive impact on the economy by increasing the employment rate and lifting the GDP. This notion is substantiated by the fact that the manufacturing sector would improve, the agricultural industry would increase, and states would gain from a tax hike. Yet, the lecturer challenges the argument found in the reading by revealing that reports found out that drones could replace $127 billion of human labor and services across multiple industries. Moreover, the lecturer elaborates this by mentioning that drones would replace commercial pilots and truck drivers; drones have already replaced soldiers and lifeguards; and most jobs that are related to human vision and judgment will be taken by drones.

The third and last point found in the reading says that drones can access hard to reach areas and improve safety. According to the reading passage, this opinion is validated by the fact that they can assist police officers, fire fighters, and even help homeowners by decreasing crimes and accidents. On the other hand, the lecturer rebuts this theory by explaining that there are some privacy concerns with this. Moreover, in contrast to the article, the lecturer asserts that the ability of the drone to reach any area opens the possibility of terrorism, cyberattacks and crimes against privacy. Another security issue is that drones can become tools for criminals, such as the Mexican smugglers who used them to drop drugs into prisons.

Thus, there is a stark difference between the reading and the listening.

PART 1

The Integrated Task

20 Trending Questions & Sample Answers

Check what questions actually appeared on the test recently!

Trending question 1: why moths are attracted to artificial lights

Moths?

The Reading

During the night time, moths seem to be charmed by porch lights, headlights or campfires even if it leads to the insects' untimely demise. Scientists have long wondered why moths are attracted to artificial lights when there is no apparent benefit, but this mystery hasn't yet been solved. While there isn't any definitive explanation for this phenomenon, now there are some convincing theories.

First, moths may confuse artificial lights with the Moon. When moths stay on tree branches or other objects, they are more vulnerable to predators unless they fly away from the predators immediately. If moths fly towards the Moon in the sky, they can escape from the predators more easily than flying towards the ground. So they fly towards artificial lights as they resemble the Moon.

Second, moths might mistake lights for flowers that they eat. Especially, nocturnal flowers with copious dilute nectar attract these pollinating insects. It is known that these flowers reflect enough light in the night. So it is reasonable to assume that moths fly towards artificial lights that look as bright as the flowers, expecting they would find food near the lights.

Finally, some entomologists believe moths zoom toward unnatural light sources because of the heat produced by artificial lights. Many artificial lights emit heat and moths need this during the cold nighttime. During the night, moths cannot use solar radiation to elevate their body temperature, so they fly towards artificial lights in order to warm up their bodies.

The Listening

Unfortunately, the theories in the reading passage have serious problems. The real reason for a moth's attraction to artificial lights will continue to remain as a mystery.

First, the Moon theory is weakened by the fact that moths are attracted to artificial lights regardless of the presence of threats. If the theory were right, moths would stay around the light only when they get attacked by a predator. But moths keep circling around and crash into the artificial lights even when there is no predator. That's not what you would expect if moths' attraction to the lights were caused by their instinct to escape from danger.

Second, although moths may be attracted to nocturnal flowers for nectar, they don't seem to really care for the light reflection from the flowers. Moths are actually less sensitive to wavelengths in low illumination. Also, moths have the ability to sense the co2 released by the flowers. This means that they can find the flowers at night without searching for the dim light from the flowers. Why do moths mistake artificial lights for flowers when the lights clearly release no carbon dioxide?

And third, the heat theory cannot explain why moths are attracted to lights that don't release any heat. Some artificial lights emit only low amount of heat. For example, fluorescent lights don't emit a lot of heat, but moths still get drawn to them. Have you ever seen moths and other flying insects swarming around your home's fluorescent lights? It turns out fluorescent lights are moths' favorite lights although they don't give out any heat. How could it be explained if moths were attracted to the heat of lights?

	Reading	Listening
Thesis		
Point 1		
Details		
Point 2		
Details		
Point 3		
Details		

Write your response here.

Student's response (5/5)

Both the reading passage and lecture discuss why moths are attracted to artificial lights. The reading states that there are three convincing theories. However, the lecture refutes the belief presented in the reading by stating that the real reason for a moth's attraction to artificial lights will continue to remain as a mystery.

To begin with, the passage claims that moths may confuse artificial lights with the Moon. The argument is supported by the fact that if moths fly towards the Moon in the sky, they can escape from the predators more easily than flying towards the ground. In other words, moths might think that artificial lights are the Moon and they have to fly towards them to survive. Nevertheless, the lecturer contradicts this idea by pointing out the Moon theory is weakened by the fact that moths are attracted to artificial lights regardless of the presence of threats. Furthermore, the lecturer states that moths keep circling around and crash into the artificial lights even when there is no predator.

Secondly, the reading mentions that moths might mistake lights for flowers that they eat. This notion is substantiated by the fact that flowers reflect enough light in the night, and hungry moths fly to artificial lights that look as bright as the flowers. Yet, the lecturer challenges the argument found in the reading by revealing that although moths may be attracted to nocturnal flowers for nectar, they don't seem to really care for the light reflection from the flowers. Moreover, the lecturer elaborates this by mentioning that moths have the ability to sense the CO_2 released by the flowers and don't need to rely on lights while looking for flowers to eat.   .

The third and last point found in the reading says that moths might zoom toward unnatural light sources because of the heat produced by artificial lights to warm up their bodies. According to the reading passage, this opinion is validated by the fact that moths cannot use sunlight to elevate their body temperature at night. On the other hand, the lecturer rebuts this theory by explaining that the heat theory cannot explain why moths are attracted to lights that don't release any heat. Moreover, the lecturer illustrates this by giving an example of fluorescent lights. They don't emit a lot of heat, but moths still get drawn to them.

Thus, there is a stark difference between the reading and the listening.

Trending question 2: building wildlife crossings for wildlife

Wildlife crossings

The Reading

The United States has a diverse array of wildlife species. However, natural areas in all regions in North America are affected by the changes brought about by urbanization. The construction of buildings, roads, and motorways can significantly fragment critical habitats and create a large barrier to movement for wildlife in all affected areas. One way of dealing with this environmental issue is called wildlife crossing, which is a general term used to describe the tunnel-like structures that facilitate the safe movement of animals across human-made barriers like highways.

First, wildlife crossings would increase animal immigration and help maintain species richness and diversity. If the animals were not able to cross the road and other types of barriers, this would cause fragmented inbreeding. As wild animals move through the wildlife crossings, diverse species would interbreed and it would effectively prevent inbreeding depression, which is often the cause of species extinction in the long term.

Second, it would provide animals an escape for movement between patches. This could reduce the number of road kills caused by motor vehicles because wild animals risk getting hit by automobiles when they cross the road, which can not only kill the animal but also could cause the people in the vehicle to lose their lives. By offering a pathway under or over the dangerous roads, wildlife crossings would contribute to wildlife conservation.

Third, wildlife crossings would provide a refuge from natural disasters. For example, when a habitat is destroyed by a wildfire, wild animals can easily escape to a safer habitat using the corridors. By connecting different habitats that might be divided otherwise, wildlife crossings would help animals increase their chances of survival.

The Listening

Constructing wildlife crossings is not necessarily the best option for animal conservation. Actually, this method has many disadvantages. Here is why.

First, sure, wildlife crossings would increase animal immigration among different habitats. But this won't necessarily lead to species richness or diversity. On the contrary, it will probably cause the extinction of many native species. I'll explain. If hundreds of random wild animals can move around, invasive species also can spread fast. So it will create more opportunities for the spread of diseases, pests, invasive and alien species. At the end, this will endanger many species and decrease the level of genetic variation among the animals.

Second, the idea that the wildlife crossings will offer an escape and save animals is not so convincing. True, the road kills might decrease. But wildlife crossings will increase the exposure to predators. This means that small animals will get attacked by big predators at a corner with nowhere to hide. Furthermore, hunters and poachers can also take advantage of the same corridors to kill wild animals. They will kill a large number of animals easily by setting up powerful traps in and around the corridors. As a result, the total number of wild animals will decline soon.

Finally, there are better and more cost effective ways to save animals at risk. When natural disasters occur, they just don't affect one habitat. For example, a wild fire usually destroys multiple habitats at the same time. So it's not likely for animals to escape from the fire by moving to a neighboring-habitat. Ultimately, species translocation method can be more effective if a habitat is completely damaged. This can be done by simply capturing and moving endangered species from a disaster area to a safer place. Because it can be completed within a day, it is also less costly than building wildlife crossings.

	Reading	Listening
Thesis		
Point 1		
Details		
Point 2		
Details		
Point 3		
Details		

Write your response here.

Student's response (5/5)

Both the reading passage and lecture discuss wildlife crossing. The reading states that natural areas and animal habitats in all regions in North America are affected by the changes brought about by urbanization and wildlife crossing is an effective way of dealing with this environmental issue. However, the lecture refutes the belief presented in the reading by stating that constructing wildlife crossings is not necessarily the best option for animal conservation, and this method has many disadvantages.

To begin with, the passage claims that wildlife crossings would increase animal immigration and help maintain species richness and diversity. The argument is supported by the fact that as wild animals move through the wildlife crossings, diverse species would interbreed and it would effectively prevent inbreeding depression. Nevertheless, the lecturer contradicts this idea by pointing out wildlife crossings won't necessarily lead to species richness or diversity and it will probably cause the extinction of many native species. Furthermore, the lecturer states that invasive species also can spread fast if hundreds of random wild animals can move around. So this will endanger many species and decrease the level of genetic variation among the animals.

Secondly, the reading mentions that it would provide animals an escape for movement between patches. This notion is substantiated by the fact that this could reduce the number of road kills caused by motor vehicles because wild animals risk getting hit by automobiles when they cross the road. Yet, the lecturer challenges the argument found in the reading by revealing that the idea that the wildlife crossings will offer an escape and save animals is not so convincing. Moreover, the lecturer elaborates this by mentioning that wildlife crossings will increase the exposure to predators, and hunters and poachers can also take advantage of the same corridors to kill wild animals

The third and last point found in the reading says that wildlife crossings would provide a refuge from natural disasters. For example, when a habitat is destroyed by a wildfire, wild animals can easily escape to a safer habitat using the corridors. On the other hand, the lecturer rebuts this theory by explaining that there are better and more cost effective ways to save animals at risk. Moreover, the lecturer asserts that a wild fire usually destroys multiple habitats at the same time, and it's not likely for animals to escape from the fire by moving to a neighboring-habitat. Therefore, other methods like species translocation method can be more effective if a habitat is completely damaged. Also, because it can be completed within a day, it is also less costly than building wildlife crossings.

Thus, there is a stark difference between the reading and the listening.

Trending question 3: the function of the cypress knee

Cypress knee ?

The Reading

A cypress knee is a unique structure forming above the roots of a cypress tree of any of various species of the subfamily Taxodioideae. They are commonly seen on trees growing in swamps. However, the mysterious function of cypress knees has long intrigued botanists. There are several theories to explain the function of cypress knees.

One theory holds that a cypress knee helps to aerate the tree's roots in very wet environments where cypress knees are most commonly found. Supporters of this theory think that it provides oxygen to the roots that grow in waters typical of a swamp. In particular, it appears strikingly similar to mangroves' underground root system that grows vertically up into the air above the soil to provide the tree with additional oxygen.

The second theory contends that it creates a barrier to catch sediment under water and reduces erosion. In fact, lowland or swamp-grown cypresses found in flooded or flood-prone areas tend to be more supported by the "knees" as opposed to cypresses grown on higher ground. Thus, this might be an adaptation to the swamp environment where water erosion occurs quite often.

A third theory proposes that a cypress knee helps stabilize the tree withstand hurricane winds. Bald cypresses which are known for their knees prefer regions that are frequently damaged by hurricanes. So the knee assists in anchoring the tree in the soft and muddy soil when strong winds are present.

The Listening

Unfortunately none of the theories about the function of cypress knees are convincing.

First, the theory about aerating the tree's roots in very wet environments. Actually, there is very little evidence that proves this claim. If this were true, the trees that have damaged or missing knees would rot in wet conditions. In fact, swamp-dwelling specimens whose knees were removed continued to thrive. Moreover, laboratory tests demonstrated that the knees are not effective at depleting oxygen in a sealed chamber.

The second theory says knees create a barrier to catch sediment and reduce erosion. Well, what about the trees that are found on land? Those cypress knees are also found on land; they don't just disappear. If the theory were true, then there would be no need for cypress knees when water is not present. Remember, water erosion cannot happen on land. In fact, they are stronger growing on land.

Finally, the third theory hypothesizes that cypress knees are used as an anchor for the tree in soft and muddy soil. This is not convincing because cypress knees are not always found in the trees growing in deeper water. If the hypothesis were true, all trees that live in hurricane prone regions should have knees, especially those in deeper water because they would need the extra support from hurricanes. But, this doesn't seem to be the case.

	Reading	Listening
Thesis		
Point 1		
Details		
Point 2		
Details		
Point 3		
Details		

Write your response here.

Student's response (5/5)

Both the reading passage and lecture discuss the function of cypress knees. The reading states that there are several compelling theories to explain the function of cypress knees. However, the lecture refutes the belief presented in the reading by stating that none of the theories about the function of cypress knees are convincing.

To begin with, the passage claims that a cypress knee might help to aerate the tree's roots in very wet environments where cypress knees are most commonly found. The argument is supported by the fact that a cypress knee appears strikingly similar to mangroves' underground root system that grows vertically up into the air above the soil to provide the tree with additional oxygen. Nevertheless, the lecturer contradicts this idea by pointing out there is very little evidence that proves this claim. Furthermore, the lecturer states that swamp-dwelling specimens whose knees were removed continued to thrive, and laboratory tests demonstrated that the knees are not effective at depleting oxygen in a sealed chamber.

Secondly, the reading mentions that a cypress knee might a special adaptation that creates a barrier to catch sediment under water and reduces erosion. This notion is substantiated by the fact that lowland or swamp-grown cypresses found in flooded or flood-prone areas tend to be more supported by the "knees" as opposed to cypresses grown on higher ground. Yet, the lecturer challenges the argument found in the reading by revealing that if the theory were true, then there would be no need for cypress knees when water is not present because water erosion cannot happen on land. Moreover, the lecturer elaborates this by mentioning that cypress knees are also found on land. They don't disappear and even become stronger growing on land.

The third and last theory found in the reading speculates that a cypress knee helps stabilize the tree withstand hurricane winds. According to the reading passage, this opinion is validated by the fact that bald cypresses which are known for their knees prefer regions that are frequently damaged by hurricanes. On the other hand, the lecturer rebuts this theory by explaining that this is not convincing because cypress knees are not always found in the trees growing in deeper water. Moreover, the lecturer asserts that if the hypothesis were true, all trees that live in hurricane prone regions should have knees, especially those in deeper water because they would need the extra support from hurricanes, but this is not the case.

Thus, there is a stark difference between the reading and the listening.

Trending question 4: how to control the Tree of Heaven

Tree of Heaven?

The Reading

Tree of Heaven (*Ailanthus altissima*) is a deciduous tree in the family Simaroubaceae. It is native to China and was brought to the United States in the late 1700's as a horticultural specimen and shade tree. Although its name sounds divine, it is an invasive species rapidly spreading in America. Its ease of establishment, fast growth and absence of insect or disease problems made it popular when planning urban landscaping, but today this invasive tree threatens to overwhelm our natural areas, agricultural fields and roadsides. Several methods may be effective in controlling this species.

One method is mechanical control which is any physical activity that inhibits the tree's growth. Mechanical, or manual, tree control techniques manage the tree populations through physical methods that remove, injure, kill, or make the growing conditions unfavorable. By removing the tree of heaven seedlings before the taproot develops or simply cutting the trees, anybody can control the invasive species without special licensing or the introduction of chemicals into the environment.

Another method is biological control by introducing toxic fungus into the trees. It would help kill the tree of heaven without damaging the surrounding environment. Studies show that inoculating invasive trees with fungus can effectively kill only the affected trees in a little more than a year as the fungus spreads its toxic substance to the attached surface.

Finally, chemical control method can be considered. The herbicides should be targeted at the roots and applied in the mid to late summer when the tree is moving carbohydrates to the roots. This method is often said to be one of the most effective and resource-efficient tools to treat invasive trees.

The Listening

The three methods suggested in the reading may appear to be effective ways of controlling the tree of heaven, but all of them have some problems in reality.

First, the mechanical treatments. They are not the easiest ways to deal with the fully grown tree of heaven. Think about how many people would be needed to remove the grown invasive trees on a mountain. Unlike pulling out small seedlings on the ground, cutting down the big trees will be highly labor intensive. Also, this can create a significant amount of site disturbance because it might cause damage to other species around the trees. While trying to cut down the trees, people might kill native plants and the disturbed areas will be the ideal condition for more invasive plants to reestablish. So its long-term effect is questionable.

Second, the biological method. It's true that this treatment is less harmful to the environment. But is this method realistic? The truth is that we can't buy the fungus in the store now. It will probably take more years of testing and navigating a series of regulations before that will happen. A company would also have to find a way to commercialize the biocontrol. If it is too expensive, nobody can afford to buy enough amount of fungus to treat many invasive trees.

Finally, the chemical control method. It only works when there are a few invasive trees. Large infestations, infestations near water, or infestations on steep slopes may be too costly or too environmentally sensitive to control by chemical means. If the herbicides spread through streams or rivers, this will surely have a negative impact on the environment.

	Reading	Listening
Thesis		
Point 1		
Details		
Point 2		
Details		
Point 3		
Details		

Write your response here.

Student's response (5/5)

Both the reading passage and lecture discuss Tree of Heaven, which is a deciduous tree in the family Simaroubaceae. The reading states that several methods may be effective in controlling this species. However, the lecture refutes the belief presented in the reading by stating that the three methods suggested in the reading may appear to be effective ways of controlling the tree of heaven, but all of them have some problems in reality.

To begin with, the passage claims that mechanical, or manual, tree control techniques can be effective to manage the tree populations through physical methods that remove, injure, kill, or make the growing conditions unfavorable. The argument is supported by the fact that removing the tree of heaven seedlings before the taproot develops or simply cutting the trees is something anybody can do to control the invasive species without special licensing or the introduction of chemicals into the environment. Nevertheless, the lecturer contradicts this idea by pointing out this is not the easiest way to deal with the fully grown tree of heaven. Furthermore, the lecturer states that unlike pulling out small seedlings on the ground, cutting down the big trees will be highly labor intensive. Also, this can create a significant amount of site disturbance because it might cause damage to other native species around the trees, so its long-term effect is questionable.

Secondly, the reading mentions that biological control by introducing toxic fungus into the trees can be useful as well. This notion is substantiated by the fact that it would help kill the tree of heaven without damaging the surrounding environment. Yet, the lecturer challenges the argument found in the reading by revealing that this method is not realistic as we can't buy the fungus in the store now. Moreover, the lecturer elaborates this by mentioning that a company would have to find a way to commercialize the biocontrol. Also, if it is too expensive, nobody can afford to buy enough amount of fungus to treat many invasive trees.

The third and last point found in the reading says that chemical control method can be also considered. According to the reading passage, this opinion is validated by the fact that when applied correctly at the right time, this method is often said to be one of the most effective and resource-efficient tools to treat invasive trees. On the other hand, the lecturer rebuts this theory by explaining that it only works when there are a few invasive trees. Moreover, the lecturer asserts that large infestations, infestations near water, or infestations on steep slopes may be too costly or too environmentally sensitive to control by chemical means.

Thus, there is a stark difference between the reading and the listening.

Trending question 5: a novel balloon-based solar-plus-storage

Solar balloon energy?

The Reading

Photovoltaic (solar) energy is becoming increasingly attractive as a renewable energy source because of its limitless supply and its eco-friendly character, in stark contrast to the finite fossil fuels coal, petroleum, and natural gas. However, the main problem with photovoltaic energy is that sunlight can be obscured by clouds, which makes electrical production intermittent and uncertain. To address this issue, experts are considering a novel balloon-based solar-plus-storage technology. By using large, levitating helium balloons containing embedded photovoltaic arrays, it will lead to higher energy yields above the cloud cover where the sun shines all day.

First, this technology could cut the cost of solar energy production significantly within a few years. With low maintenance and replacement costs, the system will considerably reduce the cost of solar energy from the current price of around $4 per watt of installed capacity to levels where it can directly compete with fossil fuel-based energy sources. This means that it is not only environmentally friendly but also practical.

Second, such a solar generator would be relatively easy and fast to install as well as to move or remove when required. Several projects have already demonstrated the feasibility of using balloons at altitudes well above 20 km. In this regard, several major companies are already planning to resort to stratospheric aircraft with the same technology as a cheaper alternative to the fleets of satellites being used for telecommunications.

Finally, it will be more productive. The main problem with photovoltaic energy is that sunlight can be obscured by clouds, which makes electrical production intermittent and uncertain. But above the cloud cover, the sun shines all day, every day, so the solar energy production will be more predictable and efficient.

The Listening

Using balloons, as mentioned in the reading, to capture solar energy from above the clouds is a novel idea. Yet, it is unrealistic.

First, could balloon technology cut costs of solar energy by 90% within 3 years? Well, this is not necessarily true. Why? Because the implementation of this technology will require overcoming major commercialization hurdles. In fact, it would cost billions of dollars to set up solar panels placed on the balloons that would be floating 3.7 miles above the earth. Moreover, the extra weight needed on the device would make it costlier to keep it afloat.

Second, the solar generator would be easier and quick to install as well as to move or maintain.   But, this solar generator would have to overcome technological feasibility. In fact, there are certain operational limitations that require frequent operations and maintenance stoppages. Moreover, hydrogen for balloons is not allowed in many places. As a result, this could impede the amount of balloons that can be used.

Finally, would these balloons be more productive? This could be true, but there are better and easier solutions. There is existing photovoltaic technology that can achieve better yields than the northern European average in locations, such as, Chile or South Africa, where there is plenty of sun. In fact, you would need to look at the full efficiency from converting solar energy to hydrogen and then back to ground electricity to verify the real productivity.

	Reading	Listening
Thesis		
Point 1		
Details		
Point 2		
Details		
Point 3		
Details		

Write your response here.

Student's response (5/5)

Both the reading passage and lecture discuss photovoltaic (solar) energy. The reading states that it will lead to higher energy yields above the cloud cover where the sun shines all day. However, the lecture refutes the belief presented in the reading by stating that using balloons to capture solar energy from above the clouds is unrealistic.

.

To begin with, the passage claims that this technology could cut the cost of solar energy production significantly within a few years. The argument is supported by the fact that with low maintenance and replacement costs, the system will considerably reduce the cost of solar energy from the current price to levels where it can directly compete with fossil fuel-based energy sources. Nevertheless, the lecturer contradicts this idea by pointing out that the implementation of this technology will require overcoming major commercialization hurdles. Furthermore, the lecturer states that it would cost billions of dollars to set up solar panels placed on the balloons that would be floating 3.7 miles above the earth, and the extra weight needed on the device would make it costlier to keep it afloat.

Secondly, the reading mentions that such a solar generator would be relatively easy and fast to install as well as to move or remove when required. This notion is substantiated by the fact that several major companies are already planning to resort to stratospheric aircraft with the same technology as a cheaper alternative to the fleets of satellites being used for telecommunications. Yet, the lecturer challenges the argument found in the reading by revealing that this solar generator would have to overcome technological feasibility. Moreover, the lecturer elaborates this by mentioning that there are certain operational limitations that require frequent operations and maintenance stoppages, and hydrogen for balloons is not allowed in many places.

The third and last point found in the reading says that it will be more productive. According to the reading passage, this opinion is validated by the fact that above the cloud cover, the sun shines all day, every day, so the solar energy production will be more predictable and efficient. On the other hand, the lecturer rebuts this theory by explaining that there are better and easier solutions. Moreover, the lecturer asserts that there is existing photovoltaic technology that can achieve better yields than the northern European average in locations, such as, Chile or South Africa, where there is plenty of sun.

Thus, there is a stark difference between the reading and the listening.

Trending question 6: the purpose of antlers

Antlers ?

The Reading

Antlers are developed in most species of deer, and the shape of the antlers has become characteristic of the species. However, the origin and primary function of antlers was debated for a long time. While there is still no universally agreed upon explanation, many interesting theories have been offered to explain why antlers evolved.

One theory is that the deer's antlers can help regulate body temperature since the antlers have blood vessels underneath a velvety skin. For example, caribou have large antlers, which have lots of surface area to allow for body temperature regulation while they are growing. The supporters of this theory claim that this is why caribou are well adapted for the cold, and they can be found in cold places like northern North America, Russia, and Scandinavia

Another theory mentions that these antlers are used to defend against predators. During the winter and into the spring, most deer retain their antlers. This is when deer are most likely to get attacked by wolves. In fact, predators, such as wolves, are more likely to kill male elks without antlers. This is because bucks can inflict deadly injuries with their antlers, and even predators like wolves would avoid them.

The last theory is that antlers are used to compete both behaviorally and physiologically against other male deer during the mating seasons. When a male encounters another male, they may fight using their antlers in order to win their mate. Also, physiologically, large antlers may be attractive for a female, and they could deter other males from the females because bucks with larger antlers display more strength, dominance and fertility.

The Listening

You've just read about three theories to explain why deer have antlers. However, none of the theories in the reading is conclusive or convincing.

First, the temperature theory. This theory is unlikely to be true because it can't explain so many things about antlers. For example, why do antlers fall off during the winter when they need thermoregulation the most? In fact, a recent study shows that antlers are more related to the deer's testosterone levels. When they don't have enough testosterone, the deer lose their antlers regardless of the temperature. But this coincidentally happens in the cold winter, and people just assume that there is a correlation between the temperature and antlers without any solid evidence.

Second, the defense theory. This theory cannot be the main purpose of antlers. Sure, deer use their antlers to protect themselves when they are in danger. But when you check most of deer species, only males have antlers. This wouldn't make any sense if the theory were right. Isn't it logical that every deer has to develop strong antlers if antlers were for defense from predators? Also, free-ranging bucks run from predators and fight with their powerful legs and hooves if necessary. This could be because antlers are not primarily normal tools to defend against a predator's attack.

Finally, the competition theory. It is doubtful that antlers are mainly for mating competition. We know female caribou never compete against each other, but both male and female caribou have antlers. Furthermore, the deer with the biggest antlers is not always the most dominant male in a group of deer. That means antlers are not essentially for competition.

	Reading	Listening
Thesis		
Point 1		
Details		
Point 2		
Details		
Point 3		
Details		

Write your response here.

Student's response (5/5)

Both the reading passage and lecture discuss antlers. The reading states that many interesting theories have been offered to explain why antlers evolved. However, the lecture refutes the belief presented in the reading by stating that none of the theories in the reading is conclusive or convincing.

To begin with, the first theory in the passage claims that the deer's antlers can help regulate body temperature since the antlers have blood vessels underneath a velvety skin. The argument is supported by the fact that this is why caribou are well adapted for the cold, and they can be found in cold places like northern North America, Russia, and Scandinavia. Nevertheless, the lecturer contradicts this idea by pointing out it can't explain so many things about antlers. For example, why do antlers fall off during the winter when they need thermoregulation the most? Furthermore, the lecturer states that a recent study shows that antlers are more related to the deer's testosterone levels. When they don't have enough testosterone, the deer lose their antlers regardless of the temperature.

The second theory in the reading mentions that antlers are used to defend against predators. This notion is substantiated by the fact that predators, such as wolves, are more likely to kill male elks without antlers. This is because bucks can inflict deadly injuries with their antlers. Yet, the lecturer challenges the argument found in the reading by revealing that this theory cannot be the main purpose of antlers as usually only male deer have antlers. Moreover, the lecturer elaborates this by mentioning that every deer, regardless of gender, has to develop strong antlers if antlers were for defense from predators, and free-ranging bucks run from predators and fight with their powerful legs and hooves.

The third theory in the reading says that antlers are used to compete both behaviorally and physiologically against other male deer during the mating seasons. According to the reading passage, this opinion is validated by the fact that males fight with other males using antlers and attract female deer by showing their big antlers. On the other hand, the lecturer rebuts this theory by explaining that it is doubtful that antlers are mainly for mating competition. Moreover, the lecturer asserts that both male and female caribou have antlers, and the deer with the biggest antlers is not always the most dominant male in a group of deer.

Thus, there is a stark difference between the reading and the listening.

Trending question 7: declining tiger population

The Reading

The largest of all the Asian big cats, tigers are one of our planet's most beautiful, awe-inspiring, and iconic animals. Unfortunately, wild tiger numbers have dropped by more than 95% since the beginning of the 20th century. No one is sure exactly what caused the decline, but chances are good that if nothing is done, tigers will soon become extinct. There are three main reasons for their decline.

First, poaching could be the major factor for the disappearance of wild tigers. Poachers illegally hunt them for their pelts, meat and body parts. Poachers killed more than 1000 wild tigers in the last ten years to supply the illicit demand for tiger parts. For example, the Bali tiger became extinct in the 1950s because hunters killed them for their body parts, which were made into jewelry.

Another major factor is the human-animal conflict. Tigers must have a large amount of space in order to survive. As humans move deeper into the territory of tigers, chances of conflict between both sides increase many folds because both the humans' and tigers' habitats intervene. Men and livestock often become the victim of tiger attacks, and this often infuriates villagers who resort to revenge killing, causing the decline of the tiger population.

Lastly, the most obvious factor is the segmentation of the habitat. While human population grows, more land is needed, resulting in less space for the tigers to wander and search for food. The habitat that remains doesn't include many huge blocks of protected land. It's mostly little "islands" of isolated forest surrounded by roads, farms, towns and other human developments. This can cause more inbreeding and genetic degradation.

The Listening

While it is true that the population of wild tigers is declining, the theories in your reading are not the most current reasons for their decline.

First, poaching. Poaching has been an issue, but tiger conservation gained global attention and many countries have banned tiger hunting.   In fact, with this ban, the tiger population has steadily increased. India houses about 70% of the world's wild tiger population, and the ban has been instrumental in increasing the tiger population there. As a result, there has been a 20% increase in tiger population within 6 years.

Second, human-animal conflict. Well, actually, these days, humans rarely encounter wild tigers. Indeed, humans may be expanding their territory, but tigers are scarce, secretive, far ranging, and they are distributed across immense geographical areas. Moreover, they are nocturnal, so they hunt at night. As a result, it wouldn't be common for farmers to encounter tigers now.

Finally, the segmentation of the habitat. Well, this isn't quite convincing since tigers are territorial and tend to live alone. If the tiger's territory is invaded, it will attack and kill the intruder. In fact, tigers respect each other's spaces. Moreover, they can adapt to a variety of habitats so long as they have three things in abundance: water, prey and vegetation.

	Reading	Listening
Thesis		
Point 1		
Details		
Point 2		
Details		
Point 3		
Details		

Write your response here.

Student's response (5/5)

Both the reading passage and lecture discuss the declining tiger population. The reading states that there are three main reasons for their decline. However, the lecture refutes the belief presented in the reading by stating that while it is true that the population of wild tigers is declining, the theories the reading are not the most current reasons for their decline .

To begin with, the passage claims that poaching could be the major factor for the disappearance of wild tigers. The argument is supported by the fact that poachers killed more than 1000 wild tigers in the last ten years to supply the illicit demand for tiger parts. For example, the Bali tiger became extinct in the 1950s because hunters killed them for their body parts, which were made into jewelry. Nevertheless, the lecturer contradicts this idea by pointing out tiger conservation gained global attention and many countries have banned tiger hunting. Furthermore, the lecturer states that the tiger population has steadily increased thanks to the ban. India, particularly, houses about 70% of the world's wild tiger population, and the ban has been instrumental in increasing the tiger population there.

Secondly, the reading mentions that another major factor is the human-animal conflict. This notion is substantiated by the fact that men and livestock often become the victim of tiger attacks, and this often infuriates villagers who resort to revenge killing, causing the decline of the tiger population. Yet, the lecturer challenges the argument found in the reading by revealing that humans rarely encounter wild tigers. Moreover, the lecturer elaborates this by mentioning that tigers are scarce, secretive, far ranging, and they are distributed across immense geographical areas. Moreover, they are nocturnal, so they hunt at night, and farmers wouldn't encounter tigers commonly.

The third and last point found in the reading says that the most obvious factor is the segmentation of the habitat. According to the reading passage, this opinion is validated by the fact that the remaining habitats for tigers are mostly little "islands" of isolated forest surrounded by roads, farms, towns and other human developments. This can cause more inbreeding and genetic degradation. On the other hand, the lecturer rebuts this theory by explaining that tigers are territorial and tend to live alone. Moreover, in contrast to the article, the lecturer asserts that if the tiger's territory is invaded, it will attack and kill the intruder. Moreover, they can adapt to a variety of habitats so long as they have three things in abundance: water, prey and vegetation.
.

Thus, there is a stark difference between the reading and the listening.

The Reading

The Mediterranean island of Malta and the neighboring island Gozo have been notable for their bewildering complex of tracks believed to be up to 6,000 years old, gouged into solid limestone along with the megalithic temples that are the oldest stone buildings in the world. Archaeologists have been trying to determine why the grooves were made. While there is still no universally agreed upon explanation, there are three competing theories that can explain the mysterious ruts on Malta Island.

First, some archeologists suggest that they were waterways. According to them, these deliberate channels were a prehistoric irrigation system stretching across the islands for farming. As Malta Island lacks rich soils and fresh water, the grooves would have been used as an innovative way to water the farm soils for better crop production.

Second, the grooves would have been built for transportation. Archaeologists presume the ruts in Malta were made by repeated use of carts, skids or sleds (wheeled or on runners) going over the same route over decades or centuries. It's thought that agricultural goods may have been transported using this system.

Finally, a less accepted theory suggests the lines served an astronomical purpose. A scholar suggests that the grooves and the megalithic temples in the middle of the grooves were built as a sign of worship or admiration to the Maltese gods. The grooves would have represented a kind of map of stars that are related to the gods.

The Listening

The evidence linking the grooves on the island of Malta to the theories in the reading passage is not at all convincing. Sure, all of the three hypotheses point to specific facts to support their arguments. But they hardly prove anything to offer a conclusive explanation.

First, the grooves may appear to be waterways for agricultural purposes. But there is contradictory evidence. You see, some of the grooves drive off the island and into the sea, continuing underwater. Why did they need sea water when they wanted to grow crops? Salt water can only damage agricultural crops and plants. And also, there is no year round river or stream on the island. This is not how irrigation works. To irrigate, there has to be a source of water.

Second, the transportation theory is quite unrealistic. If animals were used to draw the carts, their footprints might have been evident between or outside the parallel grooves, but there's no evidence of that. Also, pairs of ruts separate, combine, then separate again numerous times for seemingly no reason. This would have caused heavy traffic and accidents if the grooves were actually used as tracks for transportation.

Finally, there is no evidence to support the idea that the grooves were created for astronomical purposes. The grooves don't represent positions of stars or astronomical events. Furthermore, there are no ruts running directly to any of the temples. And in some cases, the ruts run past temples. So the association between the grooves and the temple is questionable at best.

	Reading	Listening
Thesis		
Point 1		
Details		
Point 2		
Details		
Point 3		
Details		

Student's response (5/5)

Both the reading passage and lecture discuss the grooves on the island of Malta and the neighboring island Gozo. The reading states that there are three competing theories that can explain the mysterious ruts on Malta Island. However, the lecture refutes the belief presented in the reading by stating that the evidence linking the grooves on the island of Malta to the theories in the reading passage is not at all convincing.

To begin with, the passage claims that some archeologists suggest that the grooves were waterways. The argument is supported by the fact that Malta Island lacks rich soils and fresh water. So the grooves would have been used as an innovative way to water the farm soils for better crop production. Nevertheless, the lecturer contradicts this idea by pointing out there is contradictory evidence; some of the grooves drive off the island and into the sea although farming don't require salt water. Furthermore, the lecturer states that there is no year round river or stream on the island while for irrigation, there has to be a source of water.

Secondly, the reading mentions that the grooves would have been built for transportation. This notion is substantiated by the assumption that the ruts in Malta were made by repeated use of carts, skids or sleds (wheeled or on runners) going over the same route over decades or centuries to transport agricultural products. Yet, the lecturer challenges the argument found in the reading by revealing that there's no footprints of animals that were used to draw the carts. Moreover, the lecturer elaborates this by mentioning that pairs of ruts separate, combine, then separate again numerous times for seemingly no reason. This would have caused heavy traffic and accidents.

The third and last theory found in the reading says that the lines might have served an astronomical purpose. According to the reading passage, this opinion is validated by the possibility that the grooves and the megalithic temples in the middle of the grooves were built as a sign of worship or admiration to the Maltese gods, representing a map of stars. On the other hand, the lecturer rebuts this theory by explaining that the grooves don't represent positions of stars or astronomical events. Moreover, in contrast to the article, the lecturer asserts that there are no ruts running directly to any of the temples, so the association between the groves and the temple is questionable at best.

Thus, there is a stark difference between the reading and the listening.

Write your response here.

Trending question 9: protecting the Chesapeake Bay

The Chesapeake Bay?

The Reading

The Chesapeake Bay, the largest estuary in the United States, connects rivers to the Atlantic Ocean. The area of land that drains into the bay, which is known as the Chesapeake Bay Watershed, is popular among the residents and tourists alike for fishing, crabbing, swimming, boating, kayaking, and sailing. However, the human population in the Chesapeake Bay watershed continues to grow, and the drastic development is causing the fishery declines in the region. Thus, experts are trying to figure out the best way to protect the bay ecosystem and to combat the loss of fish.

First, a set of regulations to limit the amount of the crab catch can be effective to conserve the blue crab resource and many other species that feed on the crabs in the Chesapeake Bay. Similar methods were used for bass conservation in the past, and they were proven to be highly effective.
So the crab population can be recovered in the same manner by requiring licenses, banning too invasive gears, and limiting the amount of commercial crab catch.

Second, introducing Asian oysters that are more resistant to the diseases that have killed most of the species in the Chesapeake Bay can be a great boost for the bay ecosystem. In the Chesapeake Bay, there is only one species of oyster, the native Eastern oyster, and they are known to be vulnerable to the diseases caused by the protozoan parasites in the polluted area. If Asian oysters were introduced, they would replenish the degraded native oyster population through interbreeding.

Third, reducing the use of fertilizer can also be helpful to address the root cause of the pollution in the Chesapeake Bay. By simply persuading the farmers in the region, the government can expect a significant decrease in the pollution level in the seawater.

The Listening

Hi class, my name is Shawn Brown, and I am the fisheries director for the Maryland Department of Natural Resources. Professor Spencer asked me to share with you my personal view on the Chesapeake Bay issue. Well, honestly all of the proposed methods in the reading have some problems.

First, crab catch limit might not work. Commercial crabbing is different from fishing as a sport. The bass catch limit only worked in the past because it regulated recreational fishing. The people who followed the rule were not really fishermen. They had other jobs and fishing was mainly for fun to them, which was why it was relatively easy for them to stop catching too many basses. But crabbing is mostly done by commercial fishermen, so they have to risk a huge amount of financial loss if they follow the rule. Without a doubt, this method will encounter strong resistance.

Second, Asian oysters have been proven to be fast-growing and resistant to the two most common parasitic diseases killing native bay oysters. But research in recent years has found that the imports are more vulnerable to predators and poor water quality. Just because Asian oysters are thriving in the Pacific Ocean, it doesn't mean that they are suitable for the Chesapeake Bay. Also, Asian oysters may bring new diseases which are dangerous to other species in the bay.

Finally, the farming areas surrounding the Chesapeake Bay are too large. How can the government persuade the farmers not to use any fertilizer and grow crops in almost 100.000 square meters of farmland? Moreover, the loss of the commercial gains by not using fertilizers might be more significant than the positive impact this policy might bring about. So, this cannot be realistic.

	Reading	Listening
Thesis		
Point 1		
Details		
Point 2		
Details		
Point 3		
Details		

Write your response here.

Student's response (5/5)

Both the reading passage and lecture discuss the Chesapeake Bay. The reading states that experts are trying to figure out the best way to protect the bay ecosystem and to combat the loss of fish by introducing three methods. However, the lecturer refutes the belief presented in the reading by stating that all of the proposed methods in the reading have some problems.

To begin with, the passage claims that a set of regulations to limit the amount of the crab catch can be effective to conserve the blue crab resource and many other species that feed on the crabs in the Chesapeake Bay. The argument is supported by the fact that similar methods were used for bass conservation in the past, and they were proven to be highly effective.
Nevertheless, the lecturer contradicts this idea by pointing out crab catch limit might not work as commercial crabbing is different from fishing as a sport. Furthermore, the lecturer states that the people who followed the rule were not really fishermen, which was why it was relatively easy for them to stop catching too many basses, but crabbing is mostly done by commercial fishermen, so this method will encounter strong resistance.

Secondly, the reading mentions that introducing Asian oysters that are more resistant to the diseases can be a great boost for the bay ecosystem. This notion is substantiated by the fact that the native Eastern oysters in the Bay area are known to be vulnerable to the diseases caused by the protozoan parasites in the polluted area. Yet, the lecturer challenges the argument found in the reading by revealing that research in recent years has found that the imports are more vulnerable to predators and poor water quality. Moreover, the lecturer elaborates this by mentioning that Asian oysters may not survive in the Bay and bring new diseases which are dangerous to other species.

The third and last point found in the reading says that reducing the use of fertilizer can also be helpful to address the root cause of the pollution in the Chesapeake Bay. According to the reading passage, this opinion is validated by the assumption that the government can expect a significant decrease in the pollution level in the seawater by simply persuading the farmers in the region. On the other hand, the lecturer rebuts this theory by explaining that the farming areas surrounding the Chesapeake Bay are too large. Moreover, in contrast to the article, the lecturer asserts that the loss of the commercial gains by not using fertilizers might be more significant than the positive impact this policy might bring about. So, this cannot be realistic.

Thus, there is a stark difference between the reading and the listening.

Trending question 10: is gluten bad?

The Reading

Gluten is a protein found in many grains, including wheat, barley and rye. It's common in foods such as bread, pasta, pizza and cereal. However, grocery stores and restaurants now offer gluten-free options that rival conventional foods in taste and quality as more and more people are concerned about its harmful effects on their mental or physical health. Specifically, there are three health issues that can be caused by gluten consumption.

First, gluten can cause some digestive issues in certain individuals. The digestive system would believe it to be a toxin, and then it would send antibodies from the immune system to attack it. This would cause microvilli, which separates the bloodstream and the digestive tract, to become damaged, and over time, the walls in intestines will leak into the bloodstream. As a result, a person would become bloated, constipated, or malnourished.

Second, it can cause memory problems. According to research, eating gluten could potentially increase the risk of memory loss, dementia and Alzheimer's symptoms. In fact, these side effects can affect the brain and nervous system in many people because it can trigger both inflammation and autoimmune attacks in the brain.

Third, gluten can be dangerous for those with type 1 diabetes because this disease is connected to celiac disease: celiac disease patients are often diabetic patients as well. As gluten can cause inflammation when celiac disease patients consume it, it can also cause the same problems to diabetes patients. In this case, the results can be much worse since there is a broad range of side effects associated with diabetes.

The Listening

The reading is correct in pointing out that gluten can be harmful. Yes, it can cause serious side effects in certain individuals. However, the reading does not acknowledge that not all gluten is potentially dangerous. In fact, certain whole grains that contain gluten have many health benefits.

First, the digestive problems. Well...maybe this is true, but only for a small group of people. Actually, there are greater health benefits to eating whole grains. It turns out that consuming whole grains are linked with improved health. In fact, those with the highest intake of whole grains, including wheat compared with those eating the lowest amounts were found to have lower rates of heart disease and stroke. Moreover, they also had less risk of developing type 2 diabetes and pre-mature deaths.

Second, the memory problems. Indeed, eating gluten may increase the risk of memory loss for those with celiac disease. However, only about 1 out of 133 Americans have celiac disease. If individuals who do not have celiac disease avoid gluten, they would increase their risk of heart disease because of low consumption of whole grains. So, it is better to ingest gluten found in whole grains rather than avoiding it.

Third, the diabetes. Actually, gluten is typically safe for people with diabetes. The real problem is not the gluten but the sugars and carbohydrates that are found in many foods that contain gluten. If an individual eats whole grains, it might even have some positive effects on a diabetic patient because the whole grains reduce the harmful impacts on diabetic patients.

	Reading	Listening
Thesis		
Point 1		
Details		
Point 2		
Details		
Point 3		
Details		

Write your response here.

Student's response (5/5)

Both the reading passage and lecture discuss gluten. The reading states that there are three health issues that can be caused by gluten consumption. However, the lecturer refutes the belief presented in the reading by stating that not all gluten is potentially dangerous. In fact, certain whole grains that contain gluten have many health benefits.

To begin with, the passage claims that gluten can cause some digestive issues in certain individuals. The argument is supported by the fact that gluten consumption can make the walls in intestines leak into the bloodstream. Nevertheless, the lecturer contradicts this idea by pointing out only a small group of people may actually have digestive issues when eating gluten. Furthermore, the lecturer states that there are greater health benefits to eating whole grains. In fact, those with the highest intake of whole grains, including wheat compared with those eating the lowest amounts were found to have lower rates of heart disease and stroke. Moreover, they also had less risk of developing type 2 diabetes and premature deaths.

Secondly, the reading mentions that it can cause memory problems. This notion is substantiated by the fact that it can trigger both inflammation and autoimmune attacks in the brain. Yet, the lecturer challenges the argument found in the reading by revealing that if individuals who do not have celiac disease avoid gluten, they would increase their risk of heart disease because of low consumption of whole grains. Moreover, the lecturer elaborates this by mentioning that it is better to ingest gluten found in whole grains rather than avoiding it.

The third and last point found in the reading says that gluten can be dangerous for those with type 1 diabetes because this disease is connected to celiac disease: celiac disease patients are often diabetic patients as well. According to the reading passage, this opinion is validated by the fact that as gluten can cause inflammation when celiac disease patients consume it, it can also cause the same problems to diabetes patients. On the other hand, the lecturer rebuts this theory by explaining that the real problem is not the gluten but the sugars and carbohydrates that are found in many foods that contain gluten. Moreover, in contrast to the article, the lecturer asserts that if an individual eats whole grains, it might even have some positive effects on a diabetes patient because the whole grains reduce the harmful impacts of on diabetes patients.

Thus, there is a stark difference between the reading and the listening.

Trending question 11: what were the brochs for?

The Reading

The brochs are ancient drystone hollow-walled structures or towers found only in Scotland built around 500 B.C. There were once more than 700 of these mysterious structures across the area, but their origin is a matter of some controversy. While the main purpose of these towers is uncertain, there are many theories to explain why they were built.

One theory about brochs is that they were defensive structures and places of refuge for the community and their livestock. Because they were built near the coastline, archaeologists believed that they were constructed to defend specifically against sea invaders. Many of these structures were built on Orkney Island which is located near Scandinavian countries that attacked the Scottish people frequently using their advanced shipbuilding skills.

The second theory is that the structures were dwellings for the residents. The supporters of this theory argue that the people who resided on Orkney's island were mere farmers and fishermen and needed a place to stay near the coast where they could catch fish easily. Also, during the winter, they could store the extra fish in the storage spaces inside the brochs.

Lastly, brochs might have been a symbol of high status and authority. It is suggested that wandering artisans were commissioned to create these structures for the wealthy. Since it required a considerable amount of manpower to build brochs, anyone who owned a broch must have had control or influence over a sizeable workforce. This might explain why brochs are so big and meticulous towering over the village.

The Listening

The reading contains some interesting theories about the purpose of the brochs, but none of them are quite convincing. So, the brochs' origin will remain a bit of a mystery.

First, were brochs defensive system for sea born threats? This could be possible since there was an external defense system of ramparts and ditches in and around brochs. But there is no evidence of fighting or violent destruction. If the brochs were purely built for defense purposes, then there would be signs of damage from fighting. Furthermore, the people who lived in the area were known to be peaceful fisherman.

Second, were brochs residential areas? However, there is a lack of archaeological proof for this theory. Also, some of them were built in places with a lack of good land. This is problematic. I'll explain. The interior layout of the brochs did not suggest living quarters because they were built on a slope. In fact, the ground floor was rocky and uneven. Moreover, the exit and entrance usually faced a cliff overlooking the sea. If one were to exit the broch, the individual would fall off the cliff. And, it would be simply impossible to enter in it.

Third, were brochs representative of authority and status? Well, if so, why weren't there a steady stream of them? brochs were only built over a 200-year period. Also, wouldn't something of status be built based on a personal preference? This means that each broch would differ, but that isn't the case. brochs are fairly basic standard and do not vary from one to another.

	Reading	Listening
Thesis		
Point 1		
Details		
Point 2		
Details		
Point 3		
Details		

Write your response here.

Student's response (5/5)

Both the reading passage and lecture discuss the brochs. The reading states that while the main purpose of these towers is uncertain, there are many theories to explain why they were built. However, the lecturer refutes the belief presented in the reading by stating that none of them are quite convincing, and the brochs' origin will remain a bit of a mystery.

To begin with, the first theory claims that they were defensive structures and places of refuge for the community and their livestock. The argument is supported by the fact that many of these structures were built on Orkney Island which is located near Scandinavian countries that attacked the Scottish people frequently using their advanced shipbuilding skills. Nevertheless, the lecturer contradicts this idea by pointing out there is no evidence of fighting or violent destruction. Furthermore, the lecturer states that if the brochs were purely built for defense purposes, then there would be signs of damage from fighting. Furthermore, the people who lived in the area were known to be peaceful fisherman.

The second theory in the reading speculates that the structures were dwellings for the residents who were farmers and fishermen. This notion is substantiated by the fact that during the winter, they could store the extra fish in the storage spaces inside the brochs. Yet, the lecturer challenges the argument found in the reading by revealing that there is a lack of archaeological proof for this theory. Moreover, the lecturer elaborates this by mentioning that the interior layout of the brochs did not suggest living quarters because they were built on a slope. In fact, the ground floor was rocky and uneven. Moreover, the exit and entrance usually faced a cliff overlooking the sea.

The third and last point found in the reading says that brochs might have been a symbol of high status and authority. According to the reading passage, this opinion is validated by the fact that it required a considerable amount of manpower to build brochs and wandering artisans were commissioned to create these structures for the wealthy. On the other hand, the lecturer rebuts this theory by explaining that brochs were only built over a 200-year period and it is unlikely to be related to the owner's social status. Moreover, the lecturer asserts that brochs are fairly basic standard and do not vary from one to another, which also suggests that they are not connected to the owners taste or status.

Thus, there is a stark difference between the reading and the listening.

Trending question 12: how to control the red palm weevils

Red palm weevils ?

The Reading

The red palm weevil (Rhynchophorus ferrugineus) is an invasive snout beetle that causes damage to certain palm tree species including coconut, date, oil and sago palms. This pest can cause considerable harm to the date industry in California and Arizona. In the early stages it is difficult to see in the first signs of damage, and when the damage is visible, the palm tree is already severely damaged. However, biologists have discovered some ways that could control these pests.

One method of controlling palm weevils by is cutting down the infested trees. Once palm trees are infested, they will show symptoms like yellow leaves and holes on trunks. If the infested trees are cut down, then the weevils can be prevented from spreading to other trees.

Another method is using a pheromone mixture to trap the pests. The red palm weevil is highly attracted to aggregation pheromones which male weevils release to attract other male and female weevils to palm trees that are suitable for colonization. The male produced pheromone is used since its discovery for capturing male and female insects as weevils will be attracted to pheromone mixture and be caught in the traps. Then, they will be killed by the toxic substance put in the trap without having to kill the infested trees.

The third method is using pesticides. By spraying the pesticides on tree trunks and the soil or injecting insecticides directly into palm trunks, anybody can kill weevils. The preventive spray can be repeated every 3 months, and it will ensure weevils will not appear in the future.

The Listening

The reading suggests three possible ways to control red palm weevil. However, each of these methods has some weaknesses. Thus, controlling the spread of red palm weevil is still a challenging task.

First, in the initial stages, it is hard to monitor the symptoms of infestation. Let me explain further. By the time the palm tree shows symptoms like yellow leaves, the tree has already been infected with the weevil for about a month. So, cutting them down the infested tree would be useless. This is because in one month, weevils have enough time to reproduce and spread to infest other trees.

Second, the poisonous chemicals in traps do not stay active for a long time. If they were to work, people would need to change the traps on a weekly basis. If not, then, the weevil would still survive and spread in surrounding areas. So, unless, these traps are diligently monitored and changed, the poison would be ineffective.

Third, pesticides do not guarantee a weevil's death. Why? Well, there are hundreds of weevils living deep inside the tree, and some will always survive. Even if pesticides were used, a female can lay more than 200 eggs at a time. As a result, they can produce enough offspring to do some serious damage to many trees.

	Reading	Listening
Thesis		
Point 1		
Details		
Point 2		
Details		
Point 3		
Details		

Write your response here.

Student's response (5/5)

Both the reading passage and lecture discuss the red palm weevil. The reading states that biologists have discovered several ways that could control these pests effectively. However, the lecturer refutes the belief presented in the reading by stating that controlling the spread of red palm weevil is still a challenging task.

To begin with, the passage claims that controlling palm weevils by cutting down the infested trees is a feasible method. The argument is supported by the fact that once palm trees are infested, they will show symptoms like yellow leaves and holes on trunks. If the infested trees are cut down, then the weevils can be prevented from spreading to other trees. Nevertheless, the lecturer contradicts this idea by pointing out that it is hard to monitor the symptoms of infestation in the initial stages. Furthermore, the lecturer states that cutting them down the infested tree would be useless. This is because in one month, weevils have enough time to reproduce and spread to infest other trees.

Secondly, the reading mentions that using a pheromone mixture to trap the pests is also a useful method. This notion is substantiated by the fact that the red palm weevil is highly attracted to aggregation pheromones which male weevils release to attract other male and female weevils to palm trees that are suitable for colonization. Once the insects get caught in the traps, they will be killed by the toxic substance put in the trap without having to kill the infested trees. Yet, the lecturer challenges the argument found in the reading by revealing that the poisonous chemicals in traps do not stay active for a long time. Moreover, the lecturer elaborates this by mentioning that if they were to work, people would need to change the traps on a weekly basis. If not, then, the weevil would still survive and spread in surrounding areas.

The third and last point found in the reading says that another effective method is using pesticides. According to the reading passage, this opinion is validated by the fact that the preventive spray can be repeated every 3 months, and it will ensure weevils will not appear in the future. On the other hand, the lecturer rebuts this theory by explaining that pesticides do not guarantee a weevil's death. Moreover, in contrast to the article, the lecturer asserts that even if pesticides were used, female weevils can produce enough offspring to do some serious damage to many trees and they will survive deep inside the tree.
.

Thus, there is a stark difference between the reading and the listening.

Trending question 13: why plants fold at night?

Plants fold at night?

The Reading

Plants aren't as stationary as most people would believe. Many move their tendrils, flowers or leaves in response to stimuli. Plants that open and close their flowers and leaves in response to day and night cycles are called nyctinastic. Scientists are not quite sure why some plants, particularly flowers, have evolved this way. However, there are several theories that could explain this phenomenon.

Some scientists think it happens to protect leaves from getting cold, as nyctinastic movements are associated with diurnal light and temperature changes. Nyctinastic behaviors are adaptive due to the plant being able to reduce its surface area during the nighttime, which can lead to better temperature retention. For example, some African daisies close up to protect themselves from nighttime chill and cold rain.

The second theory claims that it is a way of protection against uninvited insects and other animals. Some flowers save their nectar from nighttime nectar thieves like bats and moths by closing their flowers. Annual plants, particularly, have a limited opportunity to attract daytime pollinators, and they have to save their pollen and nectar by closing in the dark. Accordingly, nyctinasty can be regarded as a highly evolved defense mechanism against a plant's nocturnal predators.

The third theory explains that plants might close simply to avoid nighttime light. Plants can detect different types of lights. Depending on which kind of light is absorbed, some plants establish circadian cycles, which influence the opening and closing of leaves associated with nyctinastic movements. So during the nighttime, they might try not to absorb the harmful light.

The Listening

The reading is correct about some plants folding their leaves during the nighttime. However, none of the assumptions in the reading passage about the reason behind this phenomenon is convincing.

First, plants don't really have to fold their leaves when the temperature drops during the nighttime. This is because leaves contain antifreeze proteins internally. If plants folded their leaves to avoid getting frozen, why don't they fold their leaves every time it gets cold? The truth is whether they fold their leaves or not, the water inside the leaves will get frozen if it's really cold at any time of a day.

Second, the defense strategy theory. Unlike the arguments in the reading passage, the insects that attract the plants and their flowers are actually pollinators. For example, beetles and other nocturnal insects that spread pollen between plants are almost as important as daytime pollinators like bees to produce plants. So plants definitely need them to reproduce even at night. Why do they avoid the opportunities to reproduce more? This doesn't make a lot of sense from an evolutionary perspective.

Finally, do plants hate nighttime light? Well, recent research shows there is no clear relationship between night lights and plant's folding behavior. Scientists tested if plants fold their leaves and flowers during the nighttime if they completely eliminate the moonlight. Guess what? The plants still folded their leaves and flowers even though there was no nighttime light. So the idea that plants fold their leaves to avoid night lights is probably wrong.

	Reading	Listening
Thesis		
Point 1		
Details		
Point 2		
Details		
Point 3		
Details		

Write your response here.

Student's response (5/5)

Both the reading passage and lecture discuss nyctinastic plants which open and close their flowers and leaves in response to day and night cycles. The reading states that there are several theories that could explain this phenomenon. However, the lecturer refutes the belief presented in the reading by stating that none of the assumptions in the reading passage about the reason behind this phenomenon is convincing.

To begin with, some scientists think that it happens to protect leaves from getting cold, as nyctinastic movements are associated with diurnal light and temperature changes. The argument is supported by the fact that nyctinastic behaviors are adaptive due to the plant being able to reduce its surface area during the nighttime, which can lead to better temperature retention. For example, some African daisies close up to protect themselves from nighttime chill and cold rain. Nevertheless, the lecturer contradicts this idea by pointing out plants don't really have to fold their leaves when the temperature drops during the nighttime because leaves contain antifreeze proteins internally. Furthermore, the lecturer states that whether they fold their leaves or not, the water inside the leaves will get frozen if it's really cold at any time of a day.

Secondly, the reading mentions that it might be a way of protection against uninvited insects and other animals. This notion is substantiated by the fact that annual plants, particularly, have a limited opportunity to attract daytime pollinators, and they have to save their pollen and nectar by closing in the dark. Yet, the lecturer challenges the argument found in the reading by revealing that unlike the arguments in the reading passage, the insects that attract the plants and their flowers are actually pollinators. Moreover, the lecturer elaborates this by mentioning that beetles and other nocturnal insects that spread pollen between plants are almost as important as daytime pollinators like bees to produce plants.

The third and last point found in the reading says that plants might close simply to avoid nighttime light. According to the reading passage, this opinion is validated by the fact that plants can detect different types of lights, so during the nighttime, they might try not to absorb the harmful light. On the other hand, the lecturer rebuts this theory by explaining that recent research shows there is no clear relationship between night lights and plant's folding behavior. Moreover, the lecturer emphasizes that scientists tested if plants fold their leaves and flowers during the nighttime if they completely eliminate the moonlight, and they found out the plants still folded their leaves and flowers even though there was no nighttime light.

Thus, there is a stark difference between the reading and the listening.

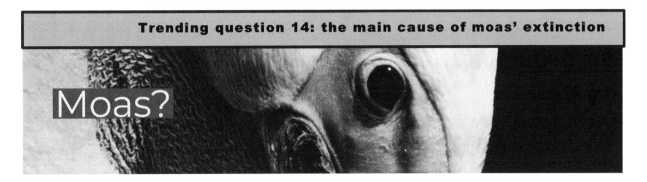

Trending question 14: the main cause of moas' extinction

Moas?

The Reading

A mere 1,000 years ago, nine species of giant, flightless birds known as moas (*Dinornithiformes*) thrived on the islands of New Zealand. The diverse species of moa became extinct about 600 years ago though little is actually known about this as the archaeological record is limited. Their extinction coincided with the arrival of the first humans on the islands in the late 13th century, and scientists have long wondered about the main cause of the moas' decline. There are three possible main causes for their demise.

First, hunting could be the major reason for the Moa birds' extinction. Research indicates that many of the flightless birds disappeared shortly after the arrival of humans to New Zealand. For example, the Maori arrived sometime before 1300, and soon after their arrival, the Moa birds were driven to extinction. This would indicate that humans overhunted the birds. Evidence confirms this as archeologists found heaps and heaps of the birds' bones in archaeological sites

Second, the Maori introduced the Polynesian rat and dog to the island. These animals could have brought diseases that affected the fowl, which shortly eradicated them. The rats also had a varied diet so they also competed with the birds for food sources. Moa birds had never experienced this kind of competition before and would have easily declined.

Third, the Moa birds might have lost their major habitat. Some scientists have pointed out that volcanic eruptions are the key reasons for the species' demise. Also, the Maori, by forest and shrub land burning, considerably altered vegetation on the islands. This action reduced the habitat of many moas.

TOEFL WRITING MASTER COURSE

The Listening

Scientists have long discussed about what caused the extinction of moas in New Zealand. They developed three theories to find the main factor of the extinction of moa birds. However, all of the three theories you read in the reading passage are unconvincing.

First, the hunting theory. Sure, the Maori hunted moas. But moas did not form a significant part of the settlers' diet. They actually preferred fish to birds. Also, a small group of people would have been incapable of wiping out the megafauna species. Using population models, scientists estimated that the founding population on New Zealand was only around 400 people. And even at the hey-day of moa hunting, the human population was only around 1,500 people. This was not enough to kill millions of moa birds in a brief period.

Second, the dogs, rats, and diseases. There isn't much direct evidence to support this theory. Well, moas' eggs were simply too big for rats or dogs to crack. And scientists are trying to identify past diseases of the extinct species by analyzing their remaining DNA samples. However, evidence of epidemic diseases is difficult to determine directly from paleoecological or archaeological remains.

Third, habitat loss. Did volcanic eruptions kill moa birds, as some scientists proposed in a recent paper? What we found out is that the major habitat destruction caused by volcanic eruptions seems to have occurred after moa populations already were depleted. Furthermore, because some habitats that could have sheltered moa populations remained intact after the volcanic eruptions, it would seem that this factor alone cannot explain the extinction of these birds.

	Reading	Listening
Thesis		
Point 1		
Details		
Point 2		
Details		
Point 3		
Details		

Write your response here.

Student's response (5/5)

Both the reading passage and lecture discuss extinct flightless birds known as moas. The reading states that there are three possible main causes for their demise. However, the lecturer refutes the belief presented in the reading by stating that all of the three theories in the reading passage are unconvincing.

To begin with, the passage claims that hunting could be the major reason for the moa birds' extinction. The argument is supported by the fact that the Maori arrived sometime before 1300, and soon after their arrival, the moa birds were driven to extinction. Also, archeologists found heaps and heaps of the birds' bones in archaeological sites. Nevertheless, the lecturer contradicts this idea by pointing out moas did not form a significant part of the settlers' diet. Furthermore, the lecturer states that a small group of people would have been incapable of wiping out the megafauna species. Even at the hey-day of moa hunting, the human population was only around 1,500 people. This was not enough to kill millions of moa birds in a brief period.

Secondly, the reading mentions that the Maori introduced the Polynesian rat and dog to the island, and these animals could have competed against the moas for the food and have brought diseases that affected the fowl, which shortly eradicated them. This notion is substantiated by the fact that moa birds had never experienced this kind of diseases and competition before. Yet, the lecturer challenges the argument found in the reading by revealing that there isn't much direct evidence to support this theory. Moreover, the lecturer elaborates this by mentioning that evidence of epidemic diseases is difficult to determine directly from paleoecological or archaeological remains.

The third and last point found in the reading says that the moa birds might have lost their major habitat. According to the reading passage, this opinion is validated by the fact that there were volcanic eruptions and the Maori, by forest and shrub land burning, considerably altered vegetation on the islands, reducing the habitat of many moas. On the other hand, the lecturer rebuts this theory by explaining that the major habitat destruction caused by volcanic eruptions seems to have occurred after moa populations already were depleted. Moreover, in contrast to the article, the lecturer asserts that because some habitats that could have sheltered moa populations remained intact after the volcanic eruptions, it would seem that this factor alone cannot explain the extinction of these birds.

Thus, there is a stark difference between the reading and the listening.

Trending question 15: banning trade of nonnative species

Nonnative species?

The Reading

Americans legally import several hundred million wild animals every year. These imports generate substantial economic benefits in many sectors of the U.S. economy. However, these benefits come at a significant cost. Some imported animals become invasive while other animals constitute a major pathway for the introduction of diseases into the U.S. In an effort to protect native species, Congress is now considering whether the country has to ban importing non-native species or not. Unfortunately, it is unlikely that such legislation could affect the country positively for several reasons.

First, many owners of exotic animals will have to turn in their pets to the authorities just because their pets are non-native species. It is obviously unethical to take the pets away from the lawful owners, and it might even cause serious social conflicts. So this strategy can have major ethical issues and should be thoroughly reassessed.

Second, the cost of implementing the law might be too high. This might cause significant economic losses in the pet industry and the farming industry. The two industries thrive on international trades of different species, and they might not be able to meet the market demand if there is the trade ban.

Finally, it is unreasonable to apply one same standard to all species. It can be very difficult to decide what non-native organisms are truly invasive in reality. Even if non-native animals are introduced into a new habitat, not all of them will kill the native species or spread diseases. In some cases, non-native species can be beneficial for the environment.

The Listening

The arguments in the reading passage don't really convey the truth about banning international trade of nonnative species. And this policy will actually help protect the environment. Here's why.

First, it's not likely that most pet owners will lose their exotic pets. According to the regulation, only commercially selling nonnative species internationally will be restricted, and you can still keep your pets if the species is not harmful to the native species. So there will be no ethical issues regarding the policy.

Second, sure, we need to consider the financial burden and economic loss for this policy. But nonnative species will cause more harm to the environment as well as the economy if we don't do anything. Because nonnative species have been spreading in the United States so quickly, they have become the major driver of species loss, so if we are worried about extinctions, then we should worry about nonnatives and invasives. Furthermore, they can cause major economic damages as well. Take red fire ants for example. They spread in the UK within several years and are now considered a multibillion-dollar risk due to their impacts on crops.

Third, the standard for the ban and related regulations to control nonnative species will be fair and reasonable. It's true that some species cannot breed or spread in cold regions, but they still might carry diseases. So banning this kind of nonnative species is only fair to protect the ecosystem in America. Also, the government will systematically investigate and evaluate whether a certain species is harmful or not before they ban the species.

	Reading	Listening
Thesis		
Point 1		
Details		
Point 2		
Details		
Point 3		
Details		

Write your response here.

Student's response (5/5)

Both the reading passage and lecture discuss banning importing non-native species to protect native species. The reading states that it is unlikely that such legislation could affect the country positively for several reasons. However, the lecture refutes the belief presented in the reading by stating that this policy will actually help protect the environment.

To begin with, the passage claims that many owners of exotic animals will have to turn in their pets to the authorities just because their pets are non-native species. The argument is supported by the fact that it is unethical to take the pets away from the lawful owners, and it might even cause serious social conflicts. Nevertheless, the lecturer contradicts this idea by pointing out that it's not likely that most pet owners will lose their exotic pets. Furthermore, the lecturer states that only commercially selling nonnative species internationally will be restricted, and you can still keep your pets if the species is not harmful to the native species.

Secondly, the reading mentions that the cost of implementing the law might be too high. This notion is substantiated by the fact that this can cause significant economic losses in the pet industry and the farming industry. Yet, the lecturer challenges the argument found in the reading by revealing that nonnative species will cause more harm to the environment as well as the economy if we don't do anything. Moreover, the lecturer elaborates this by mentioning the example of invasive red fire ants that spread in the UK within several years and are now considered a multibillion-dollar risk due to their impacts on crops. .

The third and last point found in the reading says that it is unreasonable to apply one same standard to all species. According to the reading passage, this opinion is validated by the fact that not all of non-native species will kill the native species or spread diseases. On the other hand, the lecturer rebuts this theory by explaining that the standard for the ban and related regulations to control nonnative species will be fair and reasonable. Moreover, the lecturer asserts that it's true that some species cannot breed or spread in cold regions, but they still might carry diseases. Also, the government will systematically investigate and evaluate whether a certain species is harmful or not before they ban the species.

Thus, there is a stark difference between the reading and the listening.

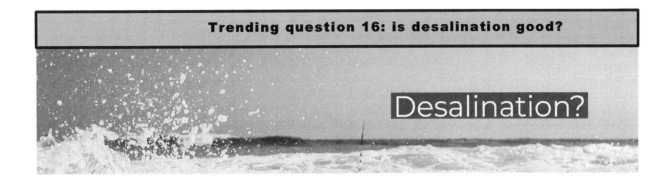

The Reading

Desalination is a process to treat saline sea water and remove dissolved salt in desalination plants with the aim of obtaining drinkable freshwater. Since fresh water shortages are becoming more prevalent worldwide, many desalination plants are being built as a solution to this problem. Although this could solve the water issue marginally, there are several reasons to believe that it causes more problems.

First, desalination can cause more harm to the environment. When the salt is removed from the water, unregulated chemicals pollute waterways and threaten marine life. The chemical from desalination can contaminate any environment where it is placed. If wildlife or vegetation comes in contact with the toxic substances, it could kill them.

Second, the desalination process contributes to the world's greenhouse gas emissions and global warming. The desalination plants could produce high amounts of greenhouse gas emissions because it takes as nine times much energy as surface water treatment and as fourteen times much energy as groundwater protection. The emissions created by desalination contribute to climate change.

Third, desalination produces exceedingly salty brine and it is hard to find a place to discard it. Desalination plants currently are being used increasingly in inland areas of many countries for supplying water for domestic purposes. If these areas are too far away from the sea, the opportunity to dispose the reject brine (also known as concentrate, reject water, or wastewater) in the ocean no longer exists, given that ocean disposal is the common practice for plants located in coastal areas. And even if it is diluted in the seawater, it can be harmful to the environment.

The Listening

Although desalination facilities have some issues, there are solutions to make the technology more sustainable and eco-friendly.

First, let's take a look at the safety of marine animals living around the desalination facilities. We can use sound generators and flashlights to disperse and scare away marine animals whenever they get too close to the facilities. As long as the animals are far away from the place where the harmful substances are released, they will be safe because the chemicals will be naturally spread in the sea water and become less harmful. This will protect marine animals from any danger.

Second, what about global warming? We can build desalination facilities in hot areas where solar energy can be directly produced and used to operate the machines without using fossil fuels. In this way, we can ensure the technology will not contribute to global warming. At the same time, this will help decrease the operational costs dramatically.

Finally, the problem with brine. We can create evaporation ponds to deal with the brine issue. They are especially suitable to dispose of reject brine from inland desalination plants in arid areas due to the abundance of solar energy. Evaporation ponds have long been used for salt production, so the produced salt can be reused or discharged without damaging the oceanic ecosystem.

	Reading	Listening
Thesis		
Point 1		
Details		
Point 2		
Details		
Point 3		
Details		

Write your response here.

Student's response (5/5)

Both the reading passage and lecture discuss desalination, which is a process to treat saline sea water and remove dissolved salt in desalination plants with the aim of obtaining drinkable freshwater. The reading states that there are several reasons to believe that it causes more problems. However, the lecture refutes the belief presented in the reading by stating that although desalination facilities have some issues, there are solutions to make the technology more sustainable and eco-friendly.   .

To begin with, the passage claims that desalination can cause more harm to the environment. The argument is supported by the fact that unregulated chemicals from the facility can pollute waterways and threaten marine life when the salt is removed from the water. Nevertheless, the lecturer contradicts this idea by pointing out We can use sound generators and flashlights to disperse and scare away marine animals whenever they get too close to the facilities. Furthermore, the lecturer states that as long as the animals are far away from the place where the harmful substances are released, they will be safe because the chemicals will be naturally spread in the sea water and become less harmful.

Secondly, the reading mentions that the desalination process contributes to the world's greenhouse gas emissions and global warming. This notion is substantiated by the fact that the desalination plants could produce high amounts of greenhouse gas emissions because it takes as nine times much energy as surface water treatment. Yet, the lecturer challenges the argument found in the reading by revealing that we can build desalination facilities in hot areas where solar energy can be directly produced and used to operate the machines without using fossil fuels. Moreover, the lecturer elaborates this by mentioning that this will help decrease the operational costs and the use of fossil fuels dramatically.

The third and last point found in the reading says that desalination produces exceedingly salty brine and it is hard to find a place to discard it. According to the reading passage, this opinion is validated by the fact that if desalination plants are located too far away from the sea, the opportunity to dispose the reject brine in the ocean no longer exists, and even if it is diluted in the seawater, it can be harmful to the environment. On the other hand, the lecturer rebuts this theory by explaining that we can create evaporation ponds to deal with the brine issue. Moreover, in contrast to the article, the lecturer asserts that they are especially suitable to dispose of reject brine from inland desalination plants in arid areas due to the abundance of solar energy. Also, evaporation ponds have long been used for salt production, so the produced salt can be reused or discharged without damaging the oceanic ecosystem.

Thus, there is a stark difference between the reading and the listening.

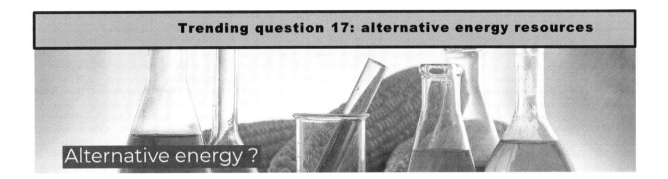

Trending question 17: alternative energy resources

Alternative energy ?

The Reading

Alternative energy is any energy source that doesn't rely on fossil fuel. Governments around the world have been seeking the best type of alternative energy in order to reduce oil dependency, slow global warming, and transition to a more sustainable future. Although scientists have found as many as eleven alternative energy sources, the US government is considering three types of alternative energy as the most feasible replacement of fossil fuels: hydrogen, biofuel-plants, and fuel from the air (CO_2).

First, hydrogen is a possible replacement for fossil fuels. It is a clean fuel, and it only produces water when consumed in a fuel cell. As a result, it can be an attractive fuel option for transportation and electricity generation application. It can also be used to store, move, and deliver energy produced from other sources.

Another affordable source of alternative energy is biofuels. They can be produced from plants or from agricultural, commercial, domestic, and industrial wastes, as long as the waste has a biological origin. Therefore, biofuels prices have been falling and have the potential to be significantly less expensive than gasoline and other fossil fuels. In fact, ethanol is already cheaper than diesel and gasoline.

Lastly, utilizing carbon dioxide from the air is another alternative energy source. By combining carbon dioxide with hydrogen from water, liquid fuel is made. This method takes the carbon dioxide out of the atmosphere to fight climate change. If the carbon dioxide were taken away from the atmosphere and reused, it could slow down global warming drastically.

The Listening

Alternative energy is a hot topic these days because nonrenewable energy like fossil fuels is limited and will be completely gone someday. But like fossil fuels, the three types of alternative energy in the reading passage have their own shortcomings.

First, hydrogen energy. Some people might think that hydrogen energy is always clean. This is not necessarily true. In order to produce hydrogen, we have to heat coal and natural gas. That process emits a lot of carbon dioxide. Also, hydrogen can be tricky to move around because it's extremely light and hard to control. So it can be very expensive to collect even little amounts of it unlike what you read in the passage.

Second, biofuel energy. It's true that the production cost for biofuel has decreased. But, still the fertilizer, water and land required to produce biofuel can create other problems, such as increased pollution and decreased access to food. Did you know that we need the land as twice as large as the entire agricultural area in America to grow corn and sugarcane to produce the amount of biofuel that would only meet 30% of the yearly energy consumption by cars? This is clearly not the best option if you consider the downsides.

Finally, using carbon dioxide from the air. Well, it certainly sounds attractive. But it's currently very inefficient, and it takes all day to collect half a liter of carbon dioxide using this technology. If we want to produce a large amount of CO_2 to replace fossil fuels, we need more advanced technology. And it will take more than a decade to achieve that goal.

	Reading	Listening
Thesis		
Point 1		
Details		
Point 2		
Details		
Point 3		
Details		

Write your response here.

Student's response (5/5)

Both the reading passage and lecture discuss alternative energy that doesn't rely on fossil fuel. The reading states that the US government is considering three types of alternative energy as the most feasible replacement of fossil fuels: hydrogen, biofuel-plants, and fuel from the air (CO2). However, the lecture refutes the belief presented in the reading by stating that like fossil fuels, the three types of alternative energy in the reading passage have their own shortcomings.   .

To begin with, the passage claims that hydrogen is a possible replacement for fossil fuels. The argument is supported by the fact that it can be an attractive fuel option for transportation and electricity generation application. It can also be used to store, move, and deliver energy produced from other sources. Nevertheless, the lecturer contradicts this idea by pointing out hydrogen energy is not necessarily always clean. Furthermore, the lecturer states that in order to produce hydrogen, we have to heat coal and natural gas. That process emits a lot of carbon dioxide. Also, hydrogen can be tricky to move around because it's extremely light and hard to control.

Secondly, the reading mentions that an affordable source of alternative energy is biofuels which can be produced from plants or from agricultural, commercial, domestic, and industrial wastes, as long as the waste has a biological origin. This notion is substantiated by the fact that ethanol is already cheaper than diesel and gasoline. Yet, the lecturer challenges the argument found in the reading by revealing that biofuels are still not affordable. Moreover, the lecturer elaborates this by mentioning that still the fertilizer, water and land required to produce biofuel can create other problems, such as increased pollution and decreased access to food.

The third and last point found in the reading says that utilizing carbon dioxide from the air is another alternative energy source. According to the reading passage, this opinion is validated by the fact that by combining carbon dioxide with hydrogen from water, liquid fuel is made, and this method takes the carbon dioxide out of the atmosphere to fight climate change. On the other hand, the lecturer rebuts this theory by explaining that it's currently very inefficient, and it takes all day to collect half a liter of carbon dioxide using this technology. Moreover, in contrast to the article, the lecturer asserts that it will take more than a decade to replace fossil fuels by using this method.

Thus, there is a stark difference between the reading and the listening.

Trending question 18: was the sabertooth cat social?

Sabertooth Cat?

The Reading

The sabertooth cat (*Smilodon fatalis*) is one of the most iconic extinct animals. The species is well-known for its extremely long canine teeth, which reached up to seven inches in length and extended below the lower jaw of the cat. Because of the anatomical features, it was once known as the saber-toothed tiger, but it is not in the tiger family. A new scientific research suggests that this species has more in common with the African lion than the tiger and is likely to be a social animal, living and hunting like lions today.

First, fossils of broken bones of sabertooth cats show that they were taken care of by group members. Their fossils contained healed injuries and debilitating arthritis. Some scientists suspect that this is a sign that old and wounded cats were supported by other group members.

Second, a large number of sabertooth cats trapped in a tar pit suggest that they hunted in groups. They were probably social cats and went to the tar pit to feed on animals trapped in the sticky goo only to be trapped there altogether. In fact, there, fossils of dire wolves and saber-toothed cats together outnumber herbivores about 9-to-1, leading scientists to speculate that both predators may have formed prides or packs, similar to modern lions and wolves.

Third, they might have needed to live in groups to successfully compete with other big social predators. As they roamed in formidable gangs, sabertooth cats easily predominated at carcasses, which would have been quite popular among other large social carnivores as well. The large number of their bones found with other giant predators show that sabertooth cats encountered dangerous competitors often and it motivated them to abandon a solitary lifestyle.

The Listening

Ever since researchers found many of fossilized Saber tooth cats in a single Tar Pit in California, people have speculated that they were social animals. However, a recent study shows that saber tooth cats indeed shared a common ancestor with all cats living today. And because most living cats are solitary, the saber tooth cats were not likely to be social animals.

First, some scientists point to the sign of recovery from bone injuries as evidence of the cat's taking care of other group members. But this could have been the result of scavenging. Even when the big cat got injured, it would have still been able to look for dead animals and eventually recovered from the injury. So the evidence is not convincing enough.

Second, what about the multiple fossilized cats that were discovered in one tar pit? Well, they could've been attracted to crying animals in the tar pit one by one. In fact, there were many other fossilized solitary animals found in the same pit. The big cats might have tried to pounce on some sinking prey in the pit individually. Then, they must have become mired in the tar. The predator and prey died together.

Finally, some scientists argue that saber tooth cats had to live in groups to compete with large predators. Then, how can you explain today's solitary animals like tigers? Tigers have to compete against other large predators, but they are territorial and usually solitary in nature. They don't need to live in groups because they know how to survive alone. This nature could apply to saber tooth cats as well.

	Reading	Listening
Thesis		
Point 1		
Details		
Point 2		
Details		
Point 3		
Details		

Write your response here.

Student's response (5/5)

Both the reading passage and lecture discuss the sabertooth cat, which is one of the most iconic extinct animals. The reading states that this species has more in common with the African lion than the tiger and is likely to be a social animal, living and hunting like lions today. However, the lecture refutes the belief presented in the reading by stating that because most living cats are solitary, the saber tooth cats were not likely to be social animals.

To begin with, the passage claims that fossils of broken bones of sabertooth cats show that they were taken care of by group members. The argument is supported by the fact that their fossils contained healed injuries and debilitating arthritis, and this is a sign that old and wounded cats were supported by other group members. Nevertheless, the lecturer contradicts this idea by pointing out this could have been the result of scavenging. Furthermore, the lecturer states that even when the big cat got injured, it would have still been able to look for dead animals and eventually recovered from the injury.

Secondly, the reading mentions that a large number of sabertooth cats trapped in a tar pit suggest that they hunted in groups. This notion is substantiated by the fact that there, fossils of dire wolves and saber-toothed cats together outnumber herbivores about 9-to-1, leading scientists to speculate that both predators may have formed prides or packs, similar to modern lions and wolves. Yet, the lecturer challenges the argument found in the reading by revealing that they could've been attracted to crying animals in the tar pit one by one. Moreover, the lecturer elaborates this by mentioning that there were many other fossilized solitary animals found in the same pit. The big cats might have tried to pounce on some sinking prey in the pit individually.

The third and last point found in the reading says that they might have needed to live in groups to successfully compete with other big social predators. According to the reading passage, this opinion is validated by the fact that the large number of their bones found with other giant predators show that sabertooth cats encountered dangerous competitors often, and it motivated them to abandon a solitary lifestyle. On the other hand, the lecturer rebuts this theory by explaining that tigers have to compete against other large predators, but they are territorial and usually solitary in nature. Moreover, in contrast to the article, the lecturer asserts that they don't need to live in groups because they know how to survive alone. This nature could apply to saber tooth cats as well.

.

Thus, there is a stark difference between the reading and the listening.

The Reading

Owl parrots (Strigops Habroptilus), also known as the kakapo, are a large species of flightless nocturnal birds commonly found in New Zealand. They are possibly one of the longest living birds; however, their population is declining. There are three probable main reasons for their decline.

One reason for the owl parrot's decline might be their low rate of reproduction. Female owl parrots do not reproduce every year because of the lack of their food supplies. They are particularly fond of the fruit of the rimu tree, and will feed on it exclusively during the breeding season. This means that the birds could lay eggs every once in a few years when trees are plentiful of fruits. This is a serious issue since they can only raise one or two owls per season.

Another reason might be the low survival rate of owl parrots' eggs due to their nocturnal nature. The mother owl parrot incubates the eggs faithfully during the daytime, but during the night she leaves to search for food since owl parrots are active at night. As a result, many of the eggs will get ill from the cold and the mother's absence. Studies found out that 40% of their eggs are infertile and 15% of them die as embryos because of the cold weather during the night.

The last possible reason might be owl parrots are hunted and eaten by a number of predators, specifically the stoats, weasel like animals brought over by European settlers. Owl parrots have become part of a stoat's regular diet. Also, if an opportunity arises, stoats may overkill owl parrots to store. Thus, predation would be one of the causes for the owl parrots decline.

The Listening

What you just read about owl parrots is no longer true. Back in the 1970s, the situation looked really bad, and owl parrot's numbers were so low that experts feared the species would not survive. But now the world's rarest parrot is on the rebound. There are many reasons to believe that these parrots will actually thrive in the future.

First, the concern about their selective food and breeding. Owl parrots do love rimu tree fruit. However, they can change their dietary staples if it's necessary. For example, they can eat apples, which are more abundant. As long as there is enough food, they will try to breed. Because they live for up to 120 years, they can have many chicks throughout their lives.

Second, the issues with their eggs. For many years, conservationists have helped the birds find better nesting places where the eggs don't get cold. Not only that, they also have taken care of the chicks and eggs during the night time when the mother birds leave the eggs unguarded. Some of the conservationists even hand-reared the chicks until they released the young birds into the wild. So every year, the birds lay more eggs, and most of them actually survive now.

Finally, the predators. Owl parrots used to be in trouble because they got hunted by feral cats called stoats. But about twenty years ago, the population was relocated to safety on three islands. The small islands are far away from the mainland and there is no predator for the birds. So the parrots have continued to bounce back and it's no longer on the verge of extinction.

	Reading	Listening
Thesis		
Point 1		
Details		
Point 2		
Details		
Point 3		
Details		

Write your response here.

Student's response (5/5)

Both the reading passage and lecture discuss owl parrots, which is a large species of flightless nocturnal birds. The reading states that there are three probable main reasons for their decline. However, the lecturer refutes the belief presented in the reading by stating that there are many reasons to believe that these parrots will actually thrive in the future.

To begin with, the passage claims that one reason for the owl parrot's decline might be their low rate of reproduction. The argument is supported by the fact that the birds could lay eggs every once in a few years when rimu trees are plentiful of fruits, and they can only raise one or two owls per season. Nevertheless, the lecturer contradicts this idea by pointing out the birds can change their dietary staples if it's necessary. Furthermore, the lecturer states that they can eat apples, which are more abundant. Also, because they live for up to 120 years, they can have many chicks throughout their lives.

Secondly, the reading mentions that another reason might be the low survival rate of owl parrots' eggs due to their nocturnal nature. This notion is substantiated by the fact that during the night, the mother owl leaves to search for food, and many of the eggs get ill from the cold and the mother's absence which is evidenced in the data. Yet, the lecturer challenges the argument found in the reading by revealing that for many years, conservationists have helped the birds find better nesting places where the eggs don't get cold. Moreover, the lecturer elaborates this by mentioning that the conservationists also have taken care of the chicks and eggs during the night time when the mother birds leave the eggs unguarded. So every year, the birds lay more eggs, and most of them actually survive now.

The third and last point found in the reading says that another possible reason might be owl parrots are hunted and eaten by a number of predators, specifically the stoats, weasel like animals brought over by European settlers. According to the reading passage, this opinion is validated by the fact that owl parrots have become part of a stoat's regular diet. On the other hand, the lecturer rebuts this theory by explaining that twenty years ago, the population was relocated to safety on three islands. Moreover, the lecturer asserts that the small islands are far away from the mainland and there is no predator for the birds. So the parrots have continued to bounce back and it's no longer on the verge of extinction.

Thus, there is a stark difference between the reading and the listening.

Trending question 20: what happened to the people on Mary Celeste

The Reading

In 1872, a newly built American ship Mary Celeste set sail from New York Harbor on its way to Italy with valuable cargo. On board were the ship's captain, his wife, their young daughter, and seven crew members. However, less than a month later, on December 5, a passing Canadian ship called Dei Gratia found Mary Celeste at full sail and adrift off the coast of Portugal, with no sign of survivors. Aside from several feet of water at the bottom of the ship and a missing lifeboat, the ship was undamaged and loaded with six months' worth of food and water. Thus, over the years, people have developed many theories to explain what might have happened to the ten people who had sailed aboard the ship.

One theory holds that pirates could have attacked the ship and killed the crew. The ship was found near the Azores, which is an archipelago known for frequent piracy, since so many ships passed through them. North African pirates or French pirates could have targeted the brand-new cargo ship with a relatively small number of crewmembers.

The second theory contends that the ship could have caught on fire because some empty inflammable alcohol bottles were found during the investigation. Whether due to turbulence or leaky barrels, toxic fumes from the alcohol may have escaped and have caused a small explosion. The captain of the ship may have then given the order to temporarily abandon ship, with everyone piling into the lifeboat to sail behind the Mary Celeste until the danger had passed.

The third theory proposes that the ship could have encountered a tornado at sea, as the bottom of the ship was filled with water when the ship was discovered. This might have caused visible damage and some waterlogging, making the captain and the crew assume that the ship was about to sink. This might have led them to decide clamber onto the lifeboat and eventually perish into the stormy sea.

The Listening

What happened to the crew of the Mary Celeste? There have been many theories on this mystery of the high seas, but none of them is convincing.

First, could North African pirates have attacked the ship and killed the crew? But the ship hadn't been looted. When the crew of the Dei Gratia discovered the Mary Celeste, there was no sign of lost items or money. There were some coins and checks in the cabin, but nobody seemed to try to get them. Also, if pirates had in reality attacked the ship, there would've had been some evidence indicating fights or intrusion. The investigators couldn't find any proof.

Second, sure, a massive explosion could have been triggered by a careless crew man who smoked near the alcohol in the cargo hold. However, there was no burn mark caused by an explosion or fire on board. Also, no one could get the smell of the alcohol fumes outside the hold when the ship was found. Keep in mind that the ship was found only ten days after it went missing. So the empty barrels of alcohol could have been actually loaded empty in New York.

Finally, it's true that when the crew of Dei Gratia salvaged the Mary Celeste, they found a lot of water in the hold. This led to the theory that Mary Celeste would have been hit by a severe storm and the captain ordered the crew to evacuate. But there was no such storm reported in that area of Atlantic during the time the Mary Celeste was abandoned. Also, the water level was not enough for the captain to order evacuation. The ship was still in sail worthy condition. So it's unreasonable to think that the experienced captain abandoned the safe ship and jumped on the small boat in the stormy sea.

	Reading	Listening
Thesis		
Point 1		
Details		
Point 2		
Details		
Point 3		
Details		

Write your response here.

Student's response (5/5)

Both the reading passage and lecture discuss American ship Mary Celeste which was at full sail and adrift off the coast of Portugal, with no sign of survivors in 1872. The reading states that over the years, people have developed many convincing theories to explain what might have happened to the ten people who had sailed aboard the ship. However, the lecture refutes the belief presented in the reading by stating that none of them is convincing.

To begin with, the passage claims that pirates could have attacked the ship and killed the crew. The argument is supported by the fact that the ship was found near the Azores, which is an archipelago known for frequent piracy, since so many ships passed through them. Nevertheless, the lecturer contradicts this idea by pointing out the ship hadn't been looted. Furthermore, the lecturer states that when the crew of the Dei Gratia discovered the Mary Celeste, there was no sign of lost items or money. There were some coins and checks in the cabin, but nobody seemed to try to get them. Also, the investigators couldn't find any sign of fights or intrusion.

Secondly, the reading mentions that the ship could have caught on fire because some empty inflammable alcohol bottles were found during the investigation. This notion is substantiated by the possibility that whether due to turbulence or leaky barrels, toxic fumes from the alcohol may have escaped and have caused a small explosion. Yet, the lecturer challenges the argument found in the reading by revealing that there was no burn mark caused by an explosion or fire on board. Moreover, the lecturer elaborates this by mentioning that no one could get the smell of the alcohol fumes outside the hold when the ship was found even though the ship was found only ten days after it went missing.

The third and last point found in the reading says that the ship could have encountered a tornado at sea, as the bottom of the ship was filled with water when the ship was discovered. According to the reading passage, this opinion is validated by the fact that there was visible damage and some waterlogging in the ship, and it might have made the captain and the crew assume that the ship was about to sink. On the other hand, the lecturer rebuts this theory by explaining that there was no such storm reported in that area of Atlantic during the time the Mary Celeste was abandoned. Moreover, in contrast to the article, the lecturer asserts that the water level was not enough for the captain to order evacuation. The ship was still in sail worthy condition. So it's unreasonable to think that the experienced captain abandoned the safe ship and jumped on the small boat in the stormy sea.

Thus, there is a stark difference between the reading and the listening.

PART 2

The Independent Task

Dirty & Simple Tips

1. The format of the question

(7) First and foremost, the TOEFL essay is not exactly required to be an academic essay although "the independent task essay" can be broadly considered to be an "argumentative essay", which is a type of essay that presents arguments about both sides of an issue to convince the readers to accept the writer's idea as true, by using anecdotes, statistics, facts, figures, and all sorts of compelling evidence.

(8) Some of the noticeable differences between the academic essay and the TOEFL essay are the following:

Argumentative essay	TOEFL independent task essay
The first paragraph must contain a clear and well-developed thesis with relevant reasons to support the argument.	The first paragraph doesn't always have to present a clear thesis with supporting arguments as long as the writer's general view on the topic is stated there and more supporting details can be found throughout the essay.
You have to provide well-researched, factual, comprehensive, and up-to-date information to support the thesis statement and consider other points of view.	You can make up any proof you want. You can choose to draw examples and evidence from history, literature, and your own life, and there will be no penalty even if your story is not accurate.
The rater will focus on the thoroughness and reliability of the essay to evaluate its quality.	The rater will focus on the level of development and flow of the narrative to evaluate its quality.
Grammatical errors are not accepted.	Grammatical errors may not affect your score if the sentences are understandable.

(9) Within 30 minutes, you are required to type your response at the computer by investigating a provided topic; gathering, generating, and assessing evidence; and establishing your position on the topic in a clear and coherent manner.

(10) The minimum number of words you can use for this essay is 300 words while there is no maximum word limit.

(11) You will be given the essay prompt with a specific topic first. You have to respond to either an open-ended topic (it is completely up to your opinion) or choose your side between two given choices.

(12) Your essay needs to address the specific topic provided in the prompt. If

you miss the point of the question and write about something irrelevant, your essay will get a score of zero even if it is well written. Hence, you have to carefully analyze the prompt and identify the key idea before writing your essay. The following are two sample prompts that have appeared on the real TOEFL tests.

Open-ended topic

(e.g.) Holidays honor people or events. If you could create a new holiday, what person or event would it honor and how would you want people to celebrate it?

A topic with two options

(e.g.) Your friend has the opportunity to study in either one of two majors (fields of study). Which one of the following two types of majors do you think is a better choice and why?

A) A major that would allow your friend to complete his or her studies and get a degree faster (so that your friend can start working full-time soon).

B) A major that would require more years of study but is likely to lead to more and better employment opportunities and job offers in the future.

(13)   Types of questions

   A) Agree/disagree

      (e.g.) Do you agree or disagree with the following statement? It is easier to become an educated person today than it was in the past. Use reasons and examples to support your position.

   B) Choice/preference

      (e.g.) Some high school teachers (teachers of students aged 14-18) spend most of their class time lecturing (speaking) while their students listen and take notes. Other high school teachers spend most of their class time on discussion and projects that require students to participate by sharing their ideas with the class.

      Which of these two approaches do you think is more effective for student learning and why?

   C) "If" questions

      (e.g.) If you had the opportunity to visit a foreign country for two weeks, which country would you like to visit?

D) Your opinion and why

(e.g.) Describe a custom from your country that you would like people from other countries to adopt.

2. Skill Development

(1) Here is an effective way to develop a relevant and strong opinion.

    A. Find the point of the task.
    B. Replace the unknown with the known (something/somebody you know well).
    C. Offer two/three reasons for your argument: consider the good things about your side and the bad things about the other option.

(e.g.) Holidays honor people or events. If you could create a new holiday, what person or event would it honor and how would you want people to celebrate it?

Find the point of the task: "Create a new holiday to celebrate somebody."

Replace the unknown with the known (something/somebody you know well): "I would like to create a new holiday to celebrate the life of Stan Lee, the writer of many Marvel comic books."

Offer two/three reasons for your argument: First, many people like Marvel characters. Second, his creativity is deeply inspiring. Finally, he revitalized the comic book industry.

(e.g.) Your friend has the opportunity to study in either one of two majors (fields of study). Which one of the following two types of majors do you think is a better choice and why?

    a) A major that would allow your friend to complete his or her studies and get a degree faster (so that your friend can start working full-time soon).

    b) A major that would require more years of study but is likely to lead to more and better employment opportunities and job offers in the future.

Find the point of the task: "I believe that my friend should choose the major that requires a longer time to complete but is likely to lead to better employment opportunities in the future."

Replace the unknown with the known (something/somebody you know well): "For example, if he goes to a medical school, he has to study for more than four years to finish his course. However, this investment and commitment can be easily justified as he will become a doctor."

Offer two/three reasons for your argument: First, an education should be beneficial and should provide the student the better future. Second, more time in school will allow him to gain more profound and specialized education. Finally, it is a once in lifetime chance to change his life and gain higher social status.

(2) The organization of your essay should look like the following.

Topic & opinion: I would like to create a new holiday to celebrate the life of Stan Lee, the writer of many Marvel comic books. 　　1.　A hook and the topic 　　2.　Point of contention 　　3.　Thesis
Argument 1 First, many people like Marvel characters. (point: topic sentence) 　　1.　Topic sentence 　　2.　Explanation 　　3.　Example or evidence 　　4.　Supporting details 　　5.　Conclusion
Argument 2 Second, his creativity is deeply inspiring. (point: topic sentence) 　　1.　Topic sentence 　　2.　Explanation 　　3.　Example or evidence 　　4.　Supporting details 　　5.　Conclusion
Argument 3 Finally, he revitalized the comic book industry. (point: topic sentence) 　　1.　Topic sentence 　　2.　Explanation 　　3.　Example or evidence 　　4.　Supporting details 　　5.　Conclusion
Conclusion: There are many reasons to create a new holiday to remember Stan Lee's contributions to the world. This will allow people to have a day of celebration of a great artist who has been extremely popular, inspiring, and revolutionary. 　　1.　Restatement of the thesis 　　2.　General summary or a big thought

(3) Does the essay always have to look like that? The answer is "no".

Your essay may have only two body paragraphs and still score high if it is thoroughly developed and meet the criteria ETS uses.

(4) What are the criteria for the essay? Your essay will be given an overall score from zero to five by two ETS raters and an automatic scoring system.

DOs

　　1.　Does your essay have a relevant and strong opinion or idea about the topic given to you?

　　2.　Does your essay have specific detailed reasons and examples to support your answer?

3. Is your essay organized with proper and effective transitions?

4. Is your essay divided into different paragraphs including introduction, body, and conclusion?

5. Does your essay use natural and intelligent (academic) vocabulary or expressions?

Don'ts

1. Does your essay repeatedly use the same idea or words?

2. Does your essay change its main opinion abruptly?

3. Does your essay have serious grammatical errors that affect the meaning of the overall argument?

(5) Key expressions

A) Positive point

1. Reading has a significant number of benefits for young learners.

2. Playing games can help you reduce stress no matter how much stress you have at work, in your personal relationships, or countless other issues faced in daily life.

3. Zoos offer visitors the chance to view animals that are confined in an enclosure.

4. Zoos provide an educational resource. The modern zoo plays a critical role in educating children and families about the different animals with whom we share this planet.

5. A national park provides a protected environment for endangered animals.

6. Computers are useful in all sorts of contexts, from crunching numeric data to typing up documents and sending emails.

7. Rewarding kids for meeting certain goals is often effective. It can help them know what to do and feel acknowledged and compensated for their hard work.

8. Classroom discussion increases students' interests and engagement; lectures mixed with discussions can help maintain students' focus.

B) Negative point

1. As for the disadvantages of a zoo, the facilities that are offered can be abused for personal or political gain.

2. Computers have disadvantages as well, contributing to sedentary lifestyles, causing eye strain and potentially interfering with childhood play.

3. Industrialization contributes to negative environmental externalities, such as pollution, increased greenhouse gas emissions, and global warming. Pollution is the most common by-product of industrialization.

4. Side effects of overworking such as added stress, staring at the computer for too long, or lack of time to unwind, all negatively impact your sleep. Chronic sleep loss raises the risk of many illnesses, such as obesity and heart disease, and also has short-term effects on your memory.

5. People struggling with video game addiction may be at a greater risk for depression, loneliness, social anxiety, anger, and feelings of shame or embarrassment for spending so much time playing games.

6. As the addiction worsens, video game addicts tend to spend more time playing and less quality time with friends, family, or significant others.

7. In the longer term, this type of sustained muscle fatigue can lead to more serious joint problems and back pain.

c) Facts

1. Studies have shown that staying mentally stimulated can slow the progress of Alzheimer's and Dementia, since keeping your brain active and engaged prevents it from losing power.

2. Computers can be used as research tools, scouring the internet and online databases for information about all different topics.

3. Classroom discussion is a practice in which the instructor and students share views on a specific topic previously lectured. Promoting and facilitating classroom discussions can not only help students learn from one another but also help students understand and retain the lecture better.

4. Now, a new study also highlights the hazards of prolonged standing at work.

D) **Examples**

1. It's true what they say about studying abroad: it's an experience you'll never forget. I just came back to the US after studying in Italy for three months and I learned so much while I was there. Not just a new culture and a new language, but also about traveling and living abroad.

2. Family relationships can set the tone for how one feels about family, and traumatic events regarding family can challenge those views and feelings. The sudden death of my mother was the event that challenged my family to see if the ties that bind were strong enough to hold. It was also an event that would determine the outcome of my feelings about my family.

3. An incident in my life involving a conflict occurred a few summers ago. It took place in a small town when my family and I were there on vacation. I had an inner conflict with decision-making.

4. *Let me take Edison for example.*

3. The advanced template

(1) Even if you don't know how to develop your essay within the time limit, fear not. If you utilize the following template well, you are likely to get the highest score in this section. This templated is developed by reflecting on all of the ETS criteria we have just learned.

(2) Depending on your preference, you might want to use just two of the body paragraphs even though the template contains three body paragraphs.

Introduction	**It is incontrovertible that** (the relevant fact to the topic)
	After all, (give a clear and ultimate reason for that)
	Yet, there could be a debate over (the specific topic)
	Some might argue that (the opposite side)
	However, I believe that (your side) **for two/three reasons**.
Body 1	**To begin with, it is important that** (the argument)
	In other words, (explain the argument)
	From my personal experience, I remember/learned that (the activity)
	This was because (the cause)
	Soon, I realized that (the effect)
	This clearly depicts that (make a point)
Body 2	**Another major consideration is that** (the argument)
	This means that (explain the argument)
	To illustrate this, one should see no further than (the activity/ a group of people)
	There are so many (cases)
	This is due to (the cause)
	Consequently, (effect)
	Therefore, we can assume that (make a point)
Body 3 (optional)	**Lastly, one should consider** (the argument)
	In view of this, (explain the argument)
	To put it simply, (effect)
	This indicates that (there is a clear causality.)
	Hence, (make a point)
Conclusion	**In summary, there are numerous reasons to believe that** (your point)
	This will allow .... (reasons)

PART 2

The Independent Task

Practice Tests

Practice 1-3: People

On the Internet – People

The following articles are about the topics that actually appear on the TOEFL test.

Roommates	
1	**I know bad roommates.** Last year my noisy, inconsiderate roommate constantly woke me up around three in the morning. Her side of the room was always messy and covered with clothes. Her suitcase from Christmas break didn't move from the middle of the room all second semester. She used my makeup. She ate my food. And she brought a kitten to live in our room (which, just by the way, is totally against dorm policies). Oh, and it gave our room fleas.
2	**Respect Each Other** First and foremost, you need to respect your roommate. I know, sometimes, it's really hard. But when you're living in tight quarters with the same person (or people), if you don't respect them first, they sure as hell won't respect you. **Be Considerate** If your roommate is sleeping or attempting to sleep, keep the noise and light levels down. If your roommate is studying, don't have loud conversations in the same room. **Keep It Clean** Seriously, I cannot emphasize how many horror stories I have heard about dirty roommates. Hair in the shower, toothpaste gelled to the sink, bathrooms littered with magazines or dirty clothes. It's gross. Respect means keeping your side of the room clean. Now, I'll admit, I'm a rather messy person. I don't like picking up my clothes, the concept of drawers, or making my bed. But at least once a week, I pick all of my stuff up off the ground and make my side of the room clean again. It's a good habit to get into and it will make you a better roommate. **Keep Your Hands Off Their Stuff** Just don't do it, especially with personal items like brushes and stuff like that. It's gross. If you really need to borrow something of theirs, always, always ask before you do. Set Ground Rules Now that we've reviewed what it means to respect each other, you and your roommate should also establish some ground rules. It may sound a little Type-A personality, but it's really just better to set up what each of your pet peeves are before the year gets rolling. For instance, I really don't like it when people have phone conversations in the room while I'm studying. https://lifehacker.com/how-to-be-a-good-roommate-and-deal-with-those-who-arent-5611551

Teachers	
1	**Teachers play vital roles in the lives of the students in their classrooms.** Teachers are best known for the role of educating the students that are placed in their care. Beyond that, teachers serve many other roles in the classroom. Teachers set the tone of their classrooms, build a warm environment, mentor and nurture students, become role models, and listen and look for signs of trouble.
2	**The most common role a teacher plays in the classroom is to teach knowledge to children.** Teachers teach in many ways including lectures, small group activities and hands-on learning activities. Teachers also play an important role in the classroom when it comes to the environment. Students often mimic a teacher's actions. If the teacher prepares a warm, happy environment, students are more likely to be happy.

	Teachers typically do not think of themselves as role models, however, inadvertently they are. Students spend a great deal of time with their teacher and therefore, the teacher becomes a role model to them. This can be a positive or negative effect depending on the teacher. Mentoring is a way a teacher encourages students to strive to be the best they can. This also includes encouraging students to enjoy learning. Part of mentoring consists of listening to students. By taking time to listen to what students say, teachers impart to students a sense of ownership in the classroom. This helps build their confidence and helps them want to be successful. Another role played by teachers is a protector role. Teachers are taught to look for signs of trouble in the students. When students' behaviors change or physical signs of abuse are noticed, teachers are required to look into the problem. Teachers must follow faculty procedures when it comes to following up on all signs of trouble. https://www.education.gov.gy/web/index.php/teachers/tips-for-teaching/item/1603-roles-of-a-teacher-in-the-classroom

Young people	
1	You, as a teenager yourself, may well have different answers than those of us who are well past our teen years. From my perspective, looking back at my teen years, I see that there were good and bad things about those years. **The major advantage of being a teen is that there are so many possibilities.** Your whole life, as they say, is ahead of you. You do not know what will happen to you in that life. There are still very few careers that you know you cannot have at this point in your life. You do not know where you will live. You do not know who you will fall in love with. All of these things are really exciting things that you still get to wonder about and will find out about.
2	**But that is also the major disadvantage of being a teen.** You don't really know what your life will be and so there is more stress, perhaps, than we older people have. At my age, I know more or less what sort of work I'll be doing the rest of my life (I think). I know who I've fallen in love with and I've been married to her for more than 20 years. I know how many kids I'll have and I know what sex they are. I'm settled and comfortable. As a teen, there is not that kind of stability and certainty in your life. There is much more in the way of worries and insecurities. What if I never find a job? What if I never find love? All of these sorts of worries are more prevalent in a teen's life. https://www.enotes.com/homework-help/what-advantages-disadvantages-being-teenager-402524

Old people	
1	**1. Seniors are one of the happiest demographics of people in the world today.** Multiple studies and surveys show that seniors are one of the happiest groups of people in the world today. Compared to the middle-aged demographics, they are significantly happier with their circumstances. Part of the reason for this perspective is that they've had more time to develop their coping mechanisms. Finances can play a role in this perspective as well. As we age, there is also more time to become comfortable with who we are. **2. You have more time to spend with loved ones.** One of the best components of a retirement is that you have additional time to spend with the people you love. Leisurely lunches with friends, overnights with the grandkids, or that trip overseas you've always wanted to take can make aging joyous.

	3. Seniors still have an opportunity to pursue their dreams. As we age, many of us put off our own dreams to care for our families. We focus on making sure that the power stays on, food gets put on the table, and having our children find success in their endeavors. It's never too late to become the person you've always wanted to be. You can still learn a new language, write a book, take a trip, or take up a new hobby, like painting. Some seniors even turn their passions from this discovery process into a second lucrative career later in life. **5. Wisdom comes from the aging process.** As we age, the wisdom of experience creates new perspectives. Older people look at the entire experience of life instead of focusing on a specific event which inspires regret. We gain more control over our emotions as we age as well, which typically deepens the relationships formed with a significant other. Aging offers better social skills, a higher emotional intelligence, and the ability to think of multiple resolutions to problems. **6. You feel a sense of accomplishment.** As the aging process continues, you can look back upon your life and feel the pride which comes when you accomplish great things. Our greatest feats in life come from the ordinary.
2	**1. Senior care comes at a higher cost.** As we get older, the cost for our healthcare needs steadily rises. If you find yourself needing a nursing home or an assisted living facility, the costs involved could be as much as the average person in the United States makes in a year. **2. There is always a safety concern for seniors.** Even seniors who are in fantastic shape have a higher risk of experience specific health conditions. You're more likely to break bones as you get older as calcium becomes harder to absorb. Eyesight quality decreases, which can make it difficult to drive places or maintain your independence. It may become difficult to walk. At some point, almost everyone needs some extra in-home care to maintain their lifestyle as they grow older. **3. It becomes difficult to maintain your property.** As you get older, you'll find that your daily living activities take longer to complete. Items that are on your to-do list that were once simple fixes become elaborate chores. Trying to find a contractor to help you take care of the lawn, clean your home, or even change your light bulbs can become a major headache quickly. **4. Aging brings about an increase in loneliness.** Seniors must make a proactive effort to maintain their social connections. Even when Facebook and other online conversations, texting and video calls are not the same as a face-to-face conversation. **5. It is more difficult to get around as you get older.** If your health declines to the point that you are no longer authorized to drive, then you're forced to rely on public transportation, family, or friends to help you get around. https://connectusfund.org/14-biggest-pros-and-cons-of-aging

Community	
1	Community is "a unified body of individuals, such as a body of persons of common and especially

	professional interests scattered through a larger society." Your neighborhood is a community, your gym or your professional organization could also be a community. It makes sense that the communities we gravitate toward, both personally and professionally, are made up of like-minded people who make us feel uplifted, encouraged, inspired, and supported.
2	**Having a community is having a support network.** As research has proven, our environment has a serious impact on who we are as a person. Motivational speaker Jim Rohn famously said, "We are the average of the five people we spend the most time with." Having a strong support network in place can influence your thinking and make you more likely to achieve your goals. **Communities are a safe space to share knowledge and can foster collective creativity and innovation.** Theodore Zeldin said, "Conversation is a meeting of minds with different memories and habits. When minds meet, they don't just exchange facts: they transform them, reshape them, draw different implications from them, engage in new trains of thought. Conversation doesn't just reshuffle the cards: it creates new cards." Communities made up of like-minded individuals can be a safe space to share and build upon knowledge and experience. In fact, many of us feel a deeper sense of satisfaction and more passion and commitment toward an idea when we are able to connect with people who have similar backgrounds. Today's technology enables knowledge to flow freely, empowering collaboration, creativity, and innovation. **Communities offer valuable networking opportunities.** Some people feel a sense of discomfort when they think about the act of networking. Think, forced small talk with complete strangers, but networking doesn't have to take place at an awkward mixer. Networking is simply the act of connecting with people. Bill Nye said, "Everyone you will ever meet knows something you don't." Networking inside your community can help you build relationships, develop your current career, and even stay up-to-date on industry trends. http://biobridges.com/blog/what-is-community-and-why-is-it-important/ Communities are helpful to join or create because they provide support to the individuals who are impacted by the daily stress, struggles and chaos of modern life. Consider the five questions that I noted as you determine what type of community you are looking to build or join. Going in with a clear intention allows you to garner exactly what it is that you want to gain from having a group of people that you can trust and rely on. https://www.huffpost.com/entry/the-importance-of-community_b_6978186 When you take a look back at history, you'll find that the most influential people in the world never got there alone. Instead they were part of a community of friends, peers, and mentors who helped push them to become the people they were destined to be. What a community of like-minded people provides, more than anything else, is a support network of people who are going through the exact same journey as you. Even if they're at different stages of the journey, they'll understand what it is you're going through and be able to give you the support you need

	to keep going. https://www.huffpost.com/entry/the-5-benefits-of-communi_b_10390826

Supervisor

1	What Are the Attributes of a Good Supervisor? Being a good supervisor starts with an honest appraisal of your leadership style to identify areas that need improvement. **Interactive Communication Skills** Without an ability to make your desires clear, your employees won't know how to accomplish the tasks you delegate. Equally important is understanding and incorporating employee feedback. A good supervisor interacts effectively with her employees, maintaining open lines of communication to ensure she stays informed about project progress and brewing problems. **Empathy and Compassion** If you can't place yourself in your employees' shoes, you can't lead them effectively. For example, a parent might not be able to work overtime, or an employee going through a hard time might need temporary special considerations. Be as accommodating as possible in the face of genuine need, and your employees will be loyal in return. **Ability to Delegate** A good supervisor excels in delegating tasks to those employees best-equipped to handle them. Proper delegation streamlines a project, ensuring efficiency and maximizing profitability. Poor delegation, on the other hand, compromises a project. For example, if you delegate a vital task to an inexperienced employee, the whole project can slow. Worse, you might have to backtrack to fix errors, an inefficient use of time and resources. **Flexibility when Possible** No single approach to management works in every situation. Rather, a good supervisor chooses tactics based on the situation. For example, as a deadline nears, you might adopt a hard-line approach to ensure the work gets done. But your employees can't operate at full-speed perpetually, so adopt a more relaxed approach during downtime between projects. This gives employees time to recover their strength. **Maintaining a Positive Attitude** Supervisors who come to work with a positive attitude make the office environment a great place to be. They use this attitude when solving problems, so the issues don't loom as large as they might. And positive attitudes are contagious. People tend to take on the attitude of their environment, and being positive is a good one to assume. Make sure to celebrate wins to acknowledge good work of the staff. https://smallbusiness.chron.com/attributes-good-supervisor-55605.html
2	8 Traits Bad Bosses Have In Common

1. Micromanagement

For people to excel, they should have the freedom to plan and execute on their own, based on the objectives set by their bosses. Micromanaging not only limits an employee's ability to deliver success, but also causes the boss to stretch themselves too thin and not lead the company well. Micromanagement leads to distrust and only serves to slow a business down long term, so it's best to avoid it.

2. A One-Size-Fits-All Approach To Management

Every employee is different, so the only way to accomplish business objects is to tailor your managing, coaching and communication to best fit that individual. Bad bosses don't show an appetite to learn, and instead offer a one-size-fits-all approach ("this is my style of being a boss"). They are impatient when an employee doesn't "get it" and they won't invest the time in learning the right way to manage each individual.

3. Doesn't Lead By Example

In my experience, the best leaders are those who are in the trenches and execute. The worst have always been those who think they are too good to get their hands dirty and who don't even know how to execute on the company's service, or don't understand or use the products. True leaders lead by example. That includes rolling up your sleeves, sitting in with different teams and departments, helping out and executing to fully understand their day to day.

4. Lack Of Empathy

If an employee makes a mistake, take the time to understand where things went wrong before passing judgment. Having empathy shows employees their leader cares and is invested in their future. Not having that quality will almost ensure high employee turnover and low productivity.

5. Focused On Blame, Rather Than Solutions And Support

Everyone makes mistakes. Good leaders minimize the damage by looking for solutions: more training, changing jobs, changing strategies or goals, etc. Good leaders do not pounce on mistakes as a way to prop up their position, casting blame so they can deflect any blame that comes their way. A worker blames the machinery, the supervisor blames the worker, the manager blames the supervisor, the head of the company blames the manager. Somewhere along this chain of denial, what's wrong with saying, "Let's focus on solutions so it doesn't happen again"?

6. Takes Credit For Others' Work

Taking credit for the work of subordinates makes for ineffective leaders because it dampens any motivation employees might have. After all, people want to be recognized and challenged with even tougher goals. Upon realizing that there's no credit for the taking, it is natural for any employee to lose their drive. A boss taking all the limelight is not just unfair to employees, but also detrimental to their careers.

7. No Respect For Employees

Ineffective leaders typically don't have mutual respect with their employees. A leader needs to do the work, listen to their employees, learn constantly and have respect for the employees they manage. Without these four elements, employees will have a difficult time giving their manager respect and the potential for a great relationship is instantly ruined. Employees want to feel that their opinions matter and that their leaders value their input. It doesn't make sense to hire someone unless they will add value to your business. Make them feel that every day by giving them responsibility and respecting them enough to step back and do what you hired them to do. When they feel respected, they will respect you in return.

8. A Sense Of Entitlement Rather Than A Sense Of Duty

A bad boss expects to be served, and the vision they share with their staff is their own rather than the company's. That kind of leadership often results in a toxic work environment, which typically stifles a business's growth.

https://www.forbes.com/sites/theyec/2018/09/25/12-traits-bad-bosses-have-in-common/#158cfedc6266

Young children	
1	The eight things every child needs to thrive

Security
Kids must feel safe and sound, with their basic survival needs met: shelter, food, clothing, medical care and protection from harm.
Stability
Stability comes from family and community. Ideally, a family remains together in a stable household, but when that's not possible, it's important to disrupt the child's life as little as possible. Kids and families should be a part of larger units to give them a sense of belonging, tradition and cultural continuity.
Consistency
No "good cop, bad cop." Parents should synchronize their parenting and make sure important values stay consistent.
Emotional support
Parents' words and actions should encourage kids' trust, respect, self-esteem and, ultimately, independence.
Love
Saying and showing you love your kids can overcome almost any parenting "mistakes" you might make. Even when your kids have disobeyed, angered, frustrated and rebelled against you, show them you love them and that you'll always love them.
Education
Make sure your kids get the best possible education for their future. This includes school, of course, but it also includes the invaluable life lessons you provide during the time you spend together.
Positive role models
Parents are their kids' first and most important role models. Instill your values and teach children empathy by being the kind of person you want them to become.
Structure
Rules, boundaries, and limits: Without them, kids are forced to be adults before they are ready, and they lose respect for you and other adults.

https://www.childrenscolorado.org/conditions-and-advice/parenting/parenting-articles/what-children-need/

Celebrities	
1	**For better or worse, celebrities have a powerful impact on how teens view themselves and how they see the world. In fact, it's easy to underestimate how much celebrities influence teenage attitudes and behavior.** Celebrities can have a positive influence on youth. In fact, they can serve as role models. But famous singers, actors, and other celebrities can also provide unhealthy examples. In particular, celebrity influence on body image and substance use is often detrimental to teen mental health. Therefore, teenagers need guidance on how to interpret celebrities' influence. Adults can engage with kids around media. In addition, they therefore support how children process what they're seeing and hearing. Moreover, parents and teachers can use celebrities' stories as entry points into important discussions about health and personal choices. Research shows that teen body image is shaped by many factors. These include friends and family, where the teen lives, and their cultural background. However, celebrity images have a profound impact on teen body image. The *Today Show* and aol.com collaborated on the "Ideal to Real" body image survey. As a result, the survey found that 80 percent of teen girls compare themselves to images they see of celebrities. Moreover, among those girls, almost half said that celebrity images make them feel dissatisfied with the way they look.
2	Celebrities influence teens in other ways as well. **When stars post images of themselves drinking or smoking on social media, they normalize substance use.** Furthermore, they make it appear attractive and cool. Moreover, teens often idolize celebrities and want to be like them. Therefore, if they see images on Instagram of a favorite singer or actor using drugs or drinking, they might be tempted to do so as well. For example, a University of Pittsburgh School of Medicine study looked at teenagers who frequently listen to music that contains references to marijuana. Subsequently, they found that these teens are more likely to use the drug than teens with less exposure to such lyrics. In addition, for every hour that American teens listen to music, they hear more than three references to different brand names of alcohol. Researchers say that this might contribute to teen drinking. In addition, researchers at Dartmouth Medical School found that movie characters who smoke cigarettes influence teens to try smoking. Therefore, media influence on youth can contribute to risk-taking behaviors. **Celebrities Can Raise Awareness and Reduce Stigma** Many celebrities are open about their struggles with addiction and mental health. As a result, they help to reduce stigma and raise awareness. For example, before reportedly entering rehab after an apparent drug overdose earlier this summer, Demi Lovato released a song about relapse, titled "Sober." Consequently, the song inspired young people nationwide to open up about their substance abuse and mental health challenges. https://www.newportacademy.com/resources/empowering-teens/celebrities-influence/

Peer pressure	
1	Who Are Your Peers? Your friends — your peers — are **people your age or close to it who have experiences and interests similar to yours.** You and your friends make dozens of decisions every day,

and you influence each other's choices and behaviors. This is often positive — it's human nature to listen to and learn from other people in your age group. As you become more independent, your peers naturally play a greater role in your life. As school and other activities take you away from home, you may spend more time with peers than you do with your parents and siblings. You'll probably develop close friendships with some of your peers, and you may feel so connected to them that they are like an extended family.

Besides close friends, your peers include other kids you know who are the same age — like people in your grade, church, sports team, or community. These peers also influence you by the way they dress and act, things they're involved in, and the attitudes they show. It's natural for people to identify with and compare themselves to their peers as they consider how they wish to be (or think they should be), or what they want to achieve. People are influenced by peers because they want to fit in, be like peers they admire, do what others are doing, or have what others have.

You might not hear a lot about it, but peers have a profoundly positive influence on each other and play important roles in each other's lives:

- **Friendship.** Among peers you can find friendship and acceptance, and share experiences that can build lasting bonds.
- **Positive examples.** Peers set plenty of good examples for each other. Having peers who are committed to doing well in school or to doing their best in a sport can influence you to be more goal-oriented, too. Peers who are kind and loyal influence you to build these qualities in yourself. Even peers you've never met can be role models! For example, watching someone your age compete in the Olympics, give a piano concert, or spearhead a community project might inspire you to go after a dream of your own.
- **Feedback and advice.** Your friends listen and give you feedback as you try out new ideas, explore belief, and discuss problems. Peers can help you make decisions, too: what courses to take; whether to get your hair cut, let it grow, or dye it; how to handle a family argument. Peers often give each other good advice. Your friends will be quick to tell you when they think you're making a mistake or doing something risky.
- **Socializing.** Your peer group gives you opportunities to try out new social skills. Getting to know lots of different people — such as classmates or teammates — gives you a chance to learn how to expand your circle of friends, build relationships, and work out differences. You may have peers you agree or disagree with, compete with, or team with, peers you admire, and peers you don't want to be like.
- **Encouragement.** Peers encourage you to work hard to get the solo in the concert, help you study, listen and support you when you're upset or troubled, and empathize with you when they've experienced similar difficulties.

2	The pressure to conform (to do what others are doing) can be powerful and hard to resist. A person might feel pressure to do something just because others are doing it (or say they are). Peer pressure can influence a person to do something that is relatively harmless — or something that has more serious consequences. Giving in to the pressure to dress a certain way is one thing — going along with the crowd to drink or smoke is another. People may feel pressure to conform so they fit in or are accepted, or so they don't feel awkward or uncomfortable. When people are unsure of what to do in a social situation, they naturally look to others for cues about what is and isn't acceptable. But these situations can be opportunities to figure out what is right for you. There's no magic to standing up to peer pressure, but it does take courage — yours: https://kidshealth.org/en/teens/peer-pressure.html?WT.ac=ctg

Peer pressure and influence might result in children:

- choosing the same clothes, hairstyle or jewellery as their friends
- listening to the same music or watching the same TV shows as their friends
- changing the way they talk, or the words they use
- doing risky things or breaking rules
- working harder at school, or not working as hard
- dating or taking part in sexual activities
- smoking or using alcohol or other drugs.

https://raisingchildren.net.au/teens/behaviour/peers-friends-trends/peer-influence

The purpose of parenting	
1	From reading to infants to helping with schoolwork to enunciating values as the child grows, parents exert enormous influence over their children's development, success, and overall happiness. They are, however, not the only influences—especially after children enter school and begin interacting with the world at large. It's especially important that parents work to give children the best start possible, but it's also important for parents to recognize that kids come into the world with their own temperaments, personalities, and goals. Ultimately, while parents may want to push their child down a certain path, a parents' job is to provide an interface with the world that eventually prepares a child for complete independence and the ability to pursue whatever path *they* choose.
2	**How to Parent Successfully** To parent effectively, it's not enough to simply avoid the obvious dangers like abuse, neglect, or overindulgence. Indeed, The National Academy of Sciences delineates four major responsibilities for parents: maintaining children's health and safety, promoting their emotional well-being, instilling social skills, and preparing children intellectually. Numerous studies suggest that the best-adjusted children are reared by parents who find a way to combine warmth and sensitivity with clear behavioral expectations. Parents may find the Four C's to be a helpful acronym: care (showing acceptance and affection), consistency (maintaining a stable environment), choices (allowing the child to develop autonomy), and consequences (applying repercussions of choices, whether positive or negative). **What Are Unhealthy Parenting Styles?** Not every parenting style is in the child's best interest. There is such a thing as overparenting, which can cripple children as they move into adulthood and render them unable to cope with the merest setbacks. Two well-known examples of overparenting styles include "helicopter parenting," in which children are excessively monitored and kept out of harm's way, and "snowplow parenting," in which potential obstacles are removed from a child's path. Both can negatively impact a child's later independence, mental health, and self-esteem. https://www.psychologytoday.com/us/basics/parenting

Day person & night person	
1	Chances are you already know whether you're a morning person or a night person (and if you don't, just ask your significant other). What you might not know is that social scientists use pretty specific—and, by academic standards, pretty casual—names for these two chronotypes. "Larks" are up and at it early in

the morning, and tend to hit the sack at a respectable evening hour; "owls" are most alert at night, and typically turn in long after dark.

Larks aren't healthier, wealthier, or wiser.

Ben Franklin, that jack-of-all-Founding Fathers, once advocated for a lark lifestyle in a famous saying: "early to bed and early to rise makes a man healthy, wealthy, and wise." But a pair of epidemiologists at Southampton University in England—perhaps still bitter over that whole Revolution thing—directly challenged Franklin's tyranny of the morning people in a 1998 paper for *BMJ*.

The researchers analyzed a national sample of men and women who'd been surveyed years earlier on sleep patterns as well as measures related to, well, health, wealth, and wisdom. There were 356 larks in the group (in bed before 11 p.m., up before 8 a.m.) and 318 owls (in bed after 11, up after 8). Contrary to Franklin's decree, night owls had larger incomes and more access to cars than did morning larks; the two chronotypes also scored roughly the same on a cognitive test and showed no self- or doctor-reported health differences.

"We found no evidence … that following Franklin's advice about going to bed and getting up early was associated with any health, socioeconomic, or cognitive advantage," the authors concluded. "If anything, owls were wealthier than larks, though there was no difference in their health or wisdom."

2

Owls are partial to bad habits—namely, smoking and drinking.

Franklin's adage about morning types being healthy does seem to hold in one regard: larks might be a little less vulnerable than owls to substance abuse.

A number of studies support these connections. One analysis of 676 adults from a Finnish twin cohort found that evening types were much more likely to be current or lifelong smokers, much less likely to stop smoking, and at much higher risk for nicotine dependence as per diagnostic criteria, compared with morning folks. Another study of 537 individuals found that owls consume more alcohol than larks.

That's not a huge surprise when you consider that nightlife is conducive to drinking and smoking. What's less clear to researchers is whether evening people are more inclined to partake because they're already out late, or whether the addictive behaviors—at least in the case of a stimulant like cigarettes—keep them up longer in the first.

Larks are persistent, cooperative, agreeable, conscientious, and proactive.

The tendency to drink and smoke among evening types is consistent with a broad personality trait that researchers call "novelty-seeking." Multiple studies have connected owls with that characteristic. In a 2011 paper notable for focusing on adolescents, Randler and a Heidelberg colleague discovered a link between night people and novelty-seeking already present among German teenagers (technically, ages 12 to 18).

The same research—which evaluated 346 test participants on both chronotype and a through character inventory—found that larks scored higher than owls (as well people who didn't fit in either category) in terms of persistence and cooperation. These positive traits among morning types built on other personality work from Randler showing that larks tended to be more agreeable and conscientious, and that they tend to be more proactive than owls. Showoffs.

Morning types may be happier.

2	This disconnect between conventional daytime expectations and nighttime preference might make life harder for owls in general. Social scientists call this outcome "social jetlag": evening types that force themselves to wake up early and perform at their peak during the day might cause themselves some sleep loss and emotional distress. They might also be less happy as a result. That's the argument put forth by two University of Toronto psychologists in a 2012 paper. After assessing a sample of 435 young adults (17 to 38) and 297 older adults (59 to 79) on their chronotypes as well as their current moods, the researchers found that morning people had higher positive affect across the board, compared with night people. Mood isn't the same as general happiness, but the findings may speak in part to the challenges owls face on a daily basis. "Waking up early may indeed make one happy as a lark," the researchers conclude in the journal *Emotion*. https://www.fastcompany.com/3046391/morning-people-vs-night-people-9-insights-backed-by-science

Neighbors	
1	**You're a Good Neighbor if:** • You welcome neighbors with a smile and introduce yourself. A simple wave or greeting when you see each other can open the lines of communication and establish a positive and friendly relationship with your neighbor. This is especially important in the very beginning as first impressions can make or break a relationship with your neighbor. • Help your neighbor carry groceries or large, heavy items that they are having trouble doing alone. It's not fun moving a couch when you only went outside to get the mail, but it will create a perfect precedent with your neighbor. • You keep your dog from barking all hours of the night and clean up after their mess. Invest in a bark collar if need be.
2	**You're a Bad Neighbor if:** • You blast your music throughout the night. • Don't clean up after your pets. • Don't mow the lawn or keep up with the exterior maintenance of your home. • If you're a condominium resident, the hallway is not a part of your residence. Keep personal belongings inside your unit. • Not returning any items you borrow from your neighbor. https://www.neighborhoods.com/blog/good-neighbors-vs-bad-neighbors

	Sons and daughters
1	Sons are still more likely than daughters to take over the family business. Haley Banwart grew up on her family's farm. She is working and getting a master's degree at Iowa State. Her brother plans to return home to farm after college. Growing up on their family farm in West Bend, Iowa, Haley Banwart and her brother Jack were like any other farm kids. They did chores, participated in 4-H and even raised cattle together. "My brother and I have had the same amount of responsibilities," says Banwart, 22. "I can drive a tractor, I can bale square hay. But it was just expected that my brother would return home." Her family never really discussed it. "It was always kind of the unwritten rule," she says. "My brother would go back and farm" — and she'd find another path. She says her grandmother always made sure the boys and the girls were all doing all the different kinds of jobs. Her mom worked on the farm alongside brothers and Riediger says her aunts were also involved. Her dad, on the other hand, would help out as needed, but had a job off-farm. Gender norms are starting to shift though, albeit slowly. The 2012 Census of Agriculture counted women as nearly a third of the nation's farmers. Some women start small vegetable operations, whereas some work on big commercial farms. Others do the books for their husbands. But all these women in farming are more likely to raise their hands and be counted as "farmers" than women of generations past. "There's this whole phenomenon of women across the country taking on greater leadership roles and...it's a little slower for agriculture," Schultz says. Many young women in agriculture say they hope to farm and raise children. As they do, the next generation of farm kids may inherit a different world, one where parents will naturally want their daughters to someday take over their family farm. https://www.npr.org/sections/thesalt/2016/08/10/488706582/sons-are-still-more-likely-than-daughters-to-take-over-the-family-farm
2	**Do parents treat sons and daughters differently?** Whilst **parents** may not intend to **treat sons and daughters differently**, research shows that they **do**. **Sons** appear to get preferential treatment in that they receive more helpful praise, more time is invested in them, and their abilities are often thought of in higher regard. https://blog.innerdrive.co.uk/do-parents-treat-their-sons-and-daughters-differently
3	Why Daughters Are Better Than Sons -- At Least Financially Ever wonder when your kid will move out of the house for good and stop treating you like an ATM? If that kid is a boy, you may have longer to wait than if you'd had a girl. After age 18, daughters are less likely than sons to move back home or need a financial hand from mom and dad, according to a new survey. And not only are those grown-up daughters more financially independent, they are also more likely to provide care for their aging parents down the road. http://money.com/money/2861530/daughter-better-investment-than-son/

Historical figures	
1	**We can learn lessons from historical figures.** Thomas A. Edison holds 1,093 patents to his name. His inventions include the phonograph, the motion picture camera, and the long-lasting, practical electric light bulb. "I have not failed; I've just found 10,000 ways that don't work." — Thomas A. Edison Fantastic lesson on persistence. Ever-curious, Thomas A. Edison, one of the greatest inventors of all times, shows that failures are not failures but rather failed experiments. In the past 12 years alone, I've started 6 businesses, and by most people's standards, they would be qualified as failures. I didn't grow the companies in size, I didn't generate sustainable revenues, and ultimately most got shut down. What people don't realize is that when you view life as a series of experiments, there is no such thing as failure, as long as you learn something from the experience. Did Edison learn from his experiences? You bet! How else would he have accomplished that much? It's not by accident that some of the most successful people of all times have failed repeatedly. Their curiosity, passion/obsession, and persistence are what made them rise above the crowd. For those of you who have read my stories before, you know I'm very much into that experimental mindset with the 3 skills I deliberately learn every month. I don't become a professional in all skills, but the lessons I learn from each is invaluable to my present or future success.
2	**Carnegie inspired many to work on themselves through his teachings.** Growing up as a poor farm-boy, he had to make his way up in the world. He is a living proof that no matter the financial background you come from, you can become what you want to become. And that starts with action. Being a poor farm-boy myself, I can attest that it's not only possible to thrive even in less-than-optimal situations but it can sometimes be a blessing in disguise. https://medium.com/epic-quotes/epic-quotes-from-epic-people-part-i-caa3e5e34d5

Family	
1	Everyone needs a family. Whether that is the one you're born into, married into, or even formed through unbreakable friendships, the truth is you need it. **But why is family important?**
2	**Family is the critical structure that allows development and autonomy.** Family is key to our psychological, identity, relational and even physical development, and it starts with the parent-infant relationship for all of us. The attachment relationship between parent and infant begins to set the neurological basis for self-regulation and coping with emotion and obstacles in life, for seeing oneself as a valuable and lovable person, for trust that others will soothe and meet your needs. As you

grow up, your family unit serves as the base for a sense of security and safety in the world, allowing you to take risks and explore the world in ways that allow you to grow, to succeed, to relate to others and to feel a stable sense of identity.

Family is the filter through which we experience, understand, get to know—and know ourselves through—culture.
In this exact sense, there are as many unique cultures (experiences of culture) as there are families. And even within each individual family, there is a variation of cultural experience because each new member of the family is born into a unique time in the life of the family. And though each cultural experience is novel and nuanced well beyond a general ability to access the myriad facets of the influences of culture, it is nonetheless there. And it is constantly influencing and causing effects that can only be understood and made use of from within the ways in which each family expresses, manifests and makes use of a more general sense of culture. For instance, a married couple will inevitably bring into their developing family their own history and expressions of their own cultural experience (ways of interacting with their family, ways of expressing love and affection, raising children and many other behaviors associated with culture). And this is true even when the people in the couple look as if they share a number of significant cultural markers (say, race, religion, sexual orientation, etc.).

Family is to teach us how to love unconditionally.
Family is to teach us how to love without conditions, without reasons, without convenience, without excuses, simply to love. And when the day is done, I wouldn't have it any other way, because my family is mine forever and that's why family's so important.

https://upjourney.com/why-is-family-important

Leader and Followers
1

"If your actions inspire others to dream more, learn more, do more and become more, you are a leader."
– John Quincy Adams

You help others without expecting anything in return.

Have you found yourself finishing tasks at work because it needs to be done not because you have been asked? Or volunteering to help someone move just because? Great leaders do things to help others and not expect anything else in return from anyone.

You treat everyone equally despite how you feel.

Whether it is at work or at school, you treat people equally regardless of your feelings. Being a leader means that you must be able to treat everyone with respect, even if you are having a bad day. If you are the kind of person to leave your personal life's luggage at the door of the establishment you work or study at, that is impressive. Not many can do that.

You are responsible, even though you don't want to be.

There are some of days where it just sucks to live and you want to just lay in bed. You want to stay there, eat your meals there and go back to sleep. Whatever has got you down, you push it aside and you force yourself out of bed because you have responsibilities. You have people counting on you and you have things to get done that will not finish themselves. There are some that don't make it out of bed, and just

2	
	push those tasks aside for another day, but not you. This is called being responsible. Leaders need be responsible when no one else wants to be.

You are approachable.

If you find yourself giving advice to your friends and coworkers more than you are taking it, it means that they value your opinion and are the go to person for help. Being approachable is an important quality for a leader to have because no one really wants to work for someone without an open door policy. People trust your judgment and confide in you: take pride in that. |
| 2 | You follow rules rather than breaking them.

There are a number of fundamental differences between leaders and followers, with their unique approach to rules providing a prominent example. While leaders are receptive to the need for change and capable of breaking rules for the greater good, followers are far more inclined to adhere to the status quo without question. There is also an issue of courage, as those with leadership potential have far greater conviction when it comes to driving change and pushing even unpopular reforms. If you have aspirations of leadership, you must therefore develop an analytical mind that can identify opportunities for change and remain strong in the face of criticism.

You are risk averse.

In the pursuit of change, you may also need to take risks in addition to breaking rules. As a result of this, the stereotypical leader has a huge appetite for risk and is willing to trust their instinct when making difficult decisions. In contrast, followers tend to be risk-averse in their nature and are unwilling to take actions or decisions that may trigger a negative reaction in some. If you wish to overcome this innate fear and emerge as a strong leader that can control individual situations, you will need to step out of your comfort zone and start taking calculated risks for the greater good.

You lack a clear and translatable vision.

Famous essayist and poet Jonathon Swift was renowned for his interpretation of being a visionary, which he described as the art 'of seeing what is invisible to others'. This also provides a clear distinction between leaders and followers, as while the former have a clear and concise understand of what they want to achieve in the long-term the latter are more inclined to live for the moment. This is why clarity of thought is such an important leadership quality, as is the willingness to make sacrifices today for the good of tomorrow. If you want to develop your leadership skills, it is imperative that you are able to prioritize clearly defined, long-term goals that can be achieved through a series of stages.

https://www.lifehack.org/287415/10-signs-youre-follower-instead-leader |

Entertainers with High Salaries	
1	**Why are some jobs more 'valuable'?**

According to Kate Phelan, a lecturer in the School of Global, Urban and Social studies at RMIT, there are two main factors affecting how much a job is "valued" and, therefore, paid: |

	1.How many people can perform the role 2.Whether the role generates revenue or prestige for the employer "A teacher can't generate as much value as an Olympic runner can — and there are more people who can do that job [teaching]," she explains. "And so … teachers can't threaten to go elsewhere and ask for more in light of that." Sports stars and celebrities are idolized for their talents and, oftentimes, their looks, so it makes sense that brands are keen to profit off their cachet through job contracts and endorsement deals. That makes their monetary value far higher than the average teacher or nurse.
2	**For Dr Ferracioli there's a fundamental flaw in our current economic system: it's unfair for some people to reap profits and others to scrape by because, ultimately, every role matters.** "It's very naive to think that when you perform well in your profession it's all due to your hard work," she says. "A surgeon can only perform surgeries if there are qualified nurses working at his or her hospital, and a CEO can only strike good deals for the company if he or she is not busy answering phone calls every day." Dr Ferracioli says, whether we realise it or not, we're able to do our jobs because of the "army of people" who clean the streets, make the train run, care for our children and perform other "less valued" tasks. "It's only if we all come together and do our bit that we as a society can provide essential services and create the conditions for us to do the things we love — [be that] brain surgery or being an executive or journalist or, in my case, a philosopher." Are we unconsciously widening the gap? If you're not a CEO, HR person or manager, the wealth gap might seem like someone else's problem, but according to our experts, we all play a part. "A lot of the time people don't realize how they are strengthening some of the more toxic aspects of capitalism," says Professor Hobbs. "People might say this is a terrible system, but they're not actually fighting against it … they're not taking their money away from the celebrity cult." https://www.abc.net.au/life/why-celebrities-make-so-much-money/11209894

Classmates/ study group	
1	**Read on to learn advantages of group study.** **1.** Procrastination Solution

Because study groups meet at regular times, attending students cannot procrastinate. If alone, a student might postpone studying until the night before class or may put off learning even longer. When in a study group, however, students must be present at a specific time, and they must be prepared to contribute to the study session. You'll stay on top of your subject throughout the semester—a real plus when exam times roll around.

2. Learn Faster

Working together, students in study groups can generally learn faster than students working alone. For instance, some part of the textbook that seems completely confusing to you could be quite clear to another student. In a study group, you can learn quickly by simply asking a question, instead of spending valuable time puzzling over the difficulty alone. In addition, you can help your fellow students when they have difficulties understanding something that you do understand.

3. Get New Perspectives

If you study by yourself, you will always see your material from the same perspective—yours. While this may not be a problem, getting fresh perspectives on a topic can help you learn it more thoroughly. As you listen and ask questions, you will soon start noticing a variety of different viewpoints on the same idea. This will force you to think more about your position and will, therefore, develop your critical thinking skills while helping you study.

https://www.speedyprep.com/blog/7-benefits-of-study-groups/

More Study Group Pros

1) Learn more as you can break down the test and study materials and split them up.
2) Pull on one another's strengths
3) Get help with your weaknesses
4) Learn to see the test and test questions in different ways
5) Pull on collective resources, such as study guides and so on.

| 2 | **Unfortunately there are some cons to forming a study group or studying with your classmates. Let's take a look a few of these cons.**
1) There will be differing levels of seriousness among your friends.
2) There is a risk that your study sessions could deviate into socializing instead of working.
3) Not everyone will pull his or her weight equally.
4) Egos may get in the way and interfere with overall progress.
5) People may not stick with the study group long enough to get the desired results and to justify the time it took to start the group in the first place.

https://mycollegeguide.org/blog/2011/12/5-pros-cons-study-groups/ |

Practice 1

Do you agree or disagree with the following statement? Playing computer games is not beneficial for a child's learning.

Write your response here.

<table>
</table>

Student's response (5/5)

It is incontrovertible that many children pass their time playing computer games as they are so prevalent today and children find these games entertaining and enjoyable. Yet, there could be a debate over the impact computer games can have on children's learning and development. Some might argue that all computer games are detrimental to children's mind and could even alter their brain performance and structure. However, I believe that some computer games can be actually instrumental to a quality education in general for two reasons.

To begin with, it is important that a child learns problem-solving skills. In other words, certain computer games could actually help children develop the analytical skills needed for their education. From my personal experiences, I observed that some of my progressive teachers would allow students to play a few selective computer games, and these games were related to something we had learned in the previous lecture. Some of these games required us to use various cognitive skills while solving a puzzle, riddle or problem in order to move to the next level. It made learning more interesting and engaging. This was because the activity was more conducive to education and enabled us to use multiple perspectives and have fun. Soon I realized that these types of computer games could be useful brain exercises. This clearly depicts that not all games are a waste of time.

Another major consideration is that there are many video games that can teach children academic subjects like history or literature. These games are not only entertaining but also very educational. To illustrate this, one should look no further than a video game called Oregon Trail. The game is set during the time when many pioneers decided to head west. The path was well known to be arduous and dangerous, and the game replicates the obstacles the pioneers had to face as they moved westward. If children played this game, they could experience going through the Oregon Trail as if they were really there surpassing perils constantly. Consequently, they would learn exactly what people in the past went through, and they may be able to remember the historical event better. It could even draw further interests on the topic that otherwise might be quite boring. Therefore, we can assume that computer games have a lot more to offer educationally.

In summary, there are numerous reasons to believe that playing certain types of computer games can have a positive impact on children. This will allow them to increase their problem solving skills and help learn about various academic subjects.

Consider the following:

Children now have a huge array of choices regarding when and how they play their computer games. Playing some types of computer games may have some minor advantages for children, according to many studies. Too much time spent playing computer games, however, also have the potential for negative impacts on emotional, physical and social development. For example, teens who spend too much time playing computer games -- particularly those games with violent content -- risk having problems with violent and aggressive behavior. Also, the level of screen brightness and the length of time that children spend focusing on the computer monitor sometimes lead to eye strain. Most importantly, too much time in front of the computer playing games reduces the time kids spend engaging in outside activities, participating in hobbies, playing with friends and using their imaginations. Computer games, even interactive gaming, fail to give children the experience of social interaction with others.

(https://www.livestrong.com/article/48504-negative-effects-computer-games-children/)

Practice 2

Do you agree or disagree with the following statement? Teenagers should get a part-time job while going to school.

Write your response here.

Student's response (5/5)

It is incontrovertible that job experiences can teach us about how the real world works as well as what we can achieve as individuals. After all, career is one of the most essential aspects of our lives, through which we contribute to our communities. Yet, there could be a debate over allowing teenagers to get a part time job while in school. Some might argue that instead of getting a job, teenagers just need to focus on school and extracurricular activities. However, I believe that teenagers should get a part-time job for two reasons.

To begin with, teenagers should learn financial responsibility. In other words, by working, they can earn their own money and appreciate the items that they might buy. From my personal experience, I had a part-time job while in high school and learned the value of earning money. This was because I wanted to become more independent and buy some items for myself, such as a bike and a computer. Soon, however, I realized that working could be tough. I had to wake up early in the morning and go to work that was far away from my place. Because I had to work so hard for my paycheck, I became very careful about my spending and learned to save money. This clearly depicts that having a job is a crucial life lesson.

Another major consideration is that a teenager must learn to balance the many tasks in life, such as work and study. This means that he or she would need to maintain his or her grades while working for extra money. To illustrate this, one should see no further than learning to prioritize the tasks we need to accomplish as a student and a part-time cashier. There are so many things he or she must accomplish that the student must learn to prioritize his or her every day activities in order to achieve the objectives like studying for a test or going to work on time. Through this process, the student will learn what is considered most important at a particular moment and try not to waste time. If teenagers don't learn to prioritize what must be done, it would be difficult for them to become completely independent since they would have to rely on someone else to complete their tasks. Therefore, we can assume that having a part-time job helps prepare a teenager for balancing the many responsibilities that an independent adult would encounter.

In summary, there are numerous reasons to believe that having a part-time job can have a positive impact on teenagers. This will allow them to appreciate the value of their money and develop effective time management skills to multitask while working and studying simultaneously.

Consider the following:

From bagging groceries to making smoothies, the first job a teenager has can provide him or her with a sense of independence, not to mention extra cash to spend on important teenage things like fast food, cool sneakers and computer games.

Working as a teenager has the obvious benefit of earning money to spend and save. But more than a simple influx of cash, working allows teens to appreciate the value of money and what it means to earn a dollar.

Parents of teens need to weigh the benefits against the potential pitfalls (like time away from schoolwork and extracurricular activities) to determine whether working is a good choice.

Having a part-time job during high school also means time away from studies and extracurricular activities. If a teen doesn't know how to prioritize, something is going to suffer

https://lifestyle.howstuffworks.com/family/parenting/tweens-teens/teens-work-part-time-while-in-school.htm

Practice 3

Do you agree or disagree with the following statement? People should choose a job that is satisfying instead of choosing a job that offers a high salary.

Write your response here.

| |
| |
| |
| |
| |

_____

Student's response (5/5)

_____

It is incontrovertible that people want to choose a great job after years of education. After all, most people spend many hours in the workplace and should gain some gratification from their professions. Yet, there could be a debate over the choice between a satisfying job and a high paying job for more fulfillments in life. Some might prefer a high paying job regardless of their job satisfaction to worry less financially. However, I believe that a satisfying job is better for three reasons.

To begin with, it is important that one is happy with his or her job whether it pays well or not. In other words, we want to feel self-motivated in terms of our career and have a well-balanced and happy life. Otherwise, we will feel miserable whenever we go to work. From my personal experience, I once had worked at a company that offered a higher salary, but I was often sick and depressed. This was because I didn't have the motivation to show up to work every morning. Soon, I realized that I was not doing my best because I did not feel inspired even though I made a decent amount of money, and I had to quit the job. This clearly depicts that money is not the ultimate key to happiness and we need to choose our professions based on our contentedness with our jobs.

Another major consideration is that when you are satisfied with your job, you are more likely to be productive and perform better professionally. It is common sense that happier employees tend to have a higher commitment to the company, would always strive to do their best, and become more prolific. To illustrate this, one should see no further than those employees who dedicate more than twenty years at a workplace and have never felt bored or tired of their work. This is due to the level of satisfaction the employees may feel at a workplace. Consequently, satisfied employees tend to become prolific producers of goods and services, leading meaningful and inspirational lives. In fact, one study found that happy employees are up to 20% more productive than unhappy employees. On the other hand, when employees are unhappy and disengaged, various issues may arise. Therefore, we can assume that satisfying jobs may lead to more professional achievements.

Lastly, one should consider that satisfied employees would try to always improve themselves and this may result it outstanding career paths. In view of this, more frequent promotions could happen when employees go above and beyond. To put it simply, if one feels satisfied at the workplace, he or she would be willing to take more initiatives, thus leading to a pay raise and possible promotion. Hence, in the end, there could be a financial reward and growth potential when employees care about their work and feel gratified.

In summary, there are numerous reasons to believe that having a satisfying job is better than a high salaried job. This will allow us to enjoy a happy life, become more productive, and ultimately have a successful career.

Consider the following:

We often tie happiness and money closely together, but that's only true to a certain extent. Research collected by the National Academy of Sciences was able to break down where the connection ended between income and overall life satisfaction.

But researchers also found something interesting: having no money (or a very low income) makes people miserable. "Low income exacerbates the emotional pain associated with such misfortunes as divorce, ill health, and being alone.

Although high income might not bring on eternal happiness, it can buy a certain threshold of happiness.

Choosing a higher paying job might mean less time spent with your kids, but more money to save up for their future. Or are you a post-college graduate with no ties to your current city? Then choosing the higher paying job might be the opportunity you need to start paying off those debts faster, for now.

https://www.classycareergirl.com/2017/02/happiness-job-big-paycheck/

Practice 4-6: Places

On the Internet – Places

The following articles are about the topics that actually appear on the TOEFL test.

Libraries	
1	**Public libraries in the United States play an essential role in providing safe, accessible, and 100% free educational resource centers for every member in communities across the country.** At a library, it doesn't matter how much money you make, because every resource there is free of charge, including books, internet access, and educational and professional training programs. Individuals and families, no matter their socioeconomic status, can count on their libraries to provide them with the resources they need to succeed and the answers to important questions they can't otherwise find. **They offer free educational resources to everyone.** Public libraries in the United States play an essential role in providing safe, accessible, and 100% free educational resource centers for every member in communities across the country. At a library, it doesn't matter how much money you make, because every resource there is free of charge, including books, internet access, and educational and professional training programs. Individuals and families, no matter their socioeconomic status, can count on their libraries to provide them with the resources they need to succeed and the answers to important questions they can't otherwise find. According to the ALA, librarians in public and academic libraries across the country answer nearly 6.6 million questions every week. If everyone who asked a question formed a line, it would span all the way from Miami, FL, to Junot, AK. These questions aren't just about card catalogs and book recommendations, either. Librarians help their patrons not only find their next reading selection, but they also answer questions about computer and internet training, job applications and resume writing, and filling out government forms, including tax and health insurance paperwork, all of it for free.
2	**Libraries help connect communities.** More so than a community center, town hall, or public park ever could, libraries connect their communities in a way that benefits everyone. They pool local resources — from educational offerings to job training to homeless outreach to ESL learning — and put them all under one welcoming roof for everyone to share. Whether you're a family looking for a fun story time, an immigrant in need of language resources, an unemployed individual searching for job help, or a community member who needs help on their taxes, you can all go to one place: the library. There, communities come together to learn, share, and celebrate where they live, who they are, and what they want to become. Libraries truly are remarkable places, and in today's world, we need them now more than ever. Find out how you can support your local library and get to work protecting one of America's most important public institutions. The country needs it. https://www.bustle.com/p/7-reasons-libraries-are-essential-now-more-than-ever-43901

Museums	
1	**Today, museums allow us to enjoy and explore history, culture and the natural world but this is nothing new.** There is evidence of people's fascination with objects from the past stretching back thousands of years; powerful Chinese emperors surrounded themselves with antiques because of their connection with earlier generations and in your home, there almost certainly are objects that belonged to members of your family. http://innovacion.educa.madrid.org/concursoprimiciasnews/docs/PrimiciasNews_Abr_18_en.pdf
	Museums provide an effective way of learning. Museums are examples of informal learning environments, which means they are devoted primarily to informal education — a lifelong process whereby individuals acquire attitudes, values, skills and knowledge from daily experience and the educative influences and resources in his or her environment. Even outside of museums, informal learning plays a pivotal role in how we take in the world around us. In fact, The U.S. Department of Labor estimates 70% or more of work-related learning occurs outside formal training. A single visit to a museum can expose visitors to in-depth information on a subject, and the nature of the museum environment is one in which you can spend as much or as little time as you like exploring exhibits. The environment allows you to form your own unique experiences and take away information that interests you. Despite the success that museums have already had in educating visitors, there **Museums are a great way to spend time with friends and family.** Museums provide a great excuse to spend time with friends and family in a positive way. Personal connections can be made with museums and also with family members during visits. A day at the museum often translates to a day spent with loved ones as fathers and mothers transform into tour guides, and the environment provides a shared learning experience. https://www.colleendilen.com/2009/07/31/10-reasons-to-visit-a-museum/

Restaurants	
1	**Restaurants have always played an essential role in the business, social, intellectual and artistic life of a thriving society.** Think of the cafes of Paris in the 20's; the three martini lunches of the 50's and 60's; we've sketched world-changing ideas and planned revolutions in restaurants. Elvis' first Las Vegas contract was written on a restaurant tablecloth. **The major events of life, personal and professional, are celebrated in restaurants**. Acquaintances become friends around a table in the safe and controlled environment of a restaurant. Individuals become lovers across a restaurant table, sometimes. **Beyond the basic purpose of restaurants to provide food and drink**, restaurants have, historically, fulfilled a human need for connection and shaped social relations. In 21st century American life restaurants occupy an increasingly important place in shaping our overall economy and the nature and makeup of our cities. https://medium.com/@EliFeldman/why-the-restaurant-industry-is-the-most-important-industry-in-todays-america-6a819f8f0ac9
2	**If you are craving for a complete meal with appetizers to dessert and everything in between, dining out is the way to go.** Can you imagine preparing all these courses for yourself at home? After preparing a big salad, you could end up calling it quits and just eating salad for dinner.

	It happens to all of us. At home, we make the same things over and over again. You often end up eating the same thing twice just because there are leftovers. **Dining out will not only give you the opportunity to eat something different or try something new**. It may also inspire you to try cooking something different at home http://tuscanhousenj.com/dining-out-the-reasons-we-like-it/

Classes	
1	**Advantage: More Interaction** A classroom environment offers students the opportunity to have face-to-face interactions with their peers and instructors. This is an added social benefit as well as an educational aid. Because students see the same peers in class every session, they get a chance to form friendships. In the case of higher learning, pupils can find potential lifelong professional connections. On the educational side, students get a chance to participate in a lecture or class discussion physically. If students don't understand something, they can always ask the instructor for clarification is always an option.
2	**Disadvantage: No Flexibility** A campus-based learning experience means the class schedule is predetermined and not subject to change. Students must shape their personal schedules around school instead of the other way around. If plans unexpectedly change or an emergency comes up, the student cannot adjust the class schedule to turn in the work at a different time. If a scheduling conflict arises between work and school, students are forced to choose between getting an education and getting a paycheck. https://www.theclassroom.com/advantages-disadvantages-classroom-learning-7922444.html

Business Development	
1	**We can all agree that land development is essential for a community's success.** While development can sometimes be frowned upon, as it changes the face of the landscape, creates more traffic, changes ecosystems and habitats, it is imperative for the prosperity of your community. It can generate more jobs, bring desired curb appeal, unite community members, and maintain or increase home values. Whether the development is residential or commercial, construction brings economic stability. Finding a balance between growth and maintaining the character of your community is key to the planning of development, as well as, weighing the pros and cons. **Construction and land development can create added waste to our landfills and not all materials are environmentally friendly.** In metropolitan or urban areas that are highly populated and built up, a heat island effect can occur. Thus, making it warmer in these areas than rural areas due to the volume of energy being consumed. Land Development can change ecosystems and force wildlife to relocate. At the same time, land development can have a positive impact on our environment. Governing entities may require developers to bring buildings up to current code or clean up contaminated sites from a previous business. Site cleanup is costly, but it brings added value to our environment. Incentives are sometimes offered for using sustainable materials or building Green or a LEED certified structure. Oftentimes developers will clear out invasive/non-native trees and replace them with native trees.

Land and Development	
1	Major land–use changes have occurred in the United States during the past 25 years. The total area of cropland, pastureland and rangeland decreased by 76 million acres in the lower 48 states from 1982 to 2003, while the total area of developed land increased by 36 million acres or 48%. What are the potential economic, social and environmental impacts of land use changes?
2	**Socioeconomic Impacts** Land is one of three major factors of production in classical economics (along with labor and capital) and an essential input for housing and food production. Thus, land use is the backbone of agricultural economies and it provides substantial economic and social benefits. Land use change is necessary and essential for economic development and social progress. Land use change, however, does not come without costs (see Table 1). Conversion of farmland and forests to urban development reduces the amount of lands available for food and timber production. Soil erosion, salinization, desertification, and other soil degradations associated with intensive agriculture and deforestation reduce the quality of land resources and future agricultural productivity (Lubowski et al. 2006). **Environmental Impacts** Land–use change is arguably the most pervasive socioeconomic force driving changes and degradation of ecosystems. Deforestation, urban development, agriculture, and other human activities have substantially altered the Earth's landscape. Such disturbance of the land affects important ecosystem processes and services, which can have wide–ranging and long–term consequences (Table 2). Farmland provides open space and valuable habitat for many wildlife species. However, intensive agriculture has potentially severe ecosystem consequences. For example, it has long been recognized that agricultural land use and practices can cause water pollution and the effect is influenced by government policies. Runoff from agricultural lands is a leading source of water pollution both in inland and coastal waters. Conversions of wetlands to crop production and irrigation water diversions have brought many wildlife species to the verge of extinction. http://www.choicesmagazine.org/magazine/article.php?article=49

Small town vs. Big Cities	
1	Small towns have plenty of great perks of their own to offer, and you may find they're a lot more affordable than a crowded city. Here are some of the reasons why small towns are great, budget-friendly places to live: • **Slower Pace:** Far away from the hustle and bustle of a big city, the slower, more relaxed pace of small towns can be a welcome change. • **Fewer Crowds:** When you go out on a Saturday night, you won't be waiting in line 45 minutes for a table or fighting to find seats in a crowded movie theater.

	• **Less Crime:** In a small town, it's safer for kids to play outside, for bicyclists to chain their bikes in front of a coffee shop, and for you to leave your car windows cracked when you're parked in your driveway over the summer. • **Lower Cost of Living:** Everything from homes to groceries is cheaper in a small town. You can get an entire house for the price of a studio apartment in a large city, and with more mom-and-pop outfits than big corporate chains, the <u>price of consumer goods</u> is often lower, too. Not to mention small towns tend to have low property taxes. https://www.thebalance.com/benefits-of-living-and-working-in-a-small-town-453928
2	**Advantages of living in a big city.** **Entertainment Options** You never have a shortage of things to see and do when you move to a major metro area. Regardless of your preferences, you'll find places which appeal to your interests, filled with like-minded people who share them. Whether you're into loud clubs or quiet bookstores, you'll find both in abundance. **Employment** As context, employment growth in several metro areas <u>has exceeded 20 percent</u> in the past five years. A combination of educational, economic and environmental factors have contributed to this, and though employment rates differ throughout the country, one thing is certain. The job market is currently strong for a wide range of industries that attract young professionals. **Transportation** Fortunately, you have a range of options for public transportation when you live in a major metro area. The subway provides a relatively fast, convenient way to get from place to place, avoiding traffic. Plus, you might be able to focus on a book rather than keeping your eyes on the road — as long as the noise isn't too distracting.
3	**Disadvantages of living in a big city.** **Higher Cost of Living** Housing costs are often higher in the city than in suburban or rural areas. While this will differ from place to place, depending on your city of choice, it's typically cheaper to live in the suburbs. This can also affect your long-term goals. Are you happy renting for a while, or is your heart set on saving for homeownership? If you're spending more income on housing year-to-year, then you might have to put off any plans for property while living in the big city. **Large Population** The large population of major metro areas can create other unforeseen challenges in your daily life. You'll find it far more difficult to find a parking space if you drive, and once you arrive at your destination, you're still not in the clear. You might have to push through a crowd, wait longer for a table at restaurants or linger in a line.

Fast Pace

Living life on the fast track can be thrilling. But it's also more likely to lead to burnout. Culture depends on the city's regional character, of course, but for the most part, city dwellers have a lot more on their plate. New York was ranked the number one most stressed out city in the U.S. due to long commutes and skyrocketing expenses.

https://www.theestateupdate.com/living-in-a-big-city/

Factories	
1	**One of the primary advantages of factories is that even a relatively small one is an engine that generates economic activity.** The factory itself may source some of its materials locally, and both the office and production staff will need to buy work clothes, lunches and many other things. They'll fill their tanks at local filling stations on their way to and from work, and trucks — whether inbound with raw materials or outbound with finished products — will do the same. Taxes paid by your company and its staff will contribute to the budgets of each level of government, helping provide services to residents and pay for the infrastructure that makes your factory possible.
2	**One factor to judge carefully is your impact on the local infrastructure.** Depending on your proposed factory's size and needs, the impact may be a non-factor or an absolute deal breaker. This impact takes many forms. If your factory increases traffic dramatically in its surrounding area, it may place an intolerable load on local traffic patterns or even physically on the roads and bridges themselves. You may also represent a competitor for limited resources: Your factory might take away a crucial swath of farmland, for example, or require a large quantity of water in an area where it's already scarce. If your company is in a position to provide infrastructure that becomes usable by the community — perhaps subsidizing an upgrade to a local highway so it can carry the added volume your factory represents — that can mitigate this problem or even turn it into a positive. https://bizfluent.com/info-8169695-advantages-disadvantages-factories.html

---

Hometown	
1	**Whatever the circumstances of your "hometown", we all have one.** It's the place that seemed to raise you right alongside your parents. It's the place that seemed to grow up right along with you. It's the place that you have the map tattooed on the back of your hand. It's the place that, even if you say don't, there is always going to be that little tiny piece of you that misses something about it whenever you leave. It's pretty magical, don't you think? As humans, part of our needs is love and belonging. I have always thought that in some situations, love and belonging are not necessarily found in people, but in places. It almost feels as if you're hometown seems to have some kind of soul that provides you with the same feelings a human provides. When you are there you know where the best places to get food, the best places to relax, the best places to think. You know the personal things too, like the house where you stood with your high school friends in dresses that cost a fortune and corsages that seemed to have taken up your entire wrist to take pictures. You know the tree next to the town library that you stood under when you got your first kiss. You know where the Sonic is where you sat in your childhood best friends' car and talked about life, and boys, and what the heck you were going to do for the rest of your life because at that point you thought you knew. You know all the side streets because you used them to get home so you would be home to get home before curfew. Looking back, you probably realize that you found yourself in all of those moments. Those little seconds, minutes, and hours that passed quicker than you probably realized in that little piece of heaven that knows all of your secrets. https://www.theodysseyonline.com/the-importance-of-home-town
2.	1. A sense nostalgia

A small thing can set off a plethora of memories, no matter how insignificant it may be. An old cafe where you hung out with your friends, that spot in the park where you got your first kiss, your school - there are just so many places in your hometown that play a huge part in growing up. And seeing them from time to time evokes a wonderful feeling.

2. Your friends are close by

When you move out, you lose touch with some friends as you don't see them very often. But when you are in your hometown, you will always be in touch with them. Meeting up now and again and catching up on each others' lives are a weekly routine. Even if some of your friends no longer live there, they will always know where to find you.

https://www.indiatimes.com/lifestyle/self/11-reasons-living-and-working-in-your-hometown-is-the-sweetest-thing-ever-244673.html

College or University	
1	**Make more money.** People who graduate from college make more money than those with just a high school diploma. A lot more money, actually. Data from the Bureau of Labor Statistics (BLS) shows that in 2016, people with a college degree made around $1,156 a week. Someone with a high school diploma earned just $692. **Have more opportunity.** People who go to college open up their choices for jobs. Many jobs these days require a college degree. Plus, college graduates have less chance of losing their jobs. In 2016, the overall unemployment rate dropped to 4 percent — but as education levels go up, unemployment rates go down. For high school graduates, the unemployment rate was 5.2 percent, but it was only 2.7 percent for college graduates. **Make connections.** In college, students make new friends and other connections that will be helpful when it's time to get started in a career. Those friends they make in college will help them get jobs, and these connections and networks will help them throughout their lives. https://owlcation.com/academia/common-problems-for-college-students

Countryside	
1	**The pros of living in the countryside** • *You will enjoy a healthier life style.* The common prejudice that countrymen live longer, healthier and better seems to be confirmed by science. It is not only a matter of clean air and more physical exercise. For example, you will get more vitamin G, a nutrient that benefits your body in several ways (for more information on this point, read <u>Five Scientific Reasons for Moving to the Country</u>). • *Prices are lower.* The cost of living in rural areas is 6-10% lower on average than the in cities. Especially housing- a key need for anyone is often discounted at least 13%. • *No problems for pets and children.* Your children and your pets will enjoy all the space they need to grow up strong and happy.

2	**The cons of living in the countryside**
	<ul><li>*You have to learn a lot of things*. Running a farm is a real job and agriculture is not as easy as it may seem.</li><li>*Isolation*. Living far away from it all is not for everybody, especially in winter, when roads get blocked by ice and snow. You may need to buy a sturdy vehicle, at least to reach the nearest grocery store or hospital.</li><li>*The countryside is toiling and requires a strong physique*. Cleaning your own driveway of tons of snow isn't the easiest task you can expect in your new location. Living in the country is beautiful, but toiling, particularly if you decide to farm.</li></ul> https://jbpropertysolutions.net/2017/10/23/some-pros-and-cons-of-living-in-the-countryside/

Movie Theaters	
1	**Sound and Picture** Experiencing a movie in a theater lets you see the film on a huge screen with plenty of detail. It also offers a surround-sound system that enhances the overall experience, making you feel as if you're actually part of the story. The downside, however, is that you have no control over either of these. The volume may be too high or too low, and the picture may be slightly blurry or too bright for your eyes. **Other People** Watching a movie in a theater full of other movie-goers can be very satisfying, especially for movies that provoke a strong reaction. The feeling of solidarity can be quite enjoyable. On the other hand, other people can be a significant source of distraction and annoyance. Despite warnings, many people talk (on cell phones or with friends nearby) or send text messages while a movie is playing. Others may kick the back of your seat, spill food or drinks, or bring unruly children to the theater. **Refreshments** Movie theater concession stands offer plenty of snacks. Movie-goers can enjoy popcorn, nachos, and a large variety of candy and soft drinks. Some theaters even offer restaurant-style food and alcohol to enjoy during a movie. Unfortunately, movie theater refreshments are notoriously overpriced; you may be charged more than twice the normal price for even a small soda. Additionally, if you want a snack during the film, you'll have to miss part of it to make a trip to the concession stand. https://ourpastimes.com/advantages-disadvantages-of-going-to-a-movie-in-the-theater-12556046.html

High School	
1	**All the things you've heard about high school are true.** It's a horrid place. It's all the bad parts of the real world thrown under one roof. You make friends and you lose friends. You meet new boys that turn into a disaster. Your teachers are always giving you a hard time. You're always wanting to pull your hair out. Four years seem to take forever. Well here is a list of 60 the things I hate about high school. Trust me, you are not alone. **1. Broken chairs** Every single classroom you walk in to in my high school has at least one broken chair or desk. You sit down

	and you one of the legs is broken and you're tipping all over the place. I didn't know this was an amusement park. I thought I was in English class. Also, you can sit down in a chair and it is cracked. It pinches my butt to no end and it just makes the class more miserable than it normally is. **2. Crowded cafeteria** Walking in to the cafeteria is like entering a maze. You have to maneuver around people, chairs, tables, backpacks, and who knows what else. First of all it is insanely stressful and my voice is gone by the time I get to my seat from saying excuse me or sorry to every single person that stands in your way. http://www.teenink.com/opinion/school_college/article/434880/60-Awful-Things-About-High-School
2	**Friends**. I can't think of anything more luxurious than spending every day with my friends. When you leave school, meeting up with even one friend can take a lot of organising. **Free knowledge.** My school was free: it cost me and my parents £0. £0 for English, maths, geography, history, art, and lots of other subjects. What a bargain! Learning can be really expensive when you leave school - especially in the UK, where university has now become almost as expensive as buying a little house. **Uniform.** In England, schoolkids wear a uniform to school. Mine was blue. It wasn't fashionable or particularly flattering, but it saved a lot of time in the mornings. Now it takes me ages to decide what to wear. **Short days**. My school days sometimes felt very long but they were, in fact, very short. The school day started at 9 and finished at 15.30. I used to think of 'home time' as the beginning of the evening, but nowadays I think of 15.30 as the middle of the afternoon. https://learnenglishteens.britishcouncil.org/magazine/life-around-world/10-reasons-why-school-was-actually-pretty-good-deal

Moving (relocation)	
1	**People relocate for their career for a number of reasons.** For some, it may be for better job prospects or the purpose of professional growth. For others, it might be just to break out of their comfort zone and to experience new things. **Pro: Bigger Job Market** Searching for a job in a new city opens the door to more opportunities, new networks, and more companies. When you begin looking at jobs in other cities, you are no longer limited to the job opportunities within your current region. You've expanded your access to job opportunities, and tapped into a bigger job market. Expanding your job search nationwide gives you to access to a broader list of options filled with positions that, otherwise, you would've missed. **Con: Stressful Relocation** Relocation is never easy. Between planning, packing, and finding a new place to stay, the entire process

can end up being more stressful than one imagined.

Depending on the industry, most job openings are for immediate hire. Meaning the company needs someone to fulfill that position as soon as possible, leaving you with a short amount of time to relocate.

This stress can overwhelm some people, causing them to be more indecisive, and even causing them to reconsider the move altogether.

Pro: New Experiences

Relocating to a new city is always good for the simple fact you get to experience new things. It gives you a look into a culture that is different from your own, and exposes you to things that, otherwise, you wouldn't have access to.

Relocation helps you meet new people and create new connections, all while exploring and discovering your new environment.

Con: Unfamiliar Places

Adjusting to a new city that you know nothing about can be a daunting task. Simple things like finding a grocery store or pharmacy can become a hard task, and requires a little bit of exploring to find. You may have to learn a new public transportation system just to find these places.

There might be tools to help make this process easier, but that does not take away from the ease of actually going out and exploring, especially if you are alone.

https://www.careermetis.com/pros-cons-relocating-your-career/

Travel

1

1. Improves Social and Communication Skills

One of the main benefits of travelling, especially to areas where your native language is not widely used, is that you learn how to communicate better with other people. Brushing up your knowledge on the most commonly used phrases or questions tourists ask can help you reach out to and relate better with the locals.

2. Ensures Peace of Mind

We all have stress and tension in our lives. Traveling forces us to temporarily disconnect from our normal routine, helping us appreciate the people and things we have around. As per a famous saying "we never know what we have until we lose it."

3. Helps You Get Original and Creative Thoughts

It is believed that if someone gets out of their comfort zone, the mind gets more creative. To develop new neural connections that trigger original and creative thoughts, you must explore new places and break out of your daily routine.

4. Broadens Your Horizons

Travelling helps you connect with different people from different cultures. This gives you the opportunity to see issues and daily life challenges from a different angle.

5. Gets You Real-life Education

Meeting different people from vast cultures and societies provides an education that is impossible to get in a traditional school, college or a university. There is no substitute for the real thing.

8. Creates Memories for Lifetime

https://www.dumblittleman.com/benefits-of-traveling/

Escapism. Travel allows you to escape. Whether it's from a bad relationship (or perhaps no relationship at all), a job you hate, or simply a boring, sedentary life, sometimes you feel like you just need to get away. Travel is the perfect form of escapism – far better than reading a book or watching a movie – because it actually means you get to leave your current situation. You can trade in whatever is making you unhappy for something different, even if it's just for a little while. A change of scenery is sometimes just what you need to get over boredom or the blues, and being far removed from a problem or stressor often allows you to look at it through new eyes.

| 2 | **Being homesick.** Even if you aren't terribly close to your family, it's likely you'll still feel some semblance of homesickness at some point during your travels. Maybe you miss your significant other. Maybe you miss a sibling or cousin. Hell, maybe you really miss your cat. Being away from home can be stimulating and wonderful, but it's not unnatural to fall into a funk every now and then when you pine for "home." The good news is that things like Skype, Facebook and e-mail make keeping in touch incredibly easy in this day and age.

https://www.dangerous-business.com/the-pros-and-cons-of-travel/ |

Dorms	
1	**The cost.** Tuition when going to Uni can be expensive as it is, but have you looked at a price of a dorm? Where I go to school, I'm paying about $2,000 a semester to live on-campus, but compared to other schools, that's nothing. For room and board at the University of Texas, undergraduate students are looking to pay about $5,000 a semester.
	Community bathrooms. Community bathrooms are gross—and that's that. People do not know how to pick up after themselves. You never know who was sitting on that toilet seat before you. And it also gets a little embarrassing for girls when it's *that* time of the month. Along with that, community showers are even worse. The fact that I have to wear shower shoes to get clean... is just not ideal.
	Weird roommates. So you're going to a new school and you don't know anyone else that's going there. You now are stuck rooming with a person that you know nothing about other than their name (you might even have more than one). Story time: My first year at Uni I started in the spring, so I only had this roommate for one semester (luckily), and then I got a new one the following fall. My roommate was the worst type of roommate I could have imagined. She was so very messy. And I don't mean the leave-your-clothes-everywhere type messy. I mean leave-your-EVERYTHING-everywhere type messy. Pizza boxes from weeks ago on your desk, a packed suitcase from where you hadn't unpacked from spring break, a distinct line on the floor on whose side was whose. Yes, she had a vacuum; no, she didn't use it.
2	**Proximity.** You're close to everything. Your class may be a five minute walk, McDonald's is probably a block down the street, and you don't have to go far to get practically anything. Now, if you're living in an

apartment you could be five to thirty minutes away from campus by car—think about it.

Community. I've always been a huge fan of living on campus because of the sense of community. You know the people you live around, you make friends, you live really close to your friends, and you get to see them *every day*. How awesome is that?

Good roommates. I know what I said before—roommates suck. But honestly, you can meet your best friend ever in college, and they could be your roommate. Two of my friends had been roommates freshman year and they were weary at first, but now they see each other every day. It's not always bad!

https://vocal.media/education/pros-and-cons-of-living-in-a-dorm

Zoos	
1	**Educational Tool** When people visit the Zoo, they are not only witnessing living and breathing animals for entertainment purposes, but also learn a lot of valuable information too. Modern zoos often provide tours, information points and actively seek to educate and teach the next generation of children the importance and value of conservation and biodiversity. Of course, individuals and children can read about animals and conservation in books, but actively engaging with animals allows them to truly empathize with their plight. **Conservation of Endangered Animals** Perhaps, it's a little obvious, but Zoo's offer a safe haven for endangered animals to live and on many occasions thrive. This is of paramount importance for some of the world's most threatened animal species and allows leading experts and researchers to discover their habits, breeding patterns and as a result learn how human's can help them survive, breed and therefore increase their dwindling numbers.
2	**Ethics of Captive Animals** Many wild animals have evolved to thrive in a certain environment, habitat, and climate and not suited to the confines and containment of captivity. Unfortunately, even though Zoos often try their best to mimic a specific species natural habitat sometimes it has little impact on their behavior and well being. For example, an Orca in the wild can survive as long as 100 years, yet in captivity, they typically don't reach 30 years of age. This illustrates that the Zoo environment does not always succeed and there are many reasons behind this. **Captive Offspring are Often Dependant** Although one of the main aims of zoos is to have successful breeding programs for some of the world's rarest animals, the resulting offspring doesn't always result in successful integration in the wild. Many animals born and raised in captivity fail to successfully make the transition from captive to wild environment, meaning that sometimes there is no choice but to keep them in the Zoo for the remainder of their lives. https://animalmentor.com/wild-life/pros-cons-zoos/

New School	
1	**Why Students Transfer**

Students transfer from one school to another for a variety of reasons, including money, campus experience, academic struggles or opportunities, or to 'trade up' to a more prestigious school. It's a decision that can have large ripple effects. Students who transfer without a plan can find themselves taking longer to graduate, owing a lot more money, and feeling no better about their new school. It's important to think carefully about the positives and negatives of changing schools.

How It Could Help

There are a variety of potential pros to transferring schools. For example, there may be more suitable degree programs, more accessible professors, and more chances for success at a new school. If you had academic or disciplinary problems at your previous college, transferring could lead to a fresh start. Keep in mind that your academic or disciplinary records will be considered for admission to a new school; however, once you get accepted somewhere, you essentially have a blank slate.

In addition, a new school could have a completely different social scene. You might participate in new activities, sports, or organizations simply not available at your previous school.

2	

How It Could Hurt

While there are plenty of pros associated with transferring, you should consider the cons as well. For example, you may not solve the problems that led you to transfer in the first place, like academic performance or community involvement. There's also a strong chance all of your previous credits won't transfer, especially if you move from a private university to a public one.

The decision to transfer could cost you in financial aid and scholarship money. If you don't plan well, you could be giving up substantial amounts of scholarship aid. You may even wind up owing your first school for a scholarship you received.

https://study.com/articles/The_Pros_and_Cons_of_Transferring_Schools.html

---

Neighborhood
1

How to Tell When You Are in a Bad Neighborhood

When scouting out a new home, you must consider whether it is a good neighborhood or not.

Random Garbage Everywhere

One obvious sign of a bad neighborhood is random garbage scattered everywhere. If the trash is not cleaned up over a long period of time, it is absolutely a red flag.

Thick Graffiti

Graffiti is a type of street art but many graffiti are drawn without the permission of houseowners. Excessive graffiti on both public and private property annoys people a lot.

Many Dilapidated or Abandoned Houses

Well maintained houses are reflections of a good neighborhood. Conversely, too many dilapidated or abandoned houses are red flags of a bad neighborhood.

https://reolink.com/signs-you-live-in-bad-neighborhood/

High Crime Rate Statistics

When you're looking into a potential neighborhood, look at the crime statistics. According to the FBI's annual crime report, there were 1,197,704 violent crimes across the country in 2015. [1]
Although crimes are often concentrated in big cities, it doesn't mean your neighborhood is necessarily safe even if it's in a small town. As you're researching online, check out sites like MyLocalCrime.com and CrimeReports.com to get a better idea of your area.

Constant Police Presence

Police officers respond to crimes. So it can be a bad sign if there's high police activity in your neighborhood. That's not to say that seeing a cop car pass through your block once in a while is something to worry about—it's part of a police officer's job to patrol different areas. But if you notice cops responding to calls multiple times a day, it might be time to move or take extra safety precautions.

Abandoned Houses and Storefronts

One of the most obvious signs of a declining neighborhood is vacant houses and storefronts. [2] If you see a lot of buildings and homes in your area that have been empty for many months to a year, it might be a sign that your neighborhood is dangerous.
According to the US Department of Housing and Urban Development, "research links foreclosed, vacant, and abandoned properties with reduced property values, increased crime, [and] increased risk to public health and welfare." [3] You can avoid moving to a declining neighborhood by looking at how many vacant buildings and homes are in the area.

All right, now that you know what to avoid when it comes to finding the right neighborhood for you and your family, check out our list of the five common signs your neighborhood is safe.

Community Events

Neighborhoods that host community events like block parties and farmers' markets tend to be closer. These types of events are a great way to bring families together and encourage people who live in the same area to get to know each other better. It's also a great way to see what people in the neighborhood are up to: some might be selling flowers or produce from their garden, while others might be into wood carving or furniture restoration. This is a great way to see what the people around you are all about.

Thriving Local Businesses

Businesses prosper when people shop. If you notice a variety of shops around your neighborhood, like family-friendly restaurants, bookstores, and coffee shops, it could be a good sign. When people are financially secure, they're more likely to spend money beyond the necessities and splurge from time to time on going out. It's worth noticing the types of businesses in your area and the people who frequent them.

Kids Playing Outside

There's comfort in the sound of kids playing. And it's also a good sign that you're in a good neighborhood. Parents are more willing to let their kids play outdoors if they feel the area is safe from potential danger. When you're scoping out the area, look around for kids biking down the street, playing ball, and laughing with friends.

https://www.safewise.com/blog/factors-to-consider-when-determining-the-safety-of-your-neighborhood/

Companies

1 **Corporatism, not capitalism, is to blame for inequality.**

Lethargic growth, depressed employment, widespread job dissatisfaction and staggering debt – such is life in a western world that seems to have lost the habit of innovation that energized it for more than a century. After a major loss of dynamism in the 1960s, productivity growth rates began dropping in most countries, falling by half in the US in the 1970s and more or less ceasing altogether in France, Germany and Britain in the late 1990s. It is urgent that these nations find a way back to their past dynamism. But some prominent voices would change the subject. The important issue is inequality, they say. In Europe, it is estimated that one-quarter of private wealth is held by the richest 1 per cent; in America, the richest 1 per cent hold one-third. This wealth has ballooned, relative to national income, in countries where growth is slow; and the share held by the rich has risen in most nations over recent decades. "Egalitarians" who complain about inequality view the wealth of the wealthiest as bad in itself: it disfigures society. They would enact a wealth tax to extirpate the offending wealth.

The blame for the losses of innovation behind slowdowns in productivity lies with the spread of corporatist values, particularly solidarity, security and stability. Politicians have introduced regulation that stifles competition; patronized interest groups through pork-barrel contracts; and lent direction to the economy through industrial policy. In the process, they have impeded those who would innovate, or reduced their incentive to try. If we can cure ourselves of these maladies, dynamism will return and the abnormal wealth inequality will wane.

https://www.ft.com/content/54411224-132c-11e4-8244-00144feabdc0

2 **Business is extremely important to a country's economy because businesses provide both goods and services and jobs.** Businesses do these things much more efficiently than individuals could on their own.

Businesses are the means by which we get most of the goods and services that we, as consumers, want and need. You will presumably be reading this answer on a computer that was produced by a business. You are buying internet access from a business. Almost everything that you use in your everyday life was produced by a business and sold by yet another business. Without these businesses, it would be very hard for us to get the things we need. Imagine, for example, how hard it would be for one person to build and sell their own computers from scratch. This is a major reason why businesses are important for a country's economy.

Businesses are also the means by which many people get their jobs. Businesses create job opportunities because they need people to produce and sell their goods and services to consumers. Without businesses, each individual would have to create his or her own way of making a living. This would be very difficult. Thus, businesses are important because they provide goods, services, and jobs. Without these things, nations' economies would be much smaller and weaker than they are.

https://www.google.com/url?sa=t&rct=j&q=&esrc=s&source=web&cd=1&ved=2ahUKEwjr4OSv2qXlAhVaL6YKHbRYA_MQFjAAegQIAhAB&url=https%3A%2F%2Fwww.enotes.com%2Fhomework-help%2Fwhy-

	buisness-important-country-economy-474583&usg=AOvVaw2iZ5kBjs-BbtL5Kf0rzUkQ
3	**A business can negatively affect society because some businesses harm the environment, and sometimes decision makers resort to unacceptable practices for their own personal benefit so yes a business can affect society.** https://www.coursehero.com/

Single Sex and Co-Ed	
1	List of Advantages of Coed Schools **1. Offers School Diversity** One of the good things about enrolling students, especially kids in mixed-gender schools is the diversity that this decision offers students. If young boys and girls are given exposed to diversity in an early age, they will find it easier to adapt in different environments when they grow up. The diversity this set-up offers is significant in teaching other forms of diversity such as cultural and social. **2. Teaches Equality** With both male and female students attending classes together and participating in class activities, these students will be able to learn about equality between men and women. As opposed to single-sex schools, coed schools treat students equally with no preference to sex, thus, when assignments are given, there are no special treatments and students are graded and evaluated on their performance and not on gender. **3. Prepares Students for the Real World** Another advantage of co-educational schools is that students are exposed to a normal environment in the sense that society is composed of both men and women. If they are taught and motivated to interact with both sexes, they can use this skill when they graduate in college and be in the real world where men and women co-exist, especially at work.
2	List of Disadvantages of Coed Schools **1. Can Result to Distraction** One of the downsides of mixed schools where there are both boys and girls is that students might not be able to concentrate with their studies. This is more possible to happen with students who are in high school and college because these are the levels where attraction among students can happen. If a boy has an infatuation on a girl or they will be in a relationship and something goes wrong, this can affect the studies of these students. Studies show that students in single sex schools are able to perform better in academics as opposed to coed students because they are not conscious about themselves and are less distracted. **2. Boys Differ from Girls** Boys are said to be better than girls when it comes to Math while females are better in communications skills and Language than males. Having said that, problems may arise when it comes to performance of students in the classroom. Say, the subject is Mathematics and the boys perform better than girls. The teacher might need to come up with techniques to teach the lesson and this can eat up much of the time intended for more lessons. Moreover, participation in class will not be balanced since one gender might be performing well than the other. This can also affect the atmosphere and the flow of lessons in the classroom. **3. Academic Performance**

Some educators who teach in single-sex schools that most students perform better academically in all-boys or all-girls schools than in coed educational institutions. This is because the co-existence of boys and girls in the classroom can lead to shyness or intimidation of some students. When these happen, students who will be intimated or embarrassed to participate in class will end up not performing well, academically.

https://connectusfund.org/12-advantages-and-disadvantages-of-coed-schools

Monuments	
1	**What is called Monument?** The definition of a **monument** is a structure, building, **statue**, gravestone or other item designed or constructed to honor someone or something. A **statue** of Abraham Lincoln designed to honor his memory is an **example** of a **monument**. https://www.yourdictionary.com/monument
2	Monuments don't mean things on their own. They mean things because we make them mean things. Monuments are not static things that have a single narrative behind them. Monuments are things that we create. Monuments are objects whose meaning and significance we create daily. https://www.npr.org/sections/codeswitch/2017/08/23/545548965/what-our-monuments-don-t-teach-us-about-remembering-the-past **Innovation in architecture is with no doubt extremely important, but preserving and restoring the old buildings is also important because those old monuments are the reflection of our history, they help us to understand and respect people who lived in different eras with different habits and traditions.** As well the existence of old monuments will help us observe the changes in the societies for a better understanding of the reasons that lead to the development of cities and societies and even traditions to the current status. Old buildings are the face of cities they reflect the changes that happened in a city over time, they reflect conflicts, wars, and the prosperity of the society, it even reflects the economic condition of the city over time. https://www.ierek.com/news/index.php/2016/10/09/importance-restoring-historical-monuments/

Architecture	
1	If you ever wondered why architecture is important—look up and around. You are likely surrounded by it right now. Architecture's grasp—that is, buildings and the designed environment—ends only in extreme conditions (the bottom of the ocean, the atmosphere, and a few dwindling spots on terrestrial earth.) Unique among creative and artistic professions, architecture must always reflect the age and cultural context that produced it. Designing and building architecture takes time, money, and collaboration (from financiers, civic officials, builders, architects, and more). It doesn't happen in a vacuum and can never truly have just one author. Architects work with dozens if not hundreds or thousands to shape their buildings, and along this chain, a deeper and richer set of values are transmitted; ones that define exactly how cultures see themselves and their world, and also how people see and experience each other. Beyond merely providing shelter, architecture becomes the stage set and context for our lives. It's the reason we feel empowered on the roof deck of an 80-story building, connected and thriving in a busy

	public plaza, and humbled in a soaring cathedral. Communities form within and at the behest of architecture, and take on their buildings' characteristics. Architecture connects to economics and the sciences, and the people that practice it can both be detail-oriented technicians (solving equations that push buildings higher into the sky, or conserving every possible electron of electricity pumped into its walls), and poets of space and form. https://www.studyarchitecture.com/blog/architecture-news/why-architecture-is-important/
2	**More 'good' architecture can bring new energy to Ottawa, experts say.** Boxy high-rises. Huge parking lots and garages. These kinds of functional, concrete structures are everywhere, it seems: Think Tunney's Pasture, or some of the behemoths in Ottawa's downtown. But they aren't on postcards. Young professionals don't see them and think, "Wow, Ottawa looks like a beautiful place to live and work." A shimmering reflection of the Chateau Laurier on the downtown Convention Centre: That's a little more inspiring. Today's architects can put beauty and functionality together, and that makes for a more engaging urban environment, according to Bill Birdsell, president of the Ontario Association of Architects. "Good" architecture interacts with the street outside and promotes a sense of community inside, Birdsell says. Cities full of this "good" stuff attract young people who want to live in an "exciting environment," he says. "Ottawa's starting to get into that." https://ottawacitizen.com/news/local-news/more-good-architecture-can-bring-new-energy-to-ottawa-experts-say

Practice 4

Some people choose to live in an apartment in a large city, while others choose to live in a large house in the countryside. Which do you prefer and why?

Write your response here.

Student's response (5/5)

It is incontrovertible that people have to choose where to live and what type of housing or accommodation to stay. After all, everybody needs a place to relax and unwind after a day's work. So, naturally, there could be a debate over the choice between living in an apartment in a large city and living in a large house in the countryside. Some might argue that living in an apartment in a large metropolitan area is more convenient. However, I believe that living in a larger house in the countryside is better for two reasons.

To begin with, it is important that one thinks about the cost of living. In other words, living in a large city can be often generally expensive, and one may feel confined due to the limited living space. From my personal experience, I had to choose to live in an area outside of a city to have a larger place with less money. This was because the city was extremely expensive, and there was a greater chance that I would live in a dangerous neighborhood. Soon I realized that there were better rewards to living outside the city. This clearly depicts that living in a larger house in the countryside is much more cost effective than in the city.

Another major consideration is that it is much quieter in the countryside than the city. This means that after working a full eight hours, it is much more enjoyable to go home and relax away from the rambunctiousness and noise that the city offers. To illustrate this, one should see no further than the amount of people, traffic, and noise pollution that accompanies city life. There are so many accidents and events in the city that one may not be able to get enough rest to start a new day. This is due to listening to the constant sounds of people yelling, car horns and sirens on a daily basis. Consequently, city life can be quite difficult and not so calm. Therefore, we can assume that living in the countryside would be more peaceful and tranquil, thus allowing a person to get the much-needed rest.

In summary, there are numerous reasons to believe that living in a large house in the country side is better than living in an apartment in a large city. This will allow us to save money and rest better.

Consider the following:

You can get pretty much anything you want, at any time of the day or night.

Public transportation (in some cities), or at least living close to amenities, saves the need – environmentally and financially – for a car.

Cities are inherently expensive. Besides the higher cost of living, something happens whenever I find myself in a city: I spend more money.

Crime is higher. The really bad kinds of crime too.

Competition for jobs is fiercer.

The rat race.

It can be a real dog-eat-dog world.

https://www.theprofessionalhobo.com/city-life-vs-country-life-an-unbiased-analysis/

Practice 5

Should cities preserve old historical buildings or destroy them and build more modern and efficient buildings?

Write your response here.

<table>
<tr><td></td></tr>
<tr><td></td></tr>
<tr><td></td></tr>
<tr><td></td></tr>
<tr><td></td></tr>
</table>

Student's response (5/5)

It is incontrovertible that city landscapes constantly change as they grow bigger and become more advanced. After all, new and tall buildings distinguish cities from rural areas. So, there could be a debate over whether or not to preserve old historical buildings in the city. Some might argue that a city needs to keep up with modernity and there isn't a place for old historical buildings. However, I believe that we should preserve these old historical buildings that have become part of the city's unique identity for two reasons.

To begin with, it is important that we understand that preserving these historical buildings are crucial to retaining a nation's heritage and history. In other words, these places help us to understand and appreciate the people who lived in different eras. From my personal experience, I went to the Notre Dame Cathedral in Paris, France. I had read about the place and seen it in pictures many times before my visit to the building. However, seeing it in real life astounded me. This was because it enabled me to imagine and feel what it might have been like to live in that time period. Soon I realized these historical buildings are unique and cannot be replicated. They were a special part of our past, and should be treasured. This clearly depicts the significance of these buildings in not only our past but also our present.

Another major consideration is that architecture can be a work of art. This means that as cultural artifacts, their value and beauty attracts people. To illustrate this, one should see no further than the unique esthetics of old buildings in the city. People are generally attracted to them because they provoke curiosity, and they stand out from the numerous modern buildings that surround them. There are so many modern buildings that are similar, and do not garner as much attention. This is due to trying to be more efficient when constructing offices and housing. Consequently, the appeal is lost and the city loses its own identity. Therefore, we can assume that keeping historical buildings in the city alive can city dwellers' lives much more fascinating than just following the trend of the generalization of urban settings.

In summary, there are numerous reasons to believe that preserving old buildings in the city is better than just replacing them with new and trendy buildings and creating boring cityscapes. This will allow us to have great opportunities to learn about history and to satisfy our biological need for intrigue.

Consider the following:

Older, smaller buildings and diverse urban fabric play a critical role in supporting robust local economies, distinctive local businesses, and unforgettable places where people connect and unwind.

It's also true, as the report points out, that older buildings tend to house more independent businesses and fewer chain stores than new buildings. Perhaps most compelling is the argument that historic buildings attract the creative class, which is essential to any dynamic urban future

It's all about balance. A city with nothing but modern skyscrapers would surely lose its aesthetic charm, its creative energy, and its urban vitality. But a city with no new construction risks turning into a museum: a beautiful but stuffy repository of artwork by dead people, frequented only by the rich and tourists.
https://grist.org/cities/we-need-old-buildings-to-make-great-cities-but-we-need-new-ones-too/

Practice 6

Do you agree or disagree with the following statement? All people should dedicate some time to helping their communities.

Write your response here.

| |
| |
| |
| |
| |
| |
| |
| |

Student's response (5/5)

It is incontrovertible that the existence of communities relies on the people living in them. After all, communities thrive when there are people actively working and living in the area. Yet, there could be a debate over whether or not people should dedicate time to helping their communities. Some might argue that the government should be responsible for maintaining the growth and prosperity of individual communities. However, I believe that people should dedicate some time to better the community by volunteering for two reasons.

To begin with, it is important to realize that communities are built on the relationship and connections of the people within them. In other words, communities prosper when there is cohesion among the inhabitants. From my personal experience, I visited a small community, and despite its poverty, I noticed that the people were happy, and seemed to have strong relationships. This was because each person dedicated a portion of their time to make a positive impact on the community. Soon I realized that communities need people just as people need communities. This clearly depicts how communities can survive when the population helps each other out.

Another major consideration is that when a community encounters a disaster, it needs people to help it revive itself. This means that through volunteering, people were able to support each other by providing hope, courage and morale. To illustrate this, one should look no further than the superstorm Hurricane Katrina. People from all around the country decided to dedicate a portion of their time to help restore the city. It took a community to make the recovery process more efficient. There are so many communities that survive because of the people who dedicate their time. This is due to feeling as if they were connected to each other and the area. Consequently, each person unites in order to create a prosperous and beautiful community. Therefore, we can assume that helping out a community has greater rewards and benefits.

In summary, there are numerous reasons to believe that all people should dedicate some time to helping their communities. This will allow people to build more solid communities and overcome challenges and disasters as one.

Consider the following:

By definition, volunteer work is unpaid, so the rewards you reap will be more emotional and perhaps spiritual rather than financial.

A number of research studies have shown that volunteering, particularly by older adults, provides health benefits.

For students who need community service hours to graduate high school or qualify for scholarships, volunteer work is a particularly important and necessary commitment of time.

The "Why People Volunteer" report, which polled numerous volunteers of all ages, found that one of the overwhelming responses from those surveyed was that volunteer work revealed interests and skills that had never been realized by the volunteers.

Once you begin to volunteer and organizers of that particular activity or program see that you're a valuable asset, you make be asked or encouraged to do more. Volunteering to clean up a park, help in a library or build a house for Habitat for Humanity can be great ways to stay busy and contribute in a positive way to your community, without much of a risk of emotional attachment to those you are helping.

In its report on "Why People Volunteer," the Voluntary Action Directorate of Multiculturalism and Citizenship Canada cites several common turnoffs to volunteering, such as poor organization, a lack of training and assignments that don't fit the volunteers' interests or skills.

https://oureverydaylife.com/what-are-the-pros-and-cons-of-volunteer-work-3952361.html

---

Practice 7-9: Things

On the Internet – Things

The following articles are about the topics that actually appear on the TOEFL test.

	Teamwork
1	Teamwork means that colleagues work well together. Have you ever wondered how some work groups exhibit effective teamwork and other teams remain dysfunctional for the life of the team? **Some organizational cultures support teamwork; others don't.** This is why so many teams struggle to get the relationships, the interaction, and the task execution right.
2	**The Team Is Clear About Its Mission** The team understands the goals and is committed to attaining them. This clear direction and agreement on mission and purpose are essential for effective teamwork. This team clarity is reinforced when the organization has clear expectations for the team's work, goals, accountability, and outcomes. **The Team Environment Encourages Reasonable Risks** The team creates an environment in which people are comfortable taking reasonable risks in communicating, advocating positions, and taking action. Team members trust each other. Team members are not punished for disagreeing; disagreement is expected and appreciated. **Respectful Communication Is the Norm** Communication is open, honest, and respectful. People feel free to express their thoughts, opinions, and potential solutions to problems. People feel as if they are heard out and listened to by team members who are attempting to understand. Team members ask questions for clarity and spend their thought time listening deeply rather than forming rebuttals while their co-worker is speaking. **Strong Sense of Group Commitment** Team members have a strong sense of belonging to the group. They experience a deep commitment to the group's decisions and actions. This sense of belonging is enhanced and reinforced when the team spends the time to develop team norms or relationship guidelines together. https://www.thebalancecareers.com/tips-for-better-teamwork-1919225

	Homework
1	**It can take kids away from computers, TVs, and mobile devices.** Today's students spend almost as much time at school as they do watching TV or using an electronic

	device. Students spend up to 4 hours per school night on electronic devices an up to 8 hours per weekend day. By encouraging homework, the amount of time being spend in front of screens can be reduced. In return, there is a lower risk of eye strain, myopia, headaches, and other issues that are associated with high levels of screen use. **It extends the learning process throughout the day.** Most school subjects are limited to 30-60 minutes of instruction per day. Specialty subjects, such as art and music, may be limited to 1-2 hours per week. Sending homework allows students to have their learning process extended in these areas, allowing them to develop a deeper knowledge, interest, or passion about certain matters. Time shortages can create knowledge gaps. Homework can help to lessen or eliminate those gaps. **It encourages discipline.** Repeating the same tasks on a daily basis is far from the definition of "fun" for the average person. Without repetition, however, it is difficult to improve personal skills or discover new talents. Homework is an opportunity to lay the framework of discipline that can last for a lifetime. Sometimes, homework isn't about the actual work that needs to be finished. It is about learning how to manage oneself so that personal goals can be consistently achieved.
2	**It eliminates play time from a child's routine.** Many children already put in the same number of hours for their schooling and activities as their parents do with their full-time jobs. Sports, clubs, Girl or Boy Scouts, church activities, and more are all part of the modern routine. There needs to be time for playing in there as well and homework can take that time away. When children aren't given time to play, they have lower levels of personal safety awareness, have lower average grades, and have a higher risk of health concerns. **It decreases the development of creative processes.** Homework is usually structured around the completion of a specific assignment. Even in art, music, or writing, the homework must be completed in a specific way to receive a good grade. That means homework is teaching concepts of compliance more than it is teaching concepts of skill development. https://brandongaille.com/24-top-pros-cons-homework/

College major	
1	Your major in college is your specialized area of study. Beyond general college requirements, you'll also take a group of courses in a subject of your choosing such as Chemistry, Comparative Literature, or Political Science. At some schools you can even design your own major.
2	Your choice of major will not lock you into a specific career for the rest of your life. That said, you WILL spend a lot of time whatever subject you choose. Here's what you need to know about college majors before you commit. **Career Prep**

Choose a major because it will prepare you for a specific career path or advanced study. Maybe you already know that you want to be a nurse, a day trader, a physical therapist, or a web developer. Before you declare, take a class or two in the relevant discipline, check out the syllabus for an advanced seminar, and talk to students in the department of your choice. Make sure you're ready for the coursework required for the career of your dreams.

Earning Potential

Future earning potential is worth considering—college is a big investment, and while college can pay you back in many ways beyond salary, this can be a major factor for students who are paying their own way or taking out loans. According to PayScale.com, the majors that lead to the highest salaries include just about any type of engineering, actuarial mathematics, computer science, physics, statistics, government, and economics. Keep your quality of life in mind, too—that six figure salary may not be worth it if you're not happy at the office.

Subjects You Love

Some students choose a major simply because they love the subject matter. If you love what you're studying, you're more likely to fully engage with your classes and college experience, and that can mean better grades and great relationships with others in your field. If your calling is philosophy, don't write it off just because you're not sure about graduate school, or what the job market holds for philosophers. Many liberal arts majors provide students with critical thinking skills and writing abilities that are highly valued by employers.

https://www.princetonreview.com/college-advice/choosing-college-majors

Automobiles	
1	Learn about Cars: All Kinds of Automobiles

Automobiles vary greatly in size, shape, color, type, available options... well you get the idea. That can make it really difficult to find which one of thousands of cars is best for you.

https://theunlimiteddriver.com/learn-about-cars-all-kinds-automobiles/

Why Cars Are Important and Why You Should Invest In One

In this fast-paced world, managing your personal and professional lives can be really hectic. If you don't have your own personal mode of transportation, life can become even more hectic. To make your life easier, you should always find an easier and reliable mode of transportation. Continue reading to learn why cars are important and why you should invest in one wisely.

Convenience and Independence

For young adults who have college and university, life without personal transportation can be frustrating. This is one of the main reasons you should invest in a car. It provides the ultimate convenience and could help you take your first step towards independence. You will not have to be dependent on your family members or public transportation, able to drive to your college without any problems.

Save Time – Save your Mind

Using public transport to take your children to school can be extremely stressful and time-consuming. You have to constantly remember the time, so that you do not miss the bus. Additionally, even if you do catch the bus, the stops made on the way can ensure you have a long journey ahead of you. However, if you own a car, you can ease the burden and stress by dropping them by yourself.

Easy Shopping and Transportation of Heavy Items

It's the start of the new month and once again, you need to head out for your monthly groceries. But, the only thing that's frustrating is carrying those heavy bags on foot or in a bus. You will not have to go through this hassle if you purchase a vehicle. Cars come with a trunk that provides sufficient space to easily transport plenty of shopping and heavy materials.

https://www.globalcarsbrands.com/why-cars-are-important-and-why-you-should-invest-in-one/

| 2 | Pollution |

Driving a car contributes significantly to air pollution. According to the U.S. Environmental Protection Agency, transportation accounts for nearly 30 percent of all greenhouse gases released into the environment, and vehicles "used primarily for personal transport account for 62 percent of total transportation emissions." The agency lists cars as major contributors of hydrocarbons, nitrogen oxides, carbon monoxide and sulfur dioxide, among other pollutants.

Costs

Purchasing a new car can be a substantial investment, and often requires taking out a loan, sometimes at high interest. You can reduce ownership costs by purchasing an inexpensive used car, but a number of costs are unavoidable, including fuel and maintenance costs. According to Insure.com, another unavoidable cost is automobile liability insurance. All but three states---New Hampshire, Wisconsin and Florida---require carrying insurance.

Safety Issues

Despite safety advancements such as seat belts and airbags, cars remain more dangerous than other major modes of transportation, including travel by air, bus and train. According to the Fatality Analysis Reporting System Encyclopedia, nearly 40,000 people die each year in car crashes. In addition, people are injured and killed in non-crash related car accidents: trapped in trunks or other compartments during hot weather; strangled by power sunroofs or windows; and suffocated by carbon monoxide released into the car.

https://itstillruns.com/disadvantages-driving-car-6386808.html

| **Grades** | |
| 1 | |

Why do schools need a grading system?

While grading systems are not a reflection of the worth of a student, they do reflect their progression through the learning material they are being taught at school. Debates about the efficacy of the examination system abound. However, the need for a grading system is obvious – there needs to be a system by which we can track the progress of a student. A grading system helps educators, parents, and students assess themselves vis a vis their peers.

	What are the pros of letter grading system in K-12?
	    1. Takes the pressure off students
	
	The most obvious effect of a letter grading system is that it takes the pressure of microscopic score comparisons between students. Since letter grading tends to group students into bands, the difference between a 90 and 92 is not fussed over.
	
	    2. More easily achievable
	
	Since the letter grading system consists of bands, the push a student might have to make to move from a high B to a low A is more easily surmountable. It is a matter of achieving a few marks to change your letter grade, in these cases – psychologically this makes it look like higher letter grades are more achievable, since the goal becomes attaining a maximum of 9 marks and have the same letter grade as the class topper, than, say, 20 to achieve the same result.
	
	    3. Better than a pass/fail system
	
	A pass/fail system that relies on one exam places too much pressure on the student and, arguably, is not an accurate reflection of the student's abilities. Letter grades look at cumulative scoring, instead of pressurising a student to deliver a stellar performance during one exam. It also reflects their abilities more holistically and encourages even those with lower scores to progress, instead of consigning an entire group of students to failure.

2	What are the cons of letter grading system in K-12?
	    1. Low levels of accuracy
	
	Letter grade systems might feel good, but they do not accurately reflect a student's performance in an exam since they tend to group students into bands. This means that a student who has managed to scrape a 91 is put on the same level as a student who achieved a perfect score.
	
	    2. Discourages competition, even when healthy
	
	Critics allege that letter grading systems also discourage healthy competition that students will anyway have to deal with in their careers. While microscopically examining every point lost is not helpful in any way, being able to chart smaller increments in scores can keep a child motivated to work towards their full potential, instead of settling for doing just a decent job.
	
	    4. Not universally applied
	
	Letter scoring systems also get a lot of flak since no standardized grading exists – some schools follow a plus or minus letter grade system over and above the simple one described above, some have different letters for different bands, etc. These variations mean that letter grades do not translate well across systems – a real issue in an increasingly globalized world.
	
	https://fedena.com/blog/2018/07/pros-and-cons-of-letter-grading-system-in-k-12.html

Computers	
1	Computers are commonly used items in many areas. It is an important thing to people, especially the people who run organizations, industry, etc. Almost anything you know is run or made by computers. Cars and jets were designed on computers, traffic signals are run by computers, most medical equipment use

	computers and space exploration was started with computers. Most of the jobs today require the use of computers. These 'mechanical brains' made a huge impact on our society. It would be hard if we didn't have the computer around.
2	Computers impacted many items in today's society. One area the computer impacted on is the business area. Business uses computers for keeping track of accounts, money, or items that they need. You may notice business people using computers a lot, especially the laptop computers, portable computers that can be taken to your work area. You may see people use things like pie-charts and graphs when they present information to other business people in meetings. Most of those charts were made by computers. The business field uses the computers a lot for their companies and organizations. Education was impacted by computers as well. Computers help out students in a lot of today's projects and essays. If a student were to do an essay on the planet Saturn, they could look in an electronic encyclopedia in the computer or they could look up their topic on the internet. They could also type their essays and reports on what's called a word-processing program. This program allows you to type anything out from a school essay to business papers. You can make your paper look very neat by adding images and neat looking text to impress your teacher. Now and days, typing out essays and reports are mandatory, especially in High School. Computers help students in any way they need, researching, typing, searching, etc. Teachers use computers as well. They use computers to keep track of grades, type out instruction for their students, and to let students use the computer for school purposes. An important field computers impacted on is the medical field. The computers helped the hospitals out very much. In pharmacies, the pharmacists use computers to keep a record of what medication to give to a patient and the amount they need. Most computers in the hospital are used to keep data of patience and their status. Computers also keep track of equipment placement and status as well. Scientists need the help of computers to find cures for diseases that need cures like cancer and STDs. Without the computers help, cures for a lot of diseases wouldn't have been found. Computer helped the medical area a lot and we are grateful for that since they keep track of our health. Other areas the computer impacted on is space exploration and designs of transportation. http://computerimpact.tripod.com/

Language	
1	Language impacts the daily lives of members of any race, creed, and region of the world. Language helps express our feelings, desires, and queries to the world around us. Words, gestures and tone are utilized in union to portray a broad spectrum of emotion. The unique and diverse methods human beings can use to communicate through written and spoken language is a large part of what allows to harness our innate ability to form lasting bonds with one another; separating mankind from the rest of the animal kingdom. The impact of multilingualism can be traced to even more fields. A doctor who can communicate with his or her patient in their native tongue is much more likely to have success at diagnosing them. A scientist or engineer capable of explaining his findings and ideas to his peers will be able to expedite and perfect their work, even if his peers could not understand him in his first language. Any hiring manager in any company in the world would tell you that the ability to speak a foreign language is a prized commodity. Learning to communicate fluently in multiple languages provides additional job security and advancement opportunities in uncertain economic times. In order to prepare our nation's children to be the next generation of future entrepreneurs, doctors, scientists, engineers, or whatever influential job they choose, we must foster an environment from a young age that promotes multilingual learning. Through this we are setting up ourselves, our children, and our children's children, for growth, success, security, and ultimately, prosperity.
2	1. Foreign Language study creates more positive attitudes and less prejudice toward people who are different.

2. Analytical skills improve when students study a foreign language.
3. Business skills plus foreign language skills make an employee more valuable in the marketplace.
4. Dealing with another culture enables people to gain a more profound understanding of their own culture.
5. Creativity is increased with the study of foreign languages.
6. Graduates often cite foreign language courses as some of the most valuable courses in college because of the communication skills developed in the process.
7. International travel is made easier and more pleasant through knowing a foreign language.
8. Skills like problem solving, dealing with abstract concepts, are increased when you study a foreign language.
9. Foreign language study enhances one's opportunities in government, business, medicine, law, technology, military, industry, marketing, etc.

https://discover.trinitydc.edu/continuing-education/2014/02/26/importance-of-language-why-learning-a-second-language-is-important/

	Customs and tradition
1	Traditions represent a critical piece of our culture. They help form the structure and foundation of our families and our society. They remind us that we are part of a history that defines our past, shapes who we are today and who we are likely to become. Once we ignore the meaning of our traditions, we're in danger of damaging the underpinning of our identity. • Tradition contributes a sense of comfort and belonging. It brings families together and enables people to reconnect with friends. • Tradition reinforces values such as freedom, faith, integrity, a good education, personal responsibility, a strong work ethic, and the value of being selfless. • Tradition provides a forum to showcase role models and celebrate the things that really matter in life. https://www.franksonnenbergonline.com/blog/7-reasons-why-traditions-are-so-important/
2	**Essay on Social Importance of Customs** They are the self-accepted rules of social life. They bind people together, assimilate their actions to the accepted standards and control their purely egoistic impulses. They are found among the preliterate as well as the literate people. They are the strongest ties in building up a social order. **Customs Constitute the Treasury of Our Social Heritage:** Customs preserve our culture and transmit it to the succeeding generations. They have added stability and certainty to our social life. They bring people together and develop social relationships among them. They provide for a feeling of security in human society. People normally obey them for their violation is always condemned and resisted. The children learn the language spoken, and the occupation followed by their parents through the customs. The imprint of custom can be found on various activities of the members of society. http://www.shareyouressays.com/essays/essay-on-social-importance-of-customs/87651

	Advertising
1	**24 Pros and Cons of Advertising** It's often said that "it takes money to make money." This often refers to the fact that a business must advertise in order to create an awareness of what is being offered to the general public. The average person is exposed to over 1,000 different brands and messages every day that promote a business or specific products. This means there are some certain advantages that can be gained by advertising, but there are certain disadvantages in the modern advertising campaign that must be considered as well. The Pros of Advertising **1. It's an easy way to create a value proposition.** Prospects need to see that something can solve a problem for them in order for them to consider making a purchase. Value is often seen as saving someone time or saving them money. Advertising is an easy way to prove that there is a value proposition to be considered with a brand or product. If the real value which is received is equal to or greater than the perceived value received in an advertising message, then a solid relationship can be built. **2. It creates a way to set brands and products apart from the competition.** People today don't just want to buy something that is "good enough." They want to purchase the best product at the best price. If someone has got $100 to spend on Champagne and there's a bottle of Dom Perignon found within that person's budget, would they spend all of their cash on the bottle of Dom or buy 5 bottles of $20 Champagne instead? Setting a brand apart gives the product extra value and that's why most people would purchase the bottle of Dom. **3. It reaches multiple demographics simultaneously.** Advertising is one of the easiest ways to reach out to multiple target groups at the same time. This action helps a business to better discover who their primary customers tend to be, the demographics to which they belong, and provides information that allows for prospect cloning. It also gives a business the chance to reach out to multiple new demographics in order to judge how influential their marketing messages happen to be.
2	The Cons of Advertising **1. It costs time and money.** Advertising doesn't come cheap. It will always cost time, money, or both to complete successfully. It may not cost someone anything to create a video, but they'll be spending time editing the content of it, use resources to upload it, and spend time responding to comments about it. This means every business must find some way to make sure there is time or money budgeted for advertising so there aren't any unhealthy surprises that come along. When money is tight, this naturally limits advertising options and that means growth options are limited as well. **2. Results are never guaranteed.** It is entirely possible for a business to spend $1 million on advertising and get $0 in return. The results of an advertising campaign are never guaranteed. This is why so much research goes into demographic research so that problems can be identified and solved by the products that a brand represents. As long as there is some sort of valid value proposition, there will always be some sort of return. Even then, however that $1 million campaign could bring a return of just $1. **3. It's a general nuisance.** Excessive advertising might have a positive effect on the economy, but it tends to have a negative effect on consumers when the same type of advertising happens over and over again. This is especially true during election cycles when political advertising takes over the landscape. Hundreds of millions of dollars

in advertising may be spent on a single election, exposing people to competing messages that get repetitive and irritating when they are seen several times per hour.

https://brandongaille.com/24-pros-and-cons-of-advertising/

The internet	
1	Pros and Cons of Internet Since the introduction of the internet, people have been able to achieve a lot by saving more time and using fewer resources. The internet brought with it sweeping changes across all industries and changed the way we do things. But with all the changes, there were benefits and shortcomings among them. ## Pros: 1. **Allows for real time communication:** The internet has brought about speed as a major factor which is very vital in terms of communication. Through such means as email and social media, you can send and receive messages almost instantaneously which makes communication real time. 2. **Get more done in less time:** The internet brought with it some level of speed that had not been experienced before. For this reason, people have been able to get more done within a very short period of time thanks to the internet. 3. **Availability of information:** The internet is averse with almost all information about everything. Through search engines such as Google, users are able to search and retrieve information about anything in the world.
2	## Cons: 1. **Decreased privacy:** The internet has also come with reduced privacy. Through the internet, people's profiles especially through social media can be accessed by everyone which leaves people exposed. 2. **It is addictive: The internet has become addictive especially through the advent of social media.** As people continue to spend more and more time online, they become addicted to the trappings of the internet which may lead to wastage of time. 9. **It exposes children to vulnerabilities:** The internet has exposed children to vulnerabilities since they are able to see what adults are doing in a different part of the world and tend to copy these habits. https://www.prosancons.com/technology/pros-cons-internet/

Discoveries	
1	Life-Changing Science Discoveries Try to imagine life without antibiotics. We wouldn't live nearly as long as we do without them. Here's a look at some discoveries that have changed the world.
2	**Electricity**

If electricity makes life easier for us, you can thank **Michael Faraday.** He made two big discoveries that changed our lives. In 1821, he discovered that when a wire carrying an electric current is placed next to a single magnetic pole, the wire will rotate. This led to the development of the electric motor. Ten years later, he became the first person to produce an electric current by moving a wire through a magnetic field. Faraday's experiment created the first generator, the forerunner of the huge generators that produce our electricity.

Penicillin

Antibiotics are powerful drugs that kill dangerous bacteria in our bodies that make us sick. In 1928, **Alexander Fleming** discovered the first antibiotic, penicillin, which he grew in his lab using mold and fungi. Without antibiotics, infections like strep throat could be deadly.

Quantum Theory

Danish physicist **Niels Bohr** is considered one of the most important figures in modern physics. He won a 1922 Nobel Prize in Physics for his research on the structure of an atom and for his work in the development of the quantum theory. Although he help develop the atomic bomb, he frequently promoted the use of atomic power for peaceful purposes.

https://www.factmonster.com/math-science/inventions-discoveries/life-changing-science-discoveries

	Types of communication (face to face vs electronic)
1	In today's digital age, it can be easy to avoid face-to-face interaction. As social media has become more and more popular in recent years, people can often find themselves having more and more interactions with friends online as opposed to in person. Job interviews can now be conducted through video chat platforms such as Skype, online classes are becoming more popular, and sometimes one can even find oneself working an entire job from online or making friends that are from far away thanks to the internet. ## What are the advantages of digital communication? There is no doubt that communicating digitally can offer a lot of benefits to everyone involved, and especially to those who are shy or experience anxiety when it comes to having high-stakes interactions in person. If the idea of asking your teacher a question in real life ties your stomach into knots and causes you to start sweating bullets, then it might be wise to take some pressure off of yourself by sending them an email. Written online communication can also be helpful because you get the chance to think about what you are going to say and proofread it before you send it out into the world. When having a conversation in person with someone you might say something that you didn't mean to say or even misspeak, while when communicating digitally there is less of a chance that your meaning will be skewed because you get the chance to actually edit and revise what you are meaning to say *before* the other person receives it.
2	## What are the disadvantages of digital communication? Obviously, while there are many upsides to communicating with people through email and other forms of nonverbal communication, there are also some downsides. To put it simply, email simply *feels* less personal than meeting with someone in person. As is mentioned above, miscommunications can

sometimes happen as a result. When you are communicating via email, you can't see the face of the other person (or people) that you are communicating with, so you might miss important body language cues or facial expressions that will clue you in to how your words and message are being received.

It is also easy to misinterpret tone in an email. If you've ever received a text from a friend that you falsely thought to be passive-aggressive because of something small—maybe the in which it was worded, or maybe even the absence or presence of certain punctuation marks—you'll understand that miscommunications simply happen. It is often easier to remedy these miscommunications in person because you can address it immediately, as opposed to over a long period of time with an email correspondence.

https://blog.collegevine.com/the-importance-of-face-to-face-communication-in-the-digital-age/

	Judgements and decisions
1	What's the best way to make a decision? Take your time and think through all your options and their consequences and then decide or go with your first reaction? Sometimes snap judgments can be best. The decision-making process can sometimes be an arduous task. As with everything, you start off identifying a problem. You lay out all the options that will address the problem. You create criteria for evaluating the options. You apply the criteria to the options and rank order them. You hold meetings with other stakeholders to get their views and opinions. Based on the meetings, you may add or subtract options, reweigh criteria, and reevaluate. You do this over and over until you finally come up with a decision, which you then implement. But is it the BEST way to come to a decision? Not necessarily. The obvious alternative to a well-studied decision-making process is to go with your first instinct. Assess the situation quickly and then react based on your knowledge and past experiences. Drawing on them, you can often come up with a decision that often parallels what you would have come up with had you dwelt on it. This is usually only successful when you have plenty of past experience and knowledge to go on. In some cases, you'll get the same results to a problem whether you carefully study all the alternatives or just go with your first reaction. Although you might not want to go around making snap decisions on a regular basis, you shouldn't be afraid to go with your gut on occasion. Trust your experience and instincts -- you'll save time and get the job done at the same time. If a decision "feels right," often it will wind up being right. https://www.techrepublic.com/blog/decision-central/snap-decisions-may-be-the-best-ones/
2	Our Brains Immediately Judge People Even if we cannot consciously see a person's face, our brain is able to make a snap decision about how trustworthy they are. According to a new study published in the *Journal of Neuroscience*, the brain immediately determines how trustworthy a face is before it's fully perceived, which supports the fact that we make very fast judgments about people. https://time.com/3083667/brain-trustworthiness/ You make decisions quicker and based on less information than you think We live in an age of information. In theory, we can learn everything about anyone or anything at the

touch of a button. All this information should allow us to make super-informed, data-driven decisions all the time. But the widespread availability of information does not mean that you actually use it even if you have it. In fact, decades of research in psychology and behavioral science find that people readily make data-poor snap judgments in a variety of instances. People form <u>lasting impressions of others</u> in the span of milliseconds, evaluators judge teachers in less than a minute and consumers make shopping decisions based on little deliberation. Even voting decisions can seemingly be predicted from preliminary impressions formed during incredibly brief time periods.

In our research, my co-author Ed O'Brien and I tested whether people can correctly anticipate how much information they and others use when making varied judgments. We consistently found that people were surprised by how quickly they make judgments and how little information they use doing so.

In one study, we asked participants to imagine having pleasant or unpleasant interactions with another person. In comparison, we asked another group of participants to predict how many of those interactions they would need to experience to determine someone's character. We found that people believed they would need many interactions to make this judgment, when in fact the first group needed few.

In plenty of cases, a quick decision is just fine.

It's not clear that quick decisions are always bad. <u>Sometimes snap judgments are remarkably accurate</u> and they can save time. It would be crippling to comb through all the available information on a topic every time a decision must be made. However, misunderstanding how much information we actually use to make our judgments has important implications beyond making good or bad decisions.

http://theconversation.com/you-make-decisions-quicker-and-based-on-less-information-than-you-think-108460

	What Would You Do With a Million Dollars?
1	If you had a million dollars (tax free), what would you do with that money? Will you invest it, take a trip, start a business, quit your job, or give it to charity?
2	**I would pay off student loans and then buy a house, though in this market I might wait a couple of years, until we know more of what is actually going to happen with real estate.** I would invest a large chunk of the rest of it, though I have no idea how, off the top of my head. That much money is beyond what I know how to invest right now, so I'd read some good books and talk to some good people. **If I added $1 million (tax free) to my assets, I would:** Start a charitable organization, perhaps structured as a foundation, perhaps not that would fund non-profits with great ideas, committed volunteers, and limited start-up resources; these non-profits could be involved in any endeavor but I would look favorably on those who would a) give Internet access and appropriate resources to senior community centers and retirement homes so that senior adults could go digital (don't laugh, once they get the hang of it, they'll be blogging away, making new friends globally, sending digital images of bingo night to their grandchildren, etc.) and b) increase green spaces and opportunities for outdoor activities, mainly for children but for all ages **Sadly, these days, a million isn't really that much, so it wouldn't go as far as I'd like. Here goes:** A 3BR house (one for me, one for my home office, and one for company) in the area I used to live, with a big kitchen, and the furniture to put in it. A new fuel-efficient car.

A vacation to London. (I haven't had a real vacation since 1997.)

The rest I'd take in cash, put in a wheel barrow, roll it in to my bank branch, dump it in front of my personal banker's desk, and say "Look at all this. I just don't know what to do with it — can you think of something?" (Based on a running joke between the two of us.)

I suppose I'd pay off my mortgage and my sister's. The rest, I'd split between investing in conservative stuff, like stocks and bonds, and I'd probably invest a hefty chunk in Wise Bread.

I would start a small venture capital fund modeled after Y Combinator. The fund will invest $10,000 to $20,000 on small startups like Reddit during their initial development stages. It will be a great opportunity to meet lots of exciting and smart people. Of course, the prospect of hitting home runs and earning billions is a nice bonus as well.

https://www.wisebread.com/what-would-you-do-with-a-million-dollars

---

Is Our Pace of Life Getting Faster?	
1	As modern technology enables instantaneous communication and being "on-call" 24 hours a day, many people have wondered: is our pace of life getting faster? New forms of technology consistently emerge to help us complete tasks faster and optimize our time management, but how are they really affecting our lives? One psychological study from 1999 compared the pace of life in 31 major cities across the world, basing its analysis on three main indicators: **the average walking speed in downtown areas, how quickly postal clerks completed basic tasks, and the accuracy of clocks in public places.** They found that the pace of life was faster in economically-developed countries, colder climates, and individualistic cultures. Japan and Western Europe were two areas that specifically stood out for having faster times.
2	Another 2007 study found that around the world, people are walking about 10% faster than they used to. Researchers identified that those who walk quickly are also more likely to speak fast and eat fast. They become impatient when waiting in lines or traffic, and they're more likely to wear a watch. Faster doesn't always equal better, as researchers found correlations between subjects with faster walking speeds and several negative health effects, like heart disease. Many business executives are concerned that they won't be able to keep up with today's rapid-fire hyperactive pace. They worry that they can't match new levels of innovation or maintain growth levels past the start-up stage. After all, the range of problems that young businesses face can seem vast. https://aligntoday.com/is-our-pace-of-life-getting-faster/ Slowing down our pace and just being for moments throughout our day gives us access to our true nature and its innate wisdom. Hurrying, on the other hand, keeps us tied to the ego, which barks its commands, pushes us harder, and shames us. The ego views life from a lens of fear and scarcity. It doesn't trust life because it isn't in touch with the truth about life. It copes with its fears and insecurities by pushing us to constantly be doing. When we are caught in the ego's world, we can never rest and just be, and we lose touch with the deep sense that all is well. When we stop long enough to notice how we may be making life about doing rather than being, we are likely to agree that life must be—has to be—about more than just getting things done, that it must be about something deeper and more mysterious, something we can't put into words but which we intuitively feel.

Here are some things you can do when you notice yourself hurrying or feeling stressed-out (taken from From Stress to Stillness: Tools for Inner Peace

- Stop whatever you're doing and take a break
- Slow down enough to really experience what you're doing
- Pay attention to your breath for a few minutes
- Take a few slow, deep breaths
- Meditate or sit quietly for a few minutes
- Notice what is aware. What is it that is conscious and aware?
- Pay attention to the sensations in your body
- Notice the aliveness that is present in your hands, arms, and entire body
- Pay attention to the sounds in your environment and the silence in between the sounds
- Pay attention to something of beauty in your environment and notice how beauty opens your heart
- Smile
- Bring to mind what you are grateful for.

https://www.radicalhappiness.com/blog/462-why-slow-is-better

Games	
1	Cognitive Benefits of Playing Video Games for Kids Contrary to the traditional belief that gaming is merely an addictive source of entertainment and diversion, recent research has proved that gaming has numerous benefits and key among them, is the development of cognitive skills in both children and adults. Just as physical exercise helps in improving and strengthening your muscles, cognitive games help to indulge one's brain in constant stimulation, thus improving the brain's performance. The following are some of the cognitive benefits of playing video games. **1. Improves coordination** When an adult or child is playing a video game, he or she is not only staring at the computer inactively. The activities and actions on the screen provide a lot of mental stimulation. For one to play, he or she will need to coordinate their visual, audial and physical movement. **2. Improves problem-solving skills** Video games involve certain rules. This means that the player has to think carefully before making any move to ensure that they stay within the required rules of that particular game. The player needs to make split- second decisions that will determine whether or not he or she will advance to the next level. **3. Enhances memory** Playing your favorite video game may require both visual and audial memory. The player is required to read or listen to the instructions which might only be provided at the beginning of the game, thus the need to remember them throughout the entire game. Mastery of the keys on your keyboard helps you easily move your characters in the game. This helps improve your memory, whether short- term or long-term. https://www.engadget.com/2017/02/09/8-cognitive-benefits-of-playing-video-games-for-kids/
2	Video Game Cons: **Violence** While every other study seems to draw opposite conclusions about the social effects of playing violent

video games, studies involving brain scans are concerning. Simply put, **children playing violent video games show decreased activity in areas of the brain dedicated to self-control and an increase in emotional arousal.** Help your children choose games you feel are appropriate. Many console game ratings include detailed information about the contents of the game's violence level, language, topics, etc.

Addiction

England's National Health Service began treating video game addiction this year, after the World Health Organization listed "gaming disorder" in its *International Classification of Disease*. What makes video games addictive? Playing releases dopamine into our systems, which gives us a feeling of pleasure and tells our brain to "do it again." In fact, video games are designed to be addictive. John Hopson, a games researcher at Microsoft Game Studios is also a doctor of behavioral and brain sciences who writes about game design. In "Behavioral Game Design" he explained how game designers can control behavior by providing simple stimulus and rewards at strategic times and places. Children with poor impulse control or who have a hard time fitting in are most vulnerable to game addiction. This may be because video games offer an easy way to fill the void created when real-world relationships are hard to form.

Social Replacement

Be aware of how much your children are playing video games and if it's replacing or negatively impacting other aspects of their lives. Kids with internet-connected games can easily "hang out" with friends after school without ever leaving home. But this type of virtual get-together is no replacement for actual face-to-face interaction. Setting aside the potential problems of online predators and cyber-bullying, virtual hangouts rob kids of the opportunity to practice their social skills and to move their bodies from one house to another.

https://www.uvpediatrics.com/topics/video-games-pros-and-cons/

	Friendship
1	Good friends are good for your health. Friends can help you celebrate good times and provide support during bad times. Friends prevent loneliness and give you a chance to offer needed companionship, too. Friends can also: • Increase your sense of belonging and purpose • Boost your happiness and reduce your stress • Improve your self-confidence and self-worth • Help you cope with traumas, such as divorce, serious illness, job loss or the death of a loved one • Encourage you to change or avoid unhealthy lifestyle habits, such as excessive drinking or lack of exercise Friends also play a significant role in promoting your overall health. Adults with strong social support have a reduced risk of many significant health problems, including depression, high blood pressure and an unhealthy body mass index (BMI). Studies have even found that older adults with a rich social life are likely to live longer than their peers with fewer connections.
2	**Why is it sometimes hard to make friends or maintain friendships?** Many adults find it hard to develop new friendships or keep up existing friendships. Friendships may take a back seat to other priorities, such as work or caring for children or aging parents. You and your friends may have grown apart due to changes in your lives or interests. Or maybe you've moved to a new

community and haven't yet found a way to meet people.

What's a healthy number of friends?

Quality counts more than quantity. While it's good to cultivate a diverse network of friends and acquaintances, you also want to nurture a few truly close friends who will be there for you through thick and thin.

What are some ways to meet new people?

It's possible that you've overlooked potential friends who are already in your social network. Think through people you've interacted with — even very casually — who made a positive impression.You may find potential friends among people with whom:

- You've worked or taken classes
- You've been friends in the past, but have since lost touch
- You've enjoyed chatting with at social gatherings

For example, try several of these ideas:

- **Attend community events.** Look for groups or clubs that gather around an interest or hobby you share. These groups are often listed in the newspaper or on community bulletin boards. There are also many websites that help you connect with new friends in your neighborhood or city. Do a Google search using terms such as [your city] + social network, or [your neighborhood] + meet-ups.
- **Volunteer.** Offer your time or talents at a hospital, place of worship, museum, community center, charitable group or other organization. You can form strong connections when you work with people who have mutual interests.
- **Extend and accept invitations.** Invite a friend to join you for coffee or lunch. When you're invited to a social gathering, say yes. Contact someone who recently invited you to an activity and return the favor.
- **Take up a new interest.** Take a college or community education course to meet people who have similar interests. Join a class at a local gym, senior center or community fitness facility.

How does social media affect friendships?

Joining a chat group or online community might help you make or maintain connections and relieve loneliness. However, research suggests that use of social networking sites doesn't necessarily translate to a larger offline network or closer offline relationships with network members. In addition, remember to exercise caution when sharing personal information or arranging an activity with someone you've only met online.

How can I nurture my friendships?

- **Be kind.** This most-basic behavior, emphasized during childhood, remains the core of successful, adult relationships. Think of friendship as an emotional bank account. Every act of kindness and every expression of gratitude are deposits into this account, while criticism and negativity draw down the account.
- **Listen up.** Ask what's going on in your friends' lives. Let the other person know you are paying close attention through eye contact, body language and occasional brief comments such as, "That sounds fun." When friends share details of hard times or difficult experiences, be

empathetic, but don't give advice unless your friends ask for it.
- **Open up.** Build intimacy with your friends by opening up about yourself. Being willing to disclose personal experiences and concerns shows that your friend holds a special place in your life, and deepens your connection.
- **Show that you can be trusted.** Being responsible, reliable and dependable is key to forming strong friendships. Keep your engagements and arrive on time. Follow through on commitments you've made to your friends. When your friends share confidential information, keep it private.

https://www.mayoclinic.org/healthy-lifestyle/adult-health/in-depth/friendships/art-20044860

	Life lessons
1	Important life lessons we are often taught too late Life is a continuous learning experience. Throughout our lives we keep rising and falling, picking up important lessons along the way. Some of these lessons come from experience, yet there are others that we learn watching others or reading in books for example. No matter how much we learn from the books there is a significant difference between practical and theoretical experience. Furthermore, there are many life lessons that we simply cannot learn until we face certain situations in our life. Most people would say that there are some lessons that come too late, catching us off-guard and unprepared. The following list unveils some of the most important lessons in life that people learn the hard way.
2	1. Walk your own path People like to judge other people. This peer pressure can make you stray from the path you started to carve for your future. Don't mind other people's aspirations, don't ever let someone else's goals and dreams influence your vision of life. It's your path and you decide where it takes you and how long it takes you to see it through. 2. Make every moment count Life goes by faster than we think. When you're in your twenties you think you'll stay there forever but before you know it you are in your thirties and it's too late for the things you wanted to do as a young person. Live your life to its full extent because life is short and we never know what tomorrow brings. 3. For every action, there's an equal opposite reaction Before you say something or act in a certain way, think about the consequences. A person could be unprepared to hear some truth or won't respond well to our gesture, no matter how good our intentions are. Treat each word with caution. https://www.theladders.com/career-advice/10-important-life-lessons-we-are-often-taught-too-late

	Entrepreneurship
1	Entrepreneurship Defined: What It Means to Be an Entrepreneur The road to entrepreneurship is often a treacherous one filled with unexpected detours, roadblocks and dead ends. There are lots of sleepless nights, plans that don't work out, funding that doesn't come through and customers that never materialize. It can be so challenging to launch a business that it may

	make you wonder why anyone willingly sets out on such a path. Yet despite all these hardships, every year, thousands of entrepreneurs embark on this journey determined to bring their vision to fruition and fill a need they see in society. They open brick-and-mortar businesses, launch tech startups, or bring a new product or service into the marketplace.
2	So what motivates entrepreneurs to venture forth when so many others would run in the other direction? Though each person's motivation is nuanced and unique, most entrepreneurs are spurred on by one or more of the following motivators: **Autonomy** – Entrepreneurs want to be their own bosses, set their own goals, control their own progress and run their businesses how they see fit. They recognize that their business's success or failure rests with them, yet they don't view this responsibility as a burden but, instead, as a marker of their freedom. **Purpose** – Many entrepreneurs have a clear vision of what they want to accomplish and feel compelled to work tirelessly to make that happen. They genuinely believe they have a product or service that fills a void and are compelled by a single-minded commitment to that goal to keep pushing ahead. They abhor stagnation and would rather fail while moving forward than languish in inactivity. **Flexibility** – Not everyone fits into the rigidity of a traditional corporate culture. Entrepreneurs are often looking to free themselves from these constraints, find a better work-life balance, or work at times and in ways that may be unconventional. This doesn't mean they are working fewer hours – oftentimes, especially in the early stages of growing a business, they are working longer and harder – but, rather, that they're working in a way that is natural and instinctual to them. https://www.businessnewsdaily.com/7275-entrepreneurship-defined.html

	Risk-taking
1	**Why risk-taking leads to success.** **Risks involve uncertainty and change.** By nature, risks involve challenging uncertainty and instituting change. If you have a desire to become more successful, it means you're at least partially unsatisfied with your current situation. Changing that situation inherently makes you more likely to escape it. **Elimination of risk is a guarantee of failure.** Mark Zuckerberg, founder of Facebook, has said that "the only strategy that is guaranteed to fail is not taking risks." If you refuse to take any risks in your life, you will pass up every opportunity in front of you in favor of a stable, certain future. That stability may be comforting, but it won't provide you with growth or advancement in any dimension. **Risk-takers are happier.** Taking risks eliminates the possibility of looking back and asking, "what if?" Even if you fail, you'll walk away with more experience and more knowledge, which can lead you to further success in other areas and at least one study shows that risk takers end up more satisfied with their lives because of it. https://www.entrepreneur.com/article/305985

	Human characteristics & qualities
1	Personality Traits & Personality Types: What is Personality? What makes someone who they are? Each person has an idea of their own personality type — if they are

	bubbly or reserved, sensitive or thick-skinned. Psychologists who try to tease out the science of who we are define personality as individual differences in the way people tend to think, feel and behave. There are many ways to measure personality, but psychologists have mostly given up on trying to divide humanity neatly into types. Instead, they focus on personality traits. https://www.livescience.com/41313-personality-traits.html
2	Reasons Your Personality Is Important **1. Because personality is what makes you interesting** Your looks can't make you interesting, at least not for long or not in a good way. Being interesting is how you grab people's attention, making personality important virtually whenever you're in a social setting. Think about the most interesting person you know, and the prettiest/most handsome person you know. Who would you rather be stuck in a room with? Being interesting is also not something that you can fake; just ask all the people who try and fail to do exactly that. Being interesting depends almost entirely on your personality, so if your personality is great then you're all set. **2. Because personality can change** Even if you don't have a great personality right now, you can acquire a better one by considering what you can do to become more likable while, of course, always staying true to yourself. To contrast, you can't acquire good looks, at least not naturally. That makes personality important in ways appearance can never be. Friends and family and partners want to see you grow as a person as you get older far more than they look forward to seeing you age. If you have a lot of anger buried inside you, for example, people close to you will be very pleased to see you change into a calmer person. No one's going to be proud of you for getting wrinkles and gray hair. **3. Because personality doesn't fade away** Good looks don't last. Eventually you grow old and gray; nothing can stop that. What makes personality important is the fact that it will stick with you, even when you're an old, old man or woman. It will even stay with you after you die. No one remembers someone who passed away by thinking about how handsome they were. They reminisces on the good times they had with them, made possible because of their compatible personalities. https://www.managementstudyguide.com/importance-of-personality-development.htm

Pets	
1	It is common for younger children to ask their parents for an animal, and if they agree, parents should make this choice responsibly, explaining their children that an animal is not a toy, but a living being that also needs care. Having an animal in the house can bring children, and the family in generates many advantages and benefits if it is not a decision made on a whim. For children, the benefits we talk about range from physical, psychological, emotional and social to educational. Children who care for a pet learn something fundamental: the importance of love and respect for animals. This will have very positive results in the social sphere of the child, as a child who learns to take care of an animal, treat it with love and patience, it could serve in the future to relate to his or her environment in a safer, more respectful and loving way with other people. In other words, child will be a person more inclined to develop not only cognitive intelligence, but also emotional intelligence. **Emotional intelligence is the ability to understand, manage and express in a clear and effective way our feelings, and interpret those of other people**, and has been considered for years as a key to the harmonious development of the quality of life of our children.

2	**Responsibility**
	In the day-to-day care of their pet, children also develops a sense of responsibility. By taking care of the animal's primary care, such as cleaning, feeding, necessities, the child learns day after day that having an animal in the house involves tasks, which must always be respected, to maintain the welfare of our animal. In doing so, our child will learn daily a sense of responsibility, knowing how to take care of a living being that is different from him. All of this forms and educates the child by bringing a sense of accomplishment that also helps him/her to feel independent and competent, slowly bringing positive feedback for self-esteem. In order to have a good coexistence between the animal and the child, education to respect is fundamental. The child should learn not to pull hair, tail, or disturb the animal while is eating or sleeping. Child will have to learn to respect a living being with characteristics and needs different from your own. http://www.oblumi.com/blog/the-importance-of-pets-for-children/

Industry	
1	The Industries Driving the U.S Economy The U.S. economy is finally recovering from the 2008 Great Recession. Jobs are being created by the millions, wage growth is picking up and foreign exports accounted for only 11.9 percent of the nation's GDP in 2016, according to the latest data by Statista. These signs indicate a prosperous recovery and a healthy, self-sufficient economy. What industries are propelling America's self-contained economy?
2	The tech sector is a huge component of the U.S. economy. Employment among computer and IT is projected to grow 13 percent from 2016 to 2026, faster than the average for all occupations. Demand for additional workers is stemming from cloud computing, the collection and storage of big data and information security. The impact of the tech industry has affected nearly every state and the industry is ranked in the top five of economic contributors in 22 states and in the top 10 of 42 states. Technology plays a role in almost all other sectors such as health care, advanced manufacturing, transportation, education and energy. The Internet of Things, artificial intelligence, machine learning, autonomous vehicles, and augmented and virtual reality are all changing society and industries. Economic growth in the United States is flourishing and continuing upward. The IT industry has been key to the economy's recovery and has influenced most other industries with digitalization and advanced technologies such as artificial intelligence and machine learning. Health care has benefited from new technologies and a demand for increased products and services due to the growing and aging population. https://www.investopedia.com/articles/investing/042915/5-industries-driving-us-economy.asp

Farming	
1	What Are the Benefits of Agriculture and Farmers? Humans once subsisted by hunting and gathering, foraging for available food wherever it could be found. These early peoples necessarily moved frequently, as food sources changed, became scarce or moved in the case of animals. This left little time to pursue anything other than survival and a peripatetic lifestyle. Human society changed dramatically approximately 12,000 years ago, possibly related to the ending of the last ice age, when agriculture began. People began planting collected seeds, harvesting them and selecting successful crops. This encouraged people to make permanent homes. With a settled lifestyle, other pursuits flourished, essentially beginning modern civilization.

	Agriculture gave people the opportunity to create civilizations, fight hunger and work to combat challenges in population growth and climate change. https://sciencing.com/benefits-agriculture-farmers-6973506.html
2	Sustainable farming is a growing practice that is vital to the health and welfare of our planet. While modern industrial agriculture is highly productive and can produce a massive amount of plants within a harvest season, it also introduces many damaging and long-term problems that can only be solved through sustainable practices. http://eatkind.net/5-reasons-sustainable-farming-important/

Skills	
1	How to Develop Your Skill Set to Advance Your Career **A skill set is a collection of skills and abilities.** Each person has a different skill set depending on their interests, natural abilities, personal qualities and technical skills. Skills can expand your professional competency and allow you to perform your job well. You can gain and improve skills with education and experience. The more advanced you are in performing certain skills, the more likely you are to get or progress in a job. **There are two main types of skills that make up your skill set—soft skills and hard skills.** Soft skills generally pertain to interpersonal skills and other personality traits that allow you to communicate and work with others. Soft skills are also transferable, which means they are valuable for any job no matter the industry. Hard skills, also known as technical skills, are capabilities you use to perform a task related to a specific job. You can gain or improve these skills through training, tutorials and practice. How to develop new skills If you want a job in an industry that requires different skills than those you currently have, there are many ways to expand your skill set or to develop your current skills for a better chance at promotions or raises. Here are several ways you can develop professional skills: 1. **Set goals for yourself.** Setting specific goals to improve your career helps you stay on track with your development. Make sure your goals are measurable, achievable and relevant to your profession or your goals. Then, consider organizing a timeline to achieve your goal by setting a beginning and end date, as well as smaller goals to achieve along the way. 2. **Seek feedback about strengths and weaknesses.** You can ask superiors, colleagues or even friends or family about your strengths and areas for improvement. It is important to seek feedback from people who will give you honest critiques rather than automatic praise. Once you identify your weaknesses, you can focus on developing those skills. 3. **Review job descriptions for positions you want.** These job descriptions will give you an idea of the transferable skills you have, as well as the job-specific skills you will need. Once you identify the skills you need, you can research job shadowing or education programs that can provide you with the necessary skill set to transition into that position. 4. **Take continuing education courses in career-related fields.** These courses are often taught by professionals with experience in their field. For some professions, continuing education courses are required to stay current in the industry. Many colleges and universities offer continuing education courses in a variety of fields. https://www.indeed.com/career-advice/career-development/how-to-develop-your-skill-set

2	**Read (or Listen to) Books, Articles, and Forums**
	Reading is fundamental, and whether you choose short blogs or books, it will make a difference. So make a plan to read content that will educate, inform, and introduce you to new tools, skills, and people. To start, dedicate 30 minutes a day to learning about your industry from top thought leaders. When reading books, use the appendix and notes to see where the author got his information and how he is researching and learning in his field.
	https://www.themuse.com/advice/6-ways-you-can-build-skills-without-asking-anyone-for-help

	TV
1	For most people, watching television is an enjoyable way to spend time. It is an undemanding activity that passes the time and there are very few families that don't own at least one television. Since so many people now own a television, there has been a proliferation in the number of channels available and shows to watch, so that you can quite easily find yourself spending hours in front of the television. Consequently, you may neglect other activities that need doing. Thus, although television may help to ease boredom, there are also some negative aspects associated with watching television.

Pros of watching television
The positive aspects of watching television include that you have something to talk to friends and relatives about. There are certain programs which are more popular than others and if you watch them you feel included and that you have something in common with the people around you.

Television can help to foster a sense of national identity, since a significant proportion of the population will be exposed to the same kinds of news programs and television shows, so that people feel that they belong to a wider community.

Plus, television can also be informative and educational, opening people's eyes up to the world outside. Educational TV programs provide priceless information that not only educate but also opens up your mind. Most of these programs teach and educate people on subjects that you may otherwise will not know and are never taught in schools. |
| 2 | **Cons of watching television**

However, there are also a lot of television shows that are not very educational, and could even be considered trash. Reality shows, for instance, offer nothing of any worth to the audience, yet people still tune in. People get hooked on shows which are poorly produced and concentrate mostly on issues of sex and violence.

Although there is no conclusive evidence that watching violence on television makes children more violent, when there is so much violence on television, it makes sense that people would become desensitized to it, and that this could make it easier for children to engage in violent activities.

Watching too much TV can lead to weight gain, poor social skills and lower academic results Unsupervised children spending too much of their time in front of a TV can have a big impact on their life. Obesity, lack of social skills and poor academic results are just some of the effects TV have on children. Some psychologist believe that too much TV time can have a major effect in the psychology of the child. Children are supposed to interact and play, not sit and watch.

https://phdessay.com/pros-cons-of-television/ |

Multimedia	
1	There are more than 32,000 broadcast radio and TV stations in the U.S., along with hundreds of cable TV and satellite radio stations. On top of that, we have daily newspapers, magazines targeting all kinds of readers, and, of course, the immeasurable breadth of the internet. All told, we have more ways to reach more people than we've ever had in the history of humankind. But is this a good thing? **The Pros of Mass Media** **It Can Keep Us Connected** Before mass media, you could live your entire life knowing nothing about the world outside of your village. Now, we are all connected. And this can be a very good thing. For instance, when a tsunami strikes, people all over the world hear about it within moments and can mobilize immediately to help. Without mass media, we would have far less ability to understand how we're all connected and how we all need each another. **It Can Spur Business** Where would business be without advertising and marketing? Thanks to the business communication made possible by mass media, businesses can reach potential consumers faster and easier than ever before. This helps keep our economy going. **It Can Spread Art and Culture** On the internet, you can see all of the world's artistic masterpieces or learn about the particularities of a culture far removed from your own. In addition, numerous TV and radio programs devote themselves to exploring the world, offering us the chance to discover new things and new ideas, and enlighten ourselves in the process.
2	**The Cons of Mass Media** **It Can Empower the Already Powerful** While mass media can create opportunities for anyone to share their story, the vast majority of our mass media is bought. And because it's bought, those with money can deeply influence what we see and hear. This gives the rich—and those connected to the rich—a far louder voice than the rest of us. At its best, this is unfair. At its worst, it's a way for a tiny minority to seize power over the vast majority. **It Can Be Used for Disinformation and Hate** How do you know what you're seeing or hearing from mass media is true? While some sources of information are far more trustworthy than others, mass media as a whole is vulnerable to propaganda and its lies. Totalitarian regimes have used mass media for nearly a century to control what their people believe. With the rise of the internet, even those in democracies can be easily exposed to media designed to drive us to hate or believe in lies. **It Can Homogenize Culture** Before mass media, art and culture were more localized, so they reflected diversity in how people spoke, dressed, and entertained themselves. Now, the entire world often sees and hears the same cultural influences. While diversity still clearly exists, there is the risk that mass media might reduce cultural variety, leaving us with less art and fewer inspirations. https://www.waldenu.edu/online-bachelors-programs/bs-in-communication/resource/the-pros-and-

	cons-of-mass-media

Face-to-face communication	
1	Face-to-face communication is one of the highly valued elements of any business, company, or workplace. Such communication comes in handy in facilitating various operations within the business while generally promoting corporate efficiency.
	1) Allows reading of body language
	Face-to-face communication allows efficiency in channeling of information from the speaker to the listener. It allows the listener to not only hear information but also observe carefully on the speaker's body language, facial expressions, and gestures. These visual cues generally improve the ability of two persons to effectively communicate with each other without missing a hint of the message.
	2) Builds trust and transparency
	Face-to-face meetings are normally effective in helping create trust and understanding between the parties communicating. This channel of communication is particularly important in businesses and in situations where important deals need to be made. Meeting face-to-face in the same room shows commitment, while dispelling any fears that may exist between the two parties.
	3) Allows discussion and conclusions
	Face-to-face meetings are normally highly effective as they allow for attendants to brainstorm together in productive discussions and constructive arguments. The likelihood of concluding the meeting with meaningful findings is therefore quite high. In cases, therefore, where a company needs to boost its ability to make resolutions, having a face-to-face meeting would ensure productivity and value for time invested in the meeting.
2	**Cons of face-to-face communication** **1) Finding appropriate time**
	Face-to-face communication can be disadvantages in situations where a large organization needs to convoke leaders from all branches. Finding common time for such leaders to meet for a face-to-face meeting may be too challenging, especially given the tight itinerary that each leader or manager has.
	2) Cost of facilitating a meeting
	The cost that goes into facilitating a meeting in a large organization with distant branches can be quite high. Mediating a face-to-face meeting would require each attendant to spend money flying from one destination to another just to attend meeting. Whereas the cost may not be much of a concern in a large organization with significant revenue, having two or three meetings every month would prove to be a logistical nightmare that may increase operational costs.
	3) Ineffective in large meetings
	In situations where face-to-face meetings are comprised of large numbers of persons in attendance, it is easy for communication to be grossly hindered. Large meetings can be quite boring, especially in situations where a single person talks for hours. The larger the meeting size, the more ineffective communication becomes because attendants easily lose their concentration.

https://smallbizclub.com/leadership/communication/7-pros-cons-face-face-communication-workplace/

Success
1	Regardless of how old you are, where you live, or what your career goals are, it's likely your ultimate goals in life are to be happy and successful. To be successful means more than just having money and making your mark. It means following your passions, living purposefully, and enjoying the present moment. **Make a list of your goals, and what you might do to achieve them.** Be sure to address both short-term and long-term goals; try to think beyond financial and career goals, such as relationship goals, personal goals for bettering yourself, things you would like to experience, or things you want to learn. Draw up a timeline that says when you want to achieve each part. **Identify your passions.** Before you can achieve success, you will have to define what success means to you. While it may take years to realize what you want to do with your life, identifying your passions, interests, and values will help you set goals and give your life a sense of meaning. If you have trouble identifying these things, then ask a friend or family member to help you. Ask yourself the following questions: **Live purposefully.** In order to achieve your dreams and be the person you want to be, you will have to start paying attention to your actions. Ask yourself, "Is what I'm doing going to lead me to where I want to be in life?" **Stick to your commitments.** Planning is not sufficient; keeping your word is also important. If you tell someone you will do something, do it. Similarly, don't tell someone you will do something if you're not sure you can. Be honest about your limits. https://www.wikihow.com/Be-Successful-in-Life
2	I've trained with some of the best coaches on the planet during my 20-year sports career, and again when I competed in the 2008 Olympics. But when I wanted to start my own company, to share my knowledge about motivational psychology and training with others, it wasn't as easy as I'd thought it would be. Launching a new business is not easy. You have to give up the comforts of a stable paycheck to delve into the unknown, an unpredictable abyss. A lot of things keep us from making the leap—things like fear and insecurity. And one thing above all the rest: motivation. When I looked back on my days as an athlete, I understood what was different. I remembered what (or who) made me push myself even when I didn't want to. The difference was, as an athlete, I had structured days and a coach to report to. Structure keeps us focused and a coach keeps pushing and challenging us. https://www.success.com/10-tips-to-achieve-anything-you-want-in-life/

Sports
1	Against a backdrop of increasing childhood obesity, the physical benefits of sports participation are clear. Kids today need to move more, and being on a team or involved in a sport is a great way to stay healthy. But there has also been more discussion of the physical risks that children face in sports, and with good reason. As a nation, we are coming to terms with the epidemic of knee (soccer and track), shoulder (tennis and baseball), and head (football) injuries related to specific sports. What's talked about less often are the psychological risks and benefits related to youth sports. **Psychological Benefits of Youth Sports** 1. **The ability to take criticism and work collaboratively.** To help young athletes improve, coaches

	must point out mistakes and faulty technique. Learning to handle this feedback establishes a foundation for adult skill-building and collaboration. In addition, with their team and coaches, athletes learn the give-and-take of working together and managing conflict. Research suggests that athletic girls become women who are better equipped than their non-athletic counterparts to handle criticism and stress. Effective coaching and competition can help build internal resources that will serve kids well into adulthood. 2. **Acquisition of a work ethic.** Sports require effort and commitment, both traits that serve us well in adulthood. I've seen how my children apply the aptitude for hard work and effort that they acquired in athletics to almost everything they do in their lives, from hobbies to academic assignments. Excelling in sport is all about the work we expend, which sets up an excellent foundation for long-term success. 3. **Resilience.** Too many tweens and teens are unable to handle the rigors of school. They are easily overwhelmed and crumble when they do poorly in class. In fact, parents often protect their children from defeat by fiercely advocating for them, doing their homework, and even asking teachers to change poor grades. Overprotection undermines the development of resilience. Youth sports provide a nice balance since parents can't protect athletes from defeat and hardship. It's good for your kids to learn how to both lose and win.
2	**Psychological Risks of Youth Sports** 1. **Self-esteem is tied to sports performance.** Who your child is as a person shouldn't be tied closely to the ability to hit home runs or score touchdowns. If it is, that's a guaranteed set-up for feelings of failure and low self-esteem. Most young athletes feel great when they win, but it's how they handle the loss that defines their long-term character. Remind your sporty kid that she's always a winner in your book, even if she loses. 2. **Delusions that sport will provide college scholarships.** Too many parents believe that their child is destined to receive a Division 1 college scholarship. This is akin to playing the lottery: Don't bank on it. Putting all your eggs in the sports basket is misguided and dangerous for your child's emotional well-being. In addition to the statistical improbability, there is a strong chance that an athlete will face a sport-ending injury or simply burn out. Make sure that your athlete has other interests and doesn't believe that sports are the only route to success. 3. **Unhealthy performance pressure.** Sports psychologists are in high demand because parents, coaches, teams, and schools put undue pressure on young athletes to perform well every time they step on the field, court, or track. Remember, they're children, not professional athletes. As a mom of five competitive tennis players, I understand the inclination to demand more, but kids are kids. Some days they will miss every serve just because, and other days they will look like they're destined for greatness. Work with them to maintain perspective and understand that it's only a game. https://www.google.com/url?sa=t&rct=j&q=&esrc=s&source=web&cd=1&ved=2ahUKEwjQm6K-1J3IAhUNyIsBHTREC7UQFjAAegQIARAB&url=https%3A%2F%2Fwww.psychologytoday.com%2Fus%2Fblog%2Fmore-women-s-work%2F201705%2Fthe-pros-and-cons-youth-sports-aren-t-only-physical&usg=AOvVaw2lvunDF90Vn78r_VVpssDt

Learning	
1	If you are like many students, your time is limited so it is important to get the most educational value out of the time you have available. Speed of learning is not the only important factor, however. Students need to be able to accurately remember the information they learn, recall it at a later time, and utilize it effectively in a wide variety of situations. Becoming an effective and efficient student is not something that happens overnight, but putting a few of these tips into daily practice can help you get more out of

	your study time.
2	**Keep Learning (and Practicing) New Things** One sure-fire way to become a more effective learner is to simply keep learning. In one article published in *Nature,* it was reported that people who learned how to juggle increased the amount of gray matter in their occipital lobes, the area of the brain is associated with visual memory. When these individuals stopped practicing their new skill, this gray matter vanished. So if you are learning a new language, it is important to keep practicing the language in order to maintain the gains you have achieved. This "use-it-or-lose-it" phenomenon involves a brain process known as "pruning." Certain pathways in the brain are maintained, while other are eliminated. If you want the new information you just learned to stay put, keep practicing and rehearsing it. **Gain Practical Experience** For many students, learning typically involves reading textbooks, attending lectures, or doing research in the library or on the Web. While seeing information and then writing it down is important, actually putting new knowledge and skills into practice can be one of the best ways to improve learning. If you are trying to acquire a new skill or ability, focus on gaining practical experience. If it is a sport or athletic skill, perform the activity on a regular basis. If you are learning a new language, practice speaking with another person and surround yourself with language-immersion experiences. Watch foreign-language films and strike up conversations with native speakers to practice your budding skills. https://www.verywellmind.com/how-to-become-a-more-effective-learner-2795162

Government spending	
1	Government spends money for a variety of reasons, including: 1. To supply goods and services that the private sector would fail to do, such as public goods, including defence, roads and bridges; merit goods, such as hospitals and schools; and welfare payments and benefits, including unemployment and disability benefit. 2. To reduce the negative effects of externalities, such as pollution controls. 3. To subsidise industries which may need financial support, and which is not available from the private sector. For example, transport infrastructure projects are unlikely to attract private finance, unless the public sector provides some of the high-risk finance, as in the case of the UKs *Private Finance Initiative* – PFI. During 2009, the UK government provided huge subsidies to the UK banking sector to help deal with the financial crisis. Agriculture is also an industry which receives large government subsidies. See: CAP. 4. To help redistribute income and achieve more equity.
2	Using public spending to stimulate economic activity has been a key option for successive governments since the 1930s when British economist, John Maynard Keynes, argued that public spending should be increased when private spending and investment were inadequate. https://www.economicsonline.co.uk/Global_economics/Fiscal_policy_government_spending.html

Public transportation	
1	Pro: Can be more productive while taking public transportation

	When you're driving, you have to focus on the road ahead of you. But if you take public transportation, you have time to finish up an assignment, read a book or let your mind wander. Plus, public transportation can help you better prepare for the day or night ahead. Pro: Environmentally friendly Using public transportation is good for the environment as you're emitting less pollution into the air. According to the Federal Transit Administration, using public transportation can: improve air quality, reduce greenhouse gas emissions, save energy and minimize impacts. And on top of being environmentally friendly, you're also beating out traffic! If public transportation isn't widely offered in your community, consider carpooling with fellow coworkers in order to save on fuel.
2	Con: Wait time/cost The first big con when it comes to public transportation is that you're stuck on the system's scheduling and pricing. It might take longer to wait for your bus, sit through multiple stops and still have to walk or drive home. Also, with fluctuating gas prices, some months it may be cheaper to hop into your car than to take public transportation. Con: Sharing the experience with others With public transit comes sharing a ride with the public. On the one hand, you can meet some really interesting people within your community and have more real world interactions on a daily basis. However, you can also see the ugly side of your community or be stuck talking to someone when you would rather read a book. Plus, after a long day in the office, the last place you'd probably want to be is in a crowded subway car. https://www.defensivedriving.com/blog/ticket-to-ride-the-pros-and-cons-of-public-transportation/

Life span	
1	The dramatic increase in average life expectancy during the twentieth century ranks as one of societys greatest achievements. While most babies born in 1900 did not live past age 50, life expectancy at birth now exceeds eighty-three years in Japan and is at least eighty-one years in several other countries (United Nations, 2011). Life expectancy is increasing so fast that half the babies born in 2007 will live to be at least 103, while half the Japanese babies born in the same year will reach the age of 107 (Boseley, 2009). It is certain that people are glad to live a longer life since longevity is the pursuit of most humans. However, longevity has also caused a lot of problems to society, such as financial burden, lack of resources and so on. This essay is to discuss both the advantages and disadvantages of the fact that people are living a longer life so that a clear picture of the situation is shown. **As for individuals, longevity has always been considered as a kind of treasure and fortune.** And wisdom is usually linked with the elder. Death has always been regarded as something frightening and most people want to live a long life. Living longer means one can stay with his or her family longer and enjoy a happy later life. People spend most of their life working and taking care of their family. **As for society, longevity allows people to contribute more to the world with their talent and wisdom.** So many prominent scientists and scholars and other elites died with regret that they could not accomplish their plan. For example, Zhu Shenghao, a talented Chinese translator of Shakespeare's works, passed away at the age of 32 due to illness. If he could live longer, there might be more Chinese versions

	of Shakespeare and more people could appreciate the Chinese translation art. Another illustration is the early death of English poets such as Byron who died at 36, Shelley at 29 and Keats at 25. All of them are supremely gifted and great treasure to the academia but die so young. **Moreover, business markets can also benefit from the reality that people live longer**. Traditionally, it is believed that a person has three major periods of life: childhood, adulthood and old age. However, old age is now evolving into two segments, a third age (young old) and a fourth age (oldest old). Recognition of the older population as a major market for business is beginning, as evidenced by an increasing number of articles about the "silver market." Because a great deal of wealth is held by the older population and the number of elders is increasing relative to other age groups, it makes sense for business to design products appealing to the older market, and to direct advertising to them. Consumption by the older population can stimulate the economy.
2	The aging population causes a series of problems to the society. **First of all, old people have to be taken care of, which leave great burden to their family as well as the society.** According to an article published in the journal Corporate Adviser, MGM Advantage calculates the current level of annual household expenditure where the main occupant is aged 75 and over at more than £6,000. So if someone lived until they were 100, between their 75th and 100th birthday not including inflation, they would need to find around £400,000 to live. This, combined with falling annuity rates, will lead to more pensioners falling below the poverty line. (Corporate Adviser 2011) Though that people live longer is good news, the fact that should not be neglected is that this has a huge financial burden on people. The great pressure to support old parents may lead to the cracks of relationship between children and parents. **Secondly, longevity does not necessary mean health.** The rate of getting illness increases with the growth of old age. In spite of the advances in medical technology, there are still many diseases that cannot be treated efficiently. For example, the prevalence of dementia increases dramatically with age, and the projected costs of caring for the growing numbers of people with dementia are daunting. **In addition, longer life expectancy and lower fertility rate may lead to lack of young working forces.** The world with less young people will become less vigorous. And the increasing population is challenging the tolerance of the planet people are living on for most of the resources people are consuming are non-renewable. So it is urgent for human beings to do the best to protect the environment and save energy. Otherwise, longevity will become meaningless if one cannot live with contentment https://www.ukessays.com/essays/sociology/advantages-and-disadvantages-of-longevity-sociology-essay.php

Jobs & work	
1	School is hard enough—classes, studying, choosing a major, getting involved in clubs and activities. The decision to add a job into the mix can be a big one—but it doesn't have to be a daunting one. There are some clear benefits to **having a job during school**, but also some drawbacks. None outweigh another, but some make more sense for you than others. See for yourself. Pros **1. Money** With rising costs of tuition, fees, housing, and supplies, it's nice to know that you can pull some of your own weight without having to rely solely on scholarships, loans, your parents, or any other outside

source.   Even if you don't make enough money to cover any of those costs, you may want the option of not having to ask for spending money.   Going out for an occasional dinner with friends, seeing a concert, going to a movie, or shopping for new clothes—having a little extra cash on hand that you earned on your own may put your mind at ease.

2. Professional Skills

If your job gives you a meaningful, professional experience in a field that interests you, then go for it.   When you graduate from your university, your future employer wants to know that you did well in school—but also that you can function appropriately and effectively in the workplace.   What better way to learn time management than to balance an on-campus job and your school work?

3. Resume Builder

Having a job in school looks great on your resume—it shows employers your diligence and ability to balance schoolwork with outside responsibilities.   It also allows you to list references that will help with that network (see #2).   Good grades, some extracurricular activities that inspire you, and a part-time job: not too bad.

2

Cons

1. Tough Balancing Act

Finding time for yourself if you work and go to school isn't easy.   Tempted by a few extra dollars?   Is it worth the cost of burnout?   Unless your schedule and personal life have room for a job, reconsider taking that job, even if it's only a few hours a week.   You might want to spend those extra hours doing something else, even if it means that you won't have that extra spending money.   If your job interferes with your success in school?   Drop it.   You're there to study and build a peer network, not make extra cash.

2. Limited Extracurricular Activities

You definitely won't have as much time to get involved with on-campus clubs and activities.   If there's a club you've always wanted to join, or a group you've been meaning to check out, you'll have to plan your extracurricular activities around your work schedule, not vice versa.   If the work opportunity is too good to pass up, don't.   If you don't need it, and want some room to explore clubs, activities, and student groups, working might not be your best option.

https://www.bachelorstudies.com/article/To-Work-or-Not-to-Work-The-Pros-and-Cons-of-Getting-a-Job-in-School/

Shopping	
1	**1. Lifts your mood.** Shopping is associated with a sense of achievement. Think about the time you scored a vintage necklace from your local neighborhood thrift shop. You were elated to find a piece of jewelry that was unique and within your budget. The heightened emotions of happiness release endorphins, known as the "feel good" chemicals in your brain. Endorphins help you refocus your mind on your body movements, improving your overall mood.

A UK study conducted at Brunel University correlated the effect of shopping on the left prefrontal cortex, a part of the brain that is linked to pleasure and positive thinking. Researchers found that levels of dopamine increase during pleasurable experiences such as window shopping.

3. Improves mental acuity.

The mental, physical, and social engagement of shopping can keep your perception intact even in old age. When you shop, you are physically active by walking, going up and down escalators, and trying on clothes. The mental component of shopping is introduced when you revise your budget, check which on-sale item is better, and calculate your total cost. Socially, you meet up with friends or you hold small-talk with an employee at a department store. It's essential to keep your mental acuity in focus as you age. Therefore, shopping can be a preventative health measure to dementia, an illness that affects many adults in the beginning of their 60s.

5. Exercise.

Ladies, it's time to go hunt for those deals and bargains in your exercise gear! Shopping from one department store to the next while you carry heavy bags has been proven to be a good workout for the heart and body. Debenhams, a department store in the UK, tested ten shoppers, five male and five female, with pedometers and surveyed 2,000 female shoppers to calculate the health benefits of a shopping trip. The study found the average person can lose up to 400 calories by walking from shop to shop carrying heavy bags. Women who spend significant amounts of time shopping have been linked to reduce risk of cardiovascular diseases and other related health issues because of the physical activity.

https://www.medicaldaily.com/memorial-day-sales-5-health-benefits-shopping-246157

Money
1	As far as I know, almost everyone wants to become wealthy and successful. Being wealthy and successful allows you to lead a comfortable life, buy anything you want to buy, do whatever you want to do and many others. However, it also brings you some disadvantages. Below I will explain them in detail. **Wealth and success can guarantee you a high quality life**. Many people are pursuing wealth and success because of this reason. Being wealthy means having a lot of money. So you will not worry about matters which are related to money. You can receive the best education, afford the best healthcare and buy anything you want. Besides, you will never worry about your work because you have enough money to feed yourself. In a word, you will be fully satisfied with your life and love your life. **Being wealthy and successful can make you more confident**. If you are a successful man, you will find that many people respect you and then you will have a feeling of victory. This will make you much more confident and your confidence and aura will be embodied in your life and work. Moreover, your accomplishments can also give you confidence and satisfaction. Some accomplishments can not be easily achieved but you are able to achieve them. Then, you will receive appreciations from other people.
2	Being wealthy and successful does have some disadvantages. **It is hard to know whether your friends or partners are interested in your money or not.** When you have gained wealth and success, many people are willing to make friends with you. So you will not know who your genuine friends are. **Perhaps you will be an open target for kidnap or blackmail**. If you have much money, some lawless person may plan to kidnap you or your relatives to earn some money.

https://ezinearticles.com/?The-Advantages-and-Disadvantages-of-Being-Wealthy-and-Successful&id=6192615

Hiring	
1	Qualities of Exceptionally Destructive Employees **1. They say, "That's not my job."** The smaller the company, the more important it is that employees can think on their feet, adapt quickly to shifting priorities, and do whatever it takes, regardless of role or position, to get things done. Even if that means a manager has to help load a truck or a machinist needs to clean up a solvent spill; or the accounting staff needs to hit the shop floor to help complete a rush order; or a CEO needs to man a customer service line during a product crisis. You get the idea. **2. They think they've paid their dues.** You did great things last year, last month, or even yesterday. We're appreciative. We're grateful. Unfortunately, today is a new day. Dues aren't *paid*. Dues *get paid*. The only real measure of any employee's value is the tangible contribution he or she makes--daily. Saying, "I've paid my dues" is like saying, "I no longer need to work hard." And suddenly, before you know it, other employees start to feel they've earned the right to coast, too. https://www.inc.com/jeff-haden/8-qualities-of-exceptionally-destructive-employees.html
2	**1.** Strong work ethic: Setting and achieving goals A strong work ethic was clearly one of the most popular qualities hiring managers look for in a candidate. Employers want to see applicants demonstrate their ability to work hard. Candidates who set high goals for themselves, or respond well to stretch goals from supervisors, indicate a willingness to do more than clock in and clock out every day. **2.** Dependable: Consistently following through Dependability can make all the difference between a candidate who usually follows through, and one who always does. Candidates who show a commitment to completing tasks on time, as assigned, during the application process will likely continue this behavior as employees. **3.** Positive attitude: Creating a good environment Positivity leads to a more productive workday, and creates a better environment for fellow employees. Great employees consistently stand out for their upbeat attitudes and earn positive reputations for themselves. One trait to look for in a candidate is their ability to acknowledge mistakes and still move forward in a positive way. This suggests they'll be equally resilient in the workplace. https://www.jibe.com/ddr/7-qualities-of-a-good-employee-and-candidate-according-to-research/

Entertainment

1	The Importance of Entertainment in Your Life In today's day and age, people are spending very hectic lives, and that does not give them enough time for extra curriculum activities. However, it is important to realize that every single human being needs to get special entertainment every so often. Entertainment comes in many shapes and forms, and everyone is free to decide which one is a better option for them. No matter if you like playing sports or watching movies, you need to do that as often as possible. Getting together with your friends is a good source of entertainment. You don't even need to worry about spending incredible sums of money when it comes to having fun. Nonetheless, the benefits are almost tangible. As long as you are spending quality time with the right people, your life will improve considerably.
2	**Less Stress** Life is stressful for everyone. No matter how much you try, you probably won't be able to eliminate stress from your life for good. Therefore, it might be a good idea to step back and have some fun. Remember the last time when enjoyed your life to the maximum? The last thing that you had on your mind was definitely not paying the bills, or completing a difficult task at work. Becoming aware of the incredible benefits of having fun motivates you to give your mind some freedom. For some, the best way of forgetting about stress and having fun is exercising. A walk at the beach is ideal regardless of your age and profession. **Increased Productivity** Taking regular breaks from your routine energizes your body and makes you more productive. Even a few minutes spent watching a funny video are enough to change your mood, lift your spirits and motivate you to continue your work. Entertainment needs to be an important part of your life. Your busy life will benefit from making an effort to have fun each day. You will soon realize that investing a few minutes in a fun activity makes you a better person from different points of view. http://www.areasofmyexpertise.com/importance-entertainment-life/

Arts	
1	The Importance of Art in the Daily Life The most common concept of art as pieces of work—whether paintings or sculptures, displayed in galleries and museums is not the case in today's modern world. In fact, people at present acknowledge that there is so much more to art than what you see displayed in intimidating art galleries. Indeed, art surrounds life, every people in every location, without us being really aware of it. Since time immemorial, art has existed as long as man. It is a huge part of our culture which shapes our ideas, and vice versa, provides us with a deeper understanding of emotions, self-awareness, and more. Many people fail to realize how art impacts their daily life. Everybody use art on a continual basis. Majority doesn't know how much of a role art plays in our lives and just how much we rely on art in all of its forms in our everyday lives. Why is art important in our daily lives? Because we are surrounded by art, and without it, the human race will not be as you know it. **Art in the Home** Arguably, almost everyone has any form of art in their home—a painting, a framed photograph, a table centerpiece, and even the main layout and design of a house is art. Art is not purely for looking at and admiring, a lot of it is functional too, especially when it comes to our homes. Everything from a delightfully patterned quilt on the bed or even your decorative tea towels and tea cupscan be considered

a form of art, our brain is just conditioned to think that it is not art when it's not only for decoration.

Art and Music

Music, same as art, is a universal language and its importance to our daily lives is undeniable. Subconsciously, we hear music through television shows, commercials, radio and through other media. Sounds, songs and music can make life extremely joyful and can have a huge effect on our mood. It has a positive impact to people's moods and perspective. It can boost productivity and boost up motivation and determination. Similarly, when stress is high, many people find that relaxing to calming music is something that eases the mind.

https://accentartandframe.com/blog/index.php/the-importance-of-art-in-the-daily-life

2	**The role of art in society**
	First, on the most basic level, art seeks to please people with beauty. In a broken world, sometimes it is important to allow people to realize that there is still beauty. Hence, art can function to refresh people and remind people of better things or transcendent realities. Second, on a deeper level, art is able to express important values within that society to people in ways that are memorable. In this way, art can be used to reinforce values and even bring people together. For instance, artwork can commemorate great accomplishments, such as military victory as in World War II. Third, art in society can also be used to challenge people. For example, a thought provoking piece of art can call into question the establishment or some other cherished ideal. This would be a more subversive use of art. In the end, art has many different functions in society. https://www.enotes.com/homework-help/what-role-art-society-283697

Science	
1	Science for Society **Science is the greatest collective endeavor.** It contributes to ensuring a longer and healthier life, monitors our health, provides medicine to cure our diseases, alleviates aches and pains, helps us to provide water for our basic needs – including our food, provides energy and makes life more fun, including sports, music, entertainment and the latest communication technology. Last but not least, it nourishes our spirit.
2	**Science generates solutions for everyday life and helps us to answer the great mysteries of the universe.** In other words, science is one of the most important channels of knowledge. It has a specific role, as well as a variety of functions for the benefit of our society: creating new knowledge, improving education, and increasing the quality of our lives. **Science must respond to societal needs and global challenges.** Public understanding and engagement with science, and citizen participation including through the popularization of science are essential to equip citizens to make informed personal and professional choices. Governments need to make decisions based on quality scientific information on issues such as health and agriculture, and parliaments need to legislate on societal issues which necessitate the latest scientific knowledge. National governments need to understand the science behind major global challenges such as climate change, ocean health, biodiversity loss and freshwater security. **Challenges today cut across the traditional boundaries of disciplines and stretch across the lifecycle of innovation** -- from research to knowledge development and its application. Science, technology and

	innovation must drive our pursuit of more equitable and sustainable development. https://en.unesco.org/themes/science-society

Movies	
1	**Film has a uniquely powerful ubiquity within human culture**. In 2009, across major territories, there were over 6.8 billion cinema admissions creating global box office revenues of over US$30 billion. When you start to then consider revenues and audience figures from those who consume digitally, via television, repeat view content they already own and view through the highly illegal but vast black-market in films, the figures become truly staggering. **The direct economic impact of film is clear, but the effect to the wider economy is also significant. The flow-on effect from film** (i.e. the use of services and purchase of goods by the industry) is thought to be that for every £1 spent on film, there is a £1.50 benefit to the economy."
	Cinema has become a powerful vehicle for culture, education, leisure and propaganda. In a 1963 report for the United Nations Educational Scientific and Cultural Organization looking at Indian Cinema and Culture, the author (Baldoon Dhingra) quoted a speech by Prime Minister Nehru who stated, "...the influence in India of films is greater than newspapers and books combined." Even at this early stage in cinema, the Indian film-market catered for over 25 million people a week- considered to be just a 'fringe' of the population.
	https://thoughteconomics.com/the-role-of-film-in-society/
2	The Role of Film in Society
	"The best films entertain us, inspire us, and reflect the world around us in thought-provoking ways," says Courtney Small of *Cinema Axis*.
	When I was 11, my father took me to see *Plan 9 From Outer Space*, the 1959 sci-fi classic sometimes called the "worst movie of all time." The screening was in a rundown high school auditorium, the seats were uncomfortable, and the audience was filled with characters odder than those on the screen. I was in heaven, which tells you all you need to know about me. That my dad took me tells you all you need to know about him. **Cinema is meant to be shared, and favorite films are like heirlooms we pass down from generation to generation.** It was his fault, after all. From the Little Rascals to the Universal Monsters, my father spent the first decade of my life introducing me to movies he loved during his childhood. More than 30 years later, I do the same thing with my nieces and nephews.
	Cinema has serious responsibilities. **The world is in deeply troubled times and cinema has a sacred trust to tell the truth.** In 2017, filmmakers around the globe must confront new threats to the values of our era. Misuse of power, corruption, and despotism rear their ugly heads. New stories must be told in ways that reflect not only what is, but what can be. No alternate facts, no fake truth. Cinema exists for the betterment of humanity.
	https://discover.wordpress.com/2017/02/23/role-of-cinema/

	Progress
1	It's been known that improvements in well-being, happiness and satisfaction can come from making progress towards our goals each day. When we track the steps we take we can begin to notice how much we're actually getting done which can be a powerful motivator. While material possessions may bring temporary moments of joy, **knowing that you're constantly developing your skills, growing and learning new things will deliver life-long fulfilment**. As you start tracking your progress you'll notice little wins, this will help to build momentum. As soon as you start building momentum you'll realize that your goals are achievable and will feel a sense of purpose, power and direction. When we are productive, we efficiently finish various tasks we set out to do and achieve better results.
2	You can start doing this by: Conducting a self-analysis **Start off by mapping out your strengths and your weaknesses**. Use your strengths to your advantage to figure out how you can apply them to the goals you're working on. Whilst at the same time paying attention on the areas that need improvement by setting aside the time to figure out what skills you need to obtain or areas you need to learn more about. Writing a to-do list **Writing lists helps you break down goals into actionable tasks that have to get done**. Once you've done this, prioritize what needs your attention and to that first. Reflect everyday **This involves checking back on what you set out to do when you were writing your list**. What tasks did you manage to complete? What took up too much of your time? Whatever didn't get done for the day, put it on your list for the following day. If you consistently repeat this process you'll notice the difference in your results and will get closer each day to achieving your goals. https://blog.etsy.com/au/achieving-goals/

	History
1	Why is it important to study history? **Studying history is important because it allows us to understand our past, which in turn allows us to understand our present.** If we want to know how and why our world is the way it is today, we have to look to history for answers. People often say that "history repeats itself," but if we study the successes and failures of the past, we may, ideally, be able to learn from our mistakes and avoid repeating them in the future. Studying history can provide us with insight into our cultures of origin as well as cultures with which we might be less familiar, thereby increasing cross-cultural awareness and understanding. **One can look at past economic and cultural trends and be able to offer reasonable predictions of what will happen next in today's world.** One can also understand why some rules exist in the modern world. For example, one can understand the importance of the social welfare programs if one looks at the Great Depression and New Deal. We can also look back on the Civil Rights movement and see why the United States puts so much effort into creating a system where everyone is equal before the law and has equal access to public amenities. History also allows us to see how the United States gradually created the Constitution after it had just fought a war against a central government that did not care for colonial interests. Without a background in history, one does not appreciate why

the Constitution was revolutionary for its time. More broadly, history enables us to understand different cultures.

If those are not good reasons for studying history, one can study history because it allows one to exercise their critical thinking skills. These critical thinking skills are important for all areas in life, academic and otherwise. Historians also write a great deal; a study of history allows one to practice writing for different audiences.

https://www.enotes.com/homework-help/why-important-study-history-explain-your-answer-389341

	Technology
1	There's no denying the fact that we live in a world which is dominated by technology. Every year, the use of new tech ideas makes the world a better place to be. We can learn more, experience new things, and stay connected with one another through technology. Parents often struggle with decisions which involve technology access. Reporting from PBS shows that kids today are getting a lot of screen time. 4% of children in 2011 spend the majority of their screen time in front of a mobile device. By 2017, that figure rose to 35%. List of the Pros of Children Using Technology **1. Technology provides a source of educational entertainment for children.** Kids become easily distracted. Taking them on a long trip or keeping them engaged while you're working as a parent is already challenging. Trying to have them learn something useful during these periods feels like an impossible task. Thanks to today's educational apps for kids that are downloadable to most devices, these moments of downtime can promote learning opportunities. Apps like Duolingo allow children to begin learning a foreign language. DragonBox teaches the fundamentals of mathematics. Science360 offers videos, photographs, and news stories to explore advanced scientific concepts. You'll find spelling games and puzzles readily available too. **2. Kids have access to more information.** Access to technology allows today's children to experience cultures in ways that could never be done before. They can watch videos showing the festivals and events held in other countries. It offers exposure to different religious and political views not always possible in a family setting. Through technology, today's children have ways to broaden their horizons like never before. That structure helps to create a smaller world where more opportunities exist.
2	List of the Cons of Children Using Technology **1. It promotes a sedentary lifestyle for kids.** Information released by the Centers for Disease Control and Prevention shows that 20% of school-aged children have a BMI which classifies them as being obese. The number of children struggling with their weight has tripled (similar to adult rates) since the 1970s. Using technology may promote new learning opportunities and provide more social connections, but it also encourages less movement. Spending more time indoors in front of a screen or using other technologies increases the risk of weight gain. **2. Technology creates new safety risks for children.** Netmums released a survey of 825 children between the ages of 7-16 in 2013, along with over 1,100 parents. The results found numerous safety risks for children when using technology. **3. It creates in-person social disconnects.**

Using technology to form relationships makes it more challenging to do the same in real life. Children who have more screen time have fewer personal interactions with others. That makes them less likely to be empathetic to the needs other people have, difficulty forming friendships, and fewer social skills that don't involve computers, tablets, or consoles.

https://connectusfund.org/16-pros-and-cons-of-children-using-technology

	Persistence
1	Persistence is the ability to maintain action regardless of your feelings. You press on even when you feel like quitting, until you achieve that important goal. I surprise myself every day. People give up too soon because they have wrong expectations of themselves and the outcome. They expect the way to be easy, and they are surprised when they find the reality to be the opposite. Their enthusiasm quickly melts and they lose heart. So start your journey with the right expectation. And don't underestimate the amount of time required either. Remember, there is no such thing as cheap success. Expect a hard way, not an easy one, and you will be mentally prepared when you encounter the reality. The size of your commitment should be proportional to the size of your desire.
2	Persistence of action comes from persistence of vision. When you're super-clear about what you want in such a way that your vision doesn't change much, you'll be more consistent — and persistent — in your actions. And that consistency of action will produce consistency of results. Every obstacle is an opportunity to improve *"I will persist until I succeed. Always will I take another step. If that is of no avail I will take another, and yet another. In truth, one step at a time is not too difficult. I know that small attempts, repeated, will complete any undertaking."* — **Og Mandino** When you work on any big goal, your motivation can wax and wane. Sometimes you'll feel motivated; sometimes you won't. But it's not your motivation that will produce results — it's your action. The decision to persist. To make progress even when you don't feel like it. Persistence allows you to keep taking action even when you don't feel motivated to do so, and therefore you keep accumulating results. Persistent people have a goal or vision in mind that motivates and drives them. Reaching this goal becomes the focal point of their life and they devote a greater percentage their energies and time toward reaching it. https://medium.com/personal-growth/persist-it-matters-7e4270f7c078

	Stress
1	The kids won't stop screaming, your boss has been hounding you because you turned a report in late, and you owe the IRS thousands of dollars you don't have. You're seriously stressed out. Stress is actually a normal part of life. At times, it serves a useful purpose. Stress can motivate you to get that promotion at work, or run the last mile of a marathon. **But if you don't get a handle on your stress and it becomes long-term, it can seriously interfere with your job, family life, and health.** More than half of Americans say they fight with friends and loved ones because of stress, and more than 70% say they experience real physical and emotional symptoms from it.
2	Everyone has different stress triggers. Work stress tops the list, according to surveys. Forty percent of U.S. workers admit to experiencing office stress, and one-quarter say work is the biggest source of stress in their lives. Your stress level will differ based on your personality and how you respond to

situations. Some people let everything roll off their back. To them, work stresses and life stresses are just minor bumps in the road. Others literally worry themselves sick.

- **Attitudes and perceptions.** How you view the world or a particular situation can determine whether it causes stress. For example, if your television set is stolen and you take the attitude, "It's OK, my insurance company will pay for a new one," you'll be far less stressed than if you think, "My TV is gone and I'll never get it back! What if the thieves come back to my house to steal again?" Similarly, people who feel like they're doing a good job at work will be less stressed out by a big upcoming project than those who worry that they are incompetent.
- **Unrealistic expectations**. No one is perfect. If you expect to do everything right all the time, you're destined to feel stressed when things don't go as expected.

Causes of work stress include:

- Being unhappy in your job
- Being insecure about your chance for advancement or risk of termination
- Having to give speeches in front of colleagues
- Loss of a job

Causes of life stress

- The death of a loved one
- Divorce
- Increase in financial obligations
- Getting married
- Emotional problems (depression, anxiety, anger, grief, guilt, low self-esteem)
- Traumatic event, such as a natural disaster, theft, rape, or violence against you or a loved one

https://www.webmd.com/balance/guide/causes-of-stress#1

	Exercise
1	You've probably heard countless times how exercise is "good for you." But did you know that it can actually help you feel good, too? Getting the right amount of exercise can rev up your energy levels and even help improve your mood.
2	Experts recommend that teens get 60 minutes or more of moderate to vigorous physical activity each day. Here are some of the reasons: • **Exercise benefits every part of the body, including the mind.** Exercising causes the body to make chemicals that can help a person to feel good. Exercise can help people sleep better. It can also help some people who have mild depression and low self-esteem. Plus, exercise can give people a real sense of accomplishment and pride at having achieved a certain goal — like beating an old time in the 100-meter dash. • **Exercise can help you look better.** People who exercise burn more calories and look more toned than those who don't. In fact, exercise can help keep your body at a healthy weight. • **Exercise helps people lose weight and lower the risk of some diseases.** Exercising regularly decreases a person's risk of developing certain diseases, including obesity, type 2 diabetes, and high blood pressure.

	• **Exercise can help a person age well.** This may not seem important now, but your body will thank you later. For example, osteoporosis (a weakening of the bones) can be a problem as people get older. Weight-bearing exercise — like jumping, running, or brisk walking — can help keep bones strong. https://kidshealth.org/en/teens/exercise-wise.html

Handmade vs machine made	
1	Handcrafted products can offer higher quality and more attention to detail – but they can give buyers some surprising side benefits as well. **Handcrafted Products Are Green.** Work done by hand takes less energy than a mass production assembly line, which makes it more environmentally sustainable. This is particularly true if the commercial good is produced overseas and needs to be shipped a very long distance to reach the consumer. **Handcrafted Products Are Worth More.** A number of experiments have shown that people value an object more highly when they are led to believe it contains an "air of authenticity," for example, if they were told it was a work of art. This means that artisan products, be they jewelry or jam, are perceived to have more value in society. **Handcrafted Products Are Unique.** One of the most prevalent, although least quantifiable, reasons people report for choosing to purchase handcrafted goods is that they just like having something that didn't come from a big company. The nature of handmade goods means that there are fewer of them, so whatever you're wearing or eating or adding to your home is as unique as you are. https://mentalfloss.com/article/577128/catherine-the-great-facts

Gifts	
1	Why Gift Giving is Important Gift giving is something that should not be a chore. It must come from the heart. When you give gifts, you are giving something willingly without wanting something in return. Making someone feel special is more than enough reason to make you give more. It tells the receiver that you were thinking about them. While it feels good to be on the receiving end, there's a feeling of self-gratification when you are the one who is doing the giving. This can't be measured by monetary value. The happiness you get from opening a gift is only temporary, but giving provides a more self-fulfilling experience that lasts for a long period of time. We learn this when we are young. As children, we give our parents good grades that make them happy. A simple act can provide a good response. It has been proven that the act of giving makes us happier than receiving. It doesn't matter how valuable the gift may be.
2	**Gifts as an expression of love** Gift giving is an act of self-gratification. It is a good way of strengthening relationships. If you are in a friendship or a relationship, you should always show the other person how much you care for him or her. You don't need to wait for an occasion in order to give a gift. Give one to show how much you

love someone.

Gifts to appreciate someone special

They say that action speaks louder than words, and there's no better way to say you appreciate someone than through gift giving. You can make someone happy with a simple gift. It doesn't need to be expensive. You can give a gift of appreciation to you father, mother, sister, brother, or anyone that has done something for you. A token of appreciation is heartfelt especially if is given sincerely. Corporates and business owners can also give gifts of appreciation to their employees for their hard work or for their special contribution to the business. It motivates the workers and makes them perform better. A token of appreciation can do wonders to the performance of your workforce.

Gifts to say "Thanks"

There are some instances when you need to give back to someone who has helped you or provided you a favor. Gift giving is an act that can show that you are thankful. Giving and receiving is the purest of reasons to give gifts. The receiver will truly feel your gratitude when you give gifts for elevating happiness and wellbeing.

Gifts for passing exams or achieving high grades

Parents can reward their kids who work hard in school to maintain high grades or for passing specific grades. Gift giving is can help inspire and motivate children to strive better in school. It will let them know that their hard work will be rewarded.

No matter what the reason is for giving a gift, the best presents are those that come from the heart.

https://lifecherish.com/2014/11/20/gift-giving/

Vacation	
1	Signs It's Time To Take a Vacation
	Debating over taking a vacation this summer? Whether it's for your health, your relationships or simply your sanity, there are hundreds of reasons to take a vacation. These are the signs it's long overdue.
	1. Working Overtime Is Your Life
	All work and no play is the surest route to burnout. If long hours are part of your job and you're not willing to find different work, book off some vacation days. "Vacations give us something to look forward to when the daily drudgeries of life are weighing us down," says Kane. Keeping your eye on the prize provides you with "a pleasant thing to focus on and feel positive about," says Kane.
	2. You're Nursing a Broken Heart
	Only time can mend a broken heart, but spending time with your best buds may speed things along. Plan a girlfriends' getaway or guys' weekend, stat!
	3. You're In a Health-Rut
	While it's possible to kick bad habits like smoking, over-eating or over-drinking at home, a trip abroad

	may make it a bit easier, says Kane. "On a vacation with healthy lifestyle habits at the centre, you're literally forced to focus on self-care and self-improvement in a way which would prove impossible at home," she explains. https://www.readersdigest.ca/travel/world/10-signs-its-time-take-vacation/

The purpose of education	
1	"The one continuing purpose of education, since ancient times, has been to bring people to as full a realization as possible of what it is to be a human being. Other statements of educational purpose have also been widely accepted: to develop the intellect, to serve social needs, to contribute to the economy, to create an effective work force, to prepare students for a job or career, to promote a particular social or political system. These purposes offered are undesirably limited in scope, and in some instances they conflict with the broad purpose I have indicated; they imply a distorted human existence. The broader humanistic purpose includes all of them, and goes beyond them, for it seeks to encompass all the dimensions of human experience." —Arthur W. Foshay, "The Curriculum Matrix: Transcendence and Mathematics," Journal of Curriculum and Supervision, 1991
2	"The function of education is to teach one to think intensively and to think critically. But education which stops with efficiency may prove the greatest menace to society. The most dangerous criminal may be the man gifted with reason but no morals. ... We must remember that intelligence is not enough. Intelligence plus character—that is the goal of true education." —Martin Luther King Jr., speech at Morehouse College, 1948

Food	
1	The **purpose of food** is to keep us alive and fueled for life. **Food** is not for pleasure. But — with the right attention to detail, you can eat healthy and have some great tasting **food** too. And you'll have a great looking body, you'll feel better, and you'll be healthier than ever. https://www.weight-lifting-complete.com/purpose-of-food/
2	Problems with food – **Waste**: Estimates vary, but between a quarter and a third of food grown around the world goes to waste. This tally includes waste from harvest all the way waste at the consumer end. Often farmers and chefs end up throwing out perfectly good food because it doesn't have a home: They can't find the right buyer, or the transaction costs of getting it to that person are too high. Sometimes food spoils in transit, or before anyone can process it into a more stable form. In home cooking waste, is related to a lack of time: Food rots when people don't have the bandwidth to cook regularly and monitor what's in the fridge. **Obesity:** Obviously, consuming too much has direct consequences. And if there's some kind of invention that can fix that, it's worth a fortune, but I have no idea what it would look like. **Overfishing:** As the world population grows, pressure will only increase on fisheries. We are currently fishing at close the maximum. If we catch too many fish, populations will collapse, and seafood levels will decline. **Fertilizer pollution:** Excess fertilizer runs off the field and pollutes waterways. Excess nitrogen fertilizer (whether it comes from manure, legumes, or a synthetic process) turns into a potent greenhouse gas. The key is getting just the right amount of fertilizer where you want it (in the plants), and keeping it away from the other spots (the water and air). https://grist.org/food/3-big-food-system-problems-begging-for-innovation/390136363/

Cooking at home vs eating at a restaurant	
1	**Cooking at Home: Healthier Ingredients** When you cook at home, you control what you put into your food. There is that old adage that "You

	are what you eat," but, for many people, your food is what you put into it. When you get food from a restaurant, you have no idea what sort of junk they put into it. How much oil is in there? How much sugar? How much heavy cream? If you're cooking at home, you have options. You can avoid high amounts of butter. You can avoid drowning your potatoes in oil. You can make healthy food that is also appetizing—I know a shocker!
2	**Eating Out: Experienced Cooks Preparing Food** Maybe you aren't certain how to cook good food. Maybe you clumsily add in too much oil, thus ruining your food by drowning it in fats. Maybe you aren't sure how to properly cook your meats, and you end up giving yourself E. coli by accident. The simple matter is that you don't know how to cook properly. While many restaurants can be fairly unhealthy, not all of them are. You can judge where to eat, what places are healthy, and expect cooks that know how to make the food for you. By eliminating your inexperience, you can have food that is appetizing, healthy, and consumable. https://vocal.media/feast/health-benefits-of-cooking-at-home-vs-eating-out

	Health
1	Tips to Stay Healthy in College Sometimes, amid classes, studying, homework, meetings and maintaining a social life, college students forget to maintain their health. Though some students may not think they need to worry about healthy habits, developing healthy habits now will make it easier for students to stay healthy throughout their lives. Here are 10 tips for college students to stay healthy:
2	**1. Eat Right** Eating a healthy diet can help boost students' immune systems, help students to maintain a healthy weight and can improve their overall health. Sometimes it may seem difficult to eat healthy in college when your meal choices consist of the cafeteria or fast food restaurants, but there are easy ways to make adjustments in your eating habits. First, always eat breakfast. This may be difficult when you're rushing out the door to get to that 8 a.m. classes, but grabbing a granola bar or banana goes a long way in keeping you from overeating throughout the day. Also, never skip meals. **2. Exercise** Fitting exercise into a busy college schedule can be difficult, but most college campuses make it easy for students to get exercise. One of the easiest ways to get exercise is to walk to class. Depending on your class schedule, this could add anywhere from 20 minutes to an hour of exercise every day. Most colleges offer physical fitness classes and intramural sports programs, so take advantage of these for a fun way to get exercise. Also, most colleges offer free or reduced memberships to gyms. This is definitely a perk that ends after graduation, so take advantage of this now. **3. Get enough sleep** Though you may be tempted to pull an all-nighter to study for an exam or stay out until 3 a.m. partying with friends, make sure you don't make that a habit. Sleep deprivation can lead to reduced brain function, fatigue, headaches and weight loss or gain. College students need between seven and nine hours of sleep and getting this amount can improve overall health. To stay rested throughout the day, try taking a short nap during the day, try to stick to a schedule, try to keep your room dark and quiet before bedtime and avoid drinking caffeine, eating and drinking right before bed. https://www.huffpost.com/entry/10-tips-to-stay-healthy-i_b_859195

	Knowledge
1	**Read. Read. Read.** You know how people say that the most successful people are always reading? It's true. Not only does reading expand your knowledge, it also keeps your brain active. You are constantly processing information, and this makes you quick on your feet when it comes to new ideas and innovations. As for the creative types out there, reading is just as important for you. Looking for new inspiration for your latest art project? Read a novel. Looking for a topic for your next short story? Read some poetry. The answers to all of your questions are written between the lines of your favorite stories. For those of us on a budget, the local library holds endless possibilities for learning something new. Bring a friend and try to find a new favorite author for the month. **Talk to a mentor.** Learning from other people is one of the most effective ways to stay educated. Also, in today's technology-driven world, having a mentor keeps you sharp with your people skills. Go to coffee with someone once a month and have a topic planned for both of you. You may be surprised at how much you can learn from one person in an hour. Don't know how to find a mentor? Ask around! One of your friends may have a boss or colleague who would love to chat with you about the topics you're interested in. https://www.elitedaily.com/life/5-ways-to-learn-after-college/1199154
2	How to Gain Wisdom Wisdom is a virtue that isn't innate, but can only be acquired through experience. Anyone who is interested in trying new things and reflecting on the process has the ability to gain wisdom. By learning as much as you can, analyzing your experiences and putting your knowledge to the test, you can become a wiser person. **Try new things.** It's hard to gain wisdom when you stay in and do the same thing day after day. You get wiser when you put yourself out there and give yourself the opportunity to learn, make mistakes and reflect on the experience. If you tend to be on the inhibited side, work on cultivating an inquisitive spirit and the willingness to put yourself in new situations. Every time you experience something new, you open yourself up to the possibility of learning and getting a little wiser for having tried it. **Step out of your comfort zone.** If you're afraid to do something, perhaps that's the very thing you should try to do. When you have to deal with an awkward or scary situation, you come out on the other side better equipped to handle fear the next time you face it. As Eleanor Roosevelt said, "We gain strength, and courage, and confidence by each experience in which we really stop to look fear in the face . . . we must do that which we think we cannot." **Make an effort to talk to people you don't know very well.** Talk to people from different backgrounds and with different perspectives from yours, and pay attention to what you can learn from them. Try not to judge them based on your own narrow point of view. The more you're able to empathize with others, the wiser you will be. https://m.wikihow.com/Gain-Wisdom

Experience	
1	Imagine that you have never seen a real lemon. You do not know what one is. If you were to look at a picture of a lemon, what would you learn from that picture? It is yellow, it is round. Even if you cannot talk about its features, you will see them. Next, you are given a plastic toy lemon. What else will you learn now? You will learn that it has small dimples on the skin, and you will be able to put the size into perspective. Finally, you are given the real thing. You will learn that you can squeeze the lemon slightly, you can dig your nails in the skin and find white underneath, you can cut it open and discover that the inside has segments, that it is wet, it is sticky and it tastes sour. You can squash the lemon and listen to the sound it makes, and let us not forget the smell! Learning opportunities are far greater when children have the chance to experience something first hand. Not only does it allow children the opportunity to use all their senses when they are exploring a new object or experience, but it also increases motivation, can improve behaviour as the child is more engaged, helps to develop communication and language skills as experiences give children something to talk about, and consequently, further develops their understanding of the world. https://www.nordangliaeducation.com/our-schools/al-khor/parent-resources/our-school-enewsletter/foundation/the-importance-of-real-life-experience
2	Work Experience placements assist students in their transition from school to work and aim to: • Provide students with an opportunity to relate school studies with a workplace • Give students an insight into the diversity of employees in the workplace • Prepare students for the demands and expectations of the working world • Help students make informed career decisions by assessing their aptitudes and interests, and exploring potential careers • Improve students' maturity, confidence and self reliance • Provide a link between school and local community • Provide students with appropriate knowledge, skills and attitudes concerning both paid and unpaid work http://www.marymount.qld.edu.au/Careers/Work%20Experience/Pages/Benefits-of-Work-Experience.aspx

1	Taking on debt is a thorny subject. Signing on an affordable mortgage is one thing. Racking up credit card debt on unnecessary purchases? Quite another. Any time you borrow money, you put your finances at risk. That's why it's important to do your research before committing to new debt. If you're not sure whether to borrow money, read our list of dos and don'ts. And if you need hands-on help managing your financial life, consider linking up with a financial advisor. Do: Comparison shop when deciding where to borrow Thinking of borrowing money? Don't just go for the first credit source you can find. Look around for a loan that meets your requirements and leaves you with monthly payments you can actually afford. If you're not happy with what lenders are offering you, it may be best to take the time to build up your credit score and then try again. Do: Go for "good debt"

	Good debt is debt you can afford that you use on something that will appreciate. That could be a home in a desirable neighborhood or an education from a reputable institution that will help your future earning power. Of course, you can't be 100% sure that your home will appreciate or your advanced degree will pay off but you can take leaps based on thorough research.
2	Don't: Just look at the interest rate Comparing loans is about more than searching for the lowest interest rate you can get. Look out for red flags like prepayment penalties. Stay away from personal loans that come with pricey insurance add-ons like credit life insurance. These insurance policies, particularly if you decide to finance them by rolling them into your loan, will raise the effective interest rate on the money you borrow. Approach payday loans and installment loans with extreme caution. Don't: Go overboard with consumer debt Consumer debt is generally considered bad debt. Why? Because it's debt taken out for something that won't appreciate. You'll spend the money and get fleeting enjoyment but you'll be making interest payments for months or years. In other words, it's generally better to save up for that new tablet or vacation than to finance it with consumer debt. https://smartasset.com/personal-loans/the-dos-and-donts-of-borrowing-money

Investment opportunities	
1	Entrepreneurs are known for taking risks. But when it comes to making personal investments, they're just as diligent as they are with their business finances, carefully balancing risk and reward -- and looking for opportunities where others are not.
2	**Real Estate** I am seeing a lot of entrepreneurs our age put their money in real estate lately. Nothing complex, just simple positive cash flow generating investment properties that are less than $250,000. It's something that we can spend some time up front, do our research, then pretty much forget about after things have been set up. The extra few thousand dollars a month is a treat and the equity upside is huge down the road. - W. Michael Hsu, Deepsky **Startups, But Diversifying Is Key** Successful entrepreneurs have a tendency to reinvest in their own startups and other businesses. That makes sense as those options have the ability to be directly affected by time and effort as opposed to uncontrollable stock market cycles. https://www.forbes.com/sites/forbesfinancecouncil/2016/05/26/six-investment-opportunities-more-entrepreneurs-are-exploring-3/#4c635448188f

Conservation	
1	**Conservation** is the care and protection of natural resources so that they can persist for future generations. It includes maintaining diversity of species, genes, and ecosystems, as well as functions of the environment, such as nutrient cycling. https://www.nationalgeographic.org › encyclopedia › conservation

Environmental problems	
1	**1. Biodiversity** Biodiversity is the most complex and vital feature of our planet. It is essentially every living thing and ecosystem that makes up the environment. From the tallest giraffe to the smallest microorganism, everything plays an important role in the maintenance of our world. But with the increase in global warming, pollution and deforestation, biodiversity is in danger. Billions of species are going or have gone extinct all over the world. Some scientists, in fact, are suggesting that we are in the beginning of a 6th mass extinction, posing issues for our planet and ourselves. Reducing our meat intake, particularly red meat, as well as making sustainable choices can help to keep our planet running smoothly. **2. Water** Water pollution is a huge concern for us and our environment. Not only is polluted water a huge financial strain but is also killing both humans and marine life. With oil spills, an abundance of plastic waste and toxic chemicals entering our waterways, we're damaging the most valuable resource our planet has to offer. By educating people on the causes and effects of water pollution, we can work together to undo the damage humans have caused. Laws also need to change to make pollution tougher, consistently across national borders. **3. Deforestation** We need plants and trees to survive. They provide oxygen, food, water and medicine for everyone, all over the globe. But if deforestation continues at the rate it's occurring, we won't have much of the valuable forestry left. With natural wildfires, illegal logging and the mass amount of timber being harvested for commercial use, our forests are decreasing at an alarming rate. As well as reducing our supply of oxygen, the loss of forests is contributing around 15% of our greenhouse gas emissions. To help, you can buy more recycled and organic products, limiting the amount of paper and cardboard you use. **4. Pollution** Pollution is one of the primary causes of many of the other environmental concerns, including climate change and biodiversity. All 7 key types of pollution – air, water, soil, noise, radioactive, light and thermal – are affecting our environment. All types of pollution, and environmental concerns, are interlinked and influence one another. So, to tackle one is to tackle them all. That's why we need to work together, as a community, to reduce the impact that pollution is having on our environment. **5. Climate Change** As pointed out by a recent UN report, without 'unprecedented changes' in our actions and behavior, our planet will suffer drastically from global warming in just 12 years. Greenhouses gases are the main cause of climate change, trapping in the sun's heat and warming the surface of the earth. An increased ocean temperature is affecting the sea life and ecosystems habituated there. The rise in global sea levels is shrinking our land, causing mass floods and freak weather incidents across the world. If we continue as we are, the world will suffer irreversibly. Saying no to driving more will reduce your carbon footprint, as will switching off electrical items when they're not in use. More importantly, we need to educate the world on the effects and severity of global warming, before it's too late. There are a wide range of initiatives in place to combat the biggest environmental concerns – from recycling schemes to major legislation reforms. Find out more about efforts to measure, model and mitigate air pollution in the article, 'Air quality networks - simplifying source apportionment, supporting pollution mitigation'. https://www.envirotech-online.com/news/air-monitoring/6/breaking-news/what-are-the-top-5-environmental-concerns-for-2019/47579

Holidays	
1	Holiday traditions are essentially ritualistic behaviors that nurture us and our relationships. They are primal parts of us, which have survived since the dawn of man. Traditional celebrations of holidays

	have been around as long as recorded history. Holiday traditions are an important part to building a strong bond between family, and our community. They give us a sense of belonging and a way to express what is important to us. They connect us to our history and help us celebrate generations of family. Most people can say, "oh this was great grandmas table cloth we always used for Thanksgiving" or "I remember stinging popcorn with my mom when I was young". They keep the memories of the past alive and help us share them with newer generations. Although holiday traditions are usually the first thing people think of when you mention traditions, they are not the only ones families have. Whether it's stringing popcorn for the Christmas tree, watching the Thanksgiving Day parade while the turkey cooks, building sand castles every summer or regularly having family movie night they are a family ritual that brings children and parents closer. These moments create positive memories for children and provide positive events for everyone to anticipate! Children crave the comfort and security that comes with traditions and predictability. This takes away the anxiety of the unknown and unpredictable. Traditions are a wonderful way to anchor family members to each other, providing a sense of unity and belonging. https://blogs.psychcentral.com/balanced-life/2013/11/why-holiday-traditions-might-be-more-important-than-you-think/
2	**Christmas** People celebrate this Christian holiday by going to church, giving gifts, and sharing the day with their families. In some parts of Europe, "star singers" go caroling — singing special Christmas songs — as they walk behind a huge star on a pole. Add these books to your classroom library to give your students a chance to learn more about different Christmas traditions can help your students **Lunar New Year** Lunar New Year is observed in many countries that follow lunar calendars, including Taiwan, Vietnam, Singapore, China, Malaysia, and more. Lunar New Year can be celebrated in January, February, March, April, September, or November, depending on the lunar calendar, but February and April are the most common times. Lunar New Year traditions vary from culture to culture. Some examples include exchanging red envelopes or silk pouches containing money, setting off fireworks, playing games, eating traditional dishes, cleaning the house, and holding parades with colorful costumes. These Lunar New Year books are excellent classroom resources to learn more about the Chinese traditions associated with the holiday. https://www.scholastic.com/teachers/articles/teaching-content/holidays-sampler-around-world/

Passing Time (leisure activities)	
1	**Mental wellness is an important part of your overall health and can impact your physical well-being.** Participating in leisure and recreation activities can help you better manage stress and reduce depression. Leisure provides you the chance to find balance in your life; it also puts you in control of how you're spending your time, which is an important consideration because you may feel overwhelmed by obligations. Taking part in leisure activities as a family is also beneficial for your kids because you're modeling healthy ways to handle stress and emotions. Participating in leisure activities regularly reduces depression; in fact, just thinking about past outdoor recreation experiences can improve mood, according to the 2005 California State Parks report. Improve Your Quality of Life. **Finding balance is also a reason why leisure and recreation can enhance your quality of life. Physical recreation, in particular, is associated with improved self-esteem. In addition, you're more likely to feel satisfied about your life when you regularly take part in recreation activities. This has significant implications for your mental health and, in turn, your physical health. In fact, 90 percent of respondents in a 2000 American Recreation Coalition**

study reported being satisfied with their health and fitness. In contrast, 60 percent of those who didn't take part in such activity reported not being satisfied with their health and fitness.

Don't: Just look at the interest rate

Comparing loans is about more than searching for the lowest interest rate you can get. Look out for red flags like prepayment penalties. Stay away from personal loans that come with pricey insurance add-ons like credit life insurance. These insurance policies, particularly if you decide to finance them by rolling them into your loan, will raise the effective interest rate on the money you borrow. Approach payday loans and installment loans with extreme caution.

Don't: Go overboard with consumer debt

Consumer debt is generally considered bad debt. Why? Because it's debt taken out for something that won't appreciate. You'll spend the money and get fleeting enjoyment but you'll be making interest payments for months or years. In other words, it's generally better to save up for that new tablet or vacation than to finance it with consumer debt.

https://smartasset.com/personal-loans/the-dos-and-donts-of-borrowing-money

2	**Outdoor Activities -**
	Pro: More strenuous, longer workouts
	Outdoor runners tend to flex their ankles more and expend more energy when compared to treadmill runners. Cyclists are also shown to burn more calories when riding outdoors.
	Another study shows that people who exercise outside do so for longer. The study participants had their activity monitored for a week; the people who exercised outside spent an average of 30 minutes more exercising than those who exercised inside.
	Pro: Vitamin D intake
	This one is simple -- going outside means exposure to the sun, which gives you vitamin D. Our bodies need vitamin D to absorb calcium for strong bone growth.
3	Con: Exposure to the elements
	You are at the whim of mother nature when you exercise outside: snow, sleet, rain, hail, freezing cold, strong winds -- you can't control any of it. If exercising outside is your go-to, you need to be prepared for any type of weather. This also means that living in a city or highly populated area will expose you to air pollutants and possible allergens.
3	**Indoor Activities-**
	Pro: Controlled environment
	Exercising in a gym or inside means you (most likely) have air conditioning and heat to make the air comfortable. You don't need to worry about rain, snow or heat. If you live in a city, escaping to the cleaner air inside a gym can also be a blessing for anyone suffering from asthma, allergies and other respiratory problems.
	Pro: Availability of group classes

	Research shows that group exercise classes help to teach accountability while giving participants a safe and effective workout. Taking classes like yoga, Zumba and kickboxing may attract people who don't like to run or walk outside.
4	Con: Cost The monthly and annual fees for gym memberships vary widely depending on location, but the average monthly fee for a gym membership ranges from $40 to $50. Adding in initiation fees can bring the total to about $800 a year https://flipbelt.com/blog/working-out-at-the-gym-vs-outdoors

Animals and Pets	
1	**They love you back.** Scientists have discovered that dogs release the 'love hormone' oxytocin when interacting with humans. We always knew they loved us too! **They make you laugh.** Whether they're accidentally doing a backward roll off the sofa or giving you the beady eye as you scoff down a bacon sandwich without offering them any, dogs will constantly have you chuckling at their antics. And nothing beats a bit of laughter.
2	**It might be tempting if you see a gorgeous pet looking longingly at you but think about whether you're really ready for the long-term commitment.** Your new pet could live for anything from two years to 20 or more and that impulse purchase might not seem like a good idea further down the line. Plus if you haven't done your research, you won't know anything about the pet's history and any health or behavioral problems that they come with. Choosing the right pet requires both planning time so don't rush in to anything. https://www.bluecross.org.uk/pet-advice/finding-right-pet

Habits	
1	**Many habits—including smoking or excess** sugar consumption—**involve the brain's dopamine (or reward) system**. Dopamine is a "feel-good" chemical that transmits signals between neurons in the brain. The first time you engage in a new, "rewarding" behavior, you get a euphoric feeling from doing it as a result of a dopamine release, notes Poldrack. This leads to changes in both the connections between neurons and the brain systems responsible for actions—and can largely account for why we start to form bad habits in the first place.
2	**Capitalizing on major life changes can also help break an unhealthy habit.** While you might think a cross-country move or a new job is no time to introduce even more changes into your life, Berkman notes that shifts in lifestyle can actually be the ideal

	opportunity for eliminating a vice. "You're going into new contexts and situations, so you don't have those same cues—it's a chance to form new habits," he says. https://time.com/5373528/break-bad-habit-science/

Hobbies	
1	**The best way to cultivate a new hobby is to try something new.** The world is full of wonderful, exciting activities that we can explore and adopt as our own. Of course, all of us are unique and, therefore, our interests and hobbies vary. But once we find a hobby that we truly enjoy and are passionate about, we become hooked. It becomes part of our lives and captivates us in a very personal way
2	**It helps to relieve stress by keeping you engaged in something you enjoy.** Hobbies give you a way to take your mind off the stresses of everyday life. They let you relax and seek pleasure in activities that aren't associated with work, chores or other responsibilities. **Having a hobby can help your social life and create a bond with others**. A hobby is something that you can frequently enjoy with other people. Whether you join a club, play in a league, or just gift others with the fruits of your labor, a hobby is a great way to meet and get closer to people who have the same interests as you do. **Hobbies help reduce or eradicate boredom**. They give you something to do when you find yourself with nothing to fill your time. They also give you an activity that you can look forward to and get excited about. http://www.skilledatlife.com/why-hobbies-are-important/
3	**Various things contribute to this, but for many of us, being legitimately busy simply isn't one of them.** Instead, we habitually waste time, creating the *illusion* of busyness. Facebook, email, Netflix – pick your poison. **Hobbies can foster new social connections.** While some hobbies are solitary endeavors, many get us out in our communities, meeting people we otherwise wouldn't, sharing our passions, and forming new bonds. Countless studies have found that social connection is a key component of happiness and a meaningful life, and hobbies have the potential to create precious new ties
3	**Hobbies help you cope with stress.** Imagine a rough day at the office, where you were harshly criticized by your boss. Coming home and turning on the TV may provide a brief distraction, but it doesn't address your damaged ego head-on. Now imagine that after work you head out to your soccer league or pottery class. These activities are more than merely distracting. They remind you that that are many facets to your self-concept. Employee, yes, but also athlete or artist. As such, a blow to one aspect of your identity is less damaging. Simply put, your eggs aren't all in one basket. https://www.psychologytoday.com/us/blog/happy-trails/201509/six-reasons-get-hobby

Clothes and Fashion	
1	The fashion industry's main reason for existence is the new collections that stomp down the runway every season, but it wasn't always this way. Fashion trends aren't an innate part of human existence; the first *homo sapiens* didn't wear a bunch of leaves for one season and then throw them out when somebody showed up wearing a fancy berry hat. They've developed. And understanding why is actually pretty amazing.

2	**There are actually two sociological theories about fashion trends and what they're for nowadays. One is a social status one:** as fashion trends trickle down from the high echelons of society (fashion houses and celebrities), across (from other countries) or up (from urban fashion, "street style," or punks), they allow us to demonstrate our wealth and hipness through emulation. We can do that seriously fast now, thanks to massive improvements in textile technology, so the fashion world needs to move faster than ever to keep one step ahead of us plebs.
	Another idea is based on conflict theory — and thinks that the rapid cycle of fashion (some fashion houses now produce eight or more collections in one year) is actually **a way of maximizing profit.** The onset of trends keeps us buying for fear of wearing "last year's stuff" — so more money goes to the fashion industry. Plus, focusing on trends apparently keeps our minds off the real problems in the world, like poverty and chocolate shortages.
	https://www.bustle.com/articles/94811-where-do-fashion-trends-start-why-people-care-about-whats-in-style-and-what-it-really

Books
1	**Reading is great fun for many people, but it also has many benefits for your mental health in the form of thinking and understanding.** By concentrating on the words and the storyline, it stimulates your brain and cognitive functions. This particular stimulation can help sharpen your mind, especially the part of the brain that is responsible for concentration and critical analysis. It sharpens this part of the brain much like you would sharpen a knife. This sharpening of the mind will eventually heighten your focus when concentrating on something important.
	By causing you to focus intensely on the words, your brain takes in a significant amount of information, which can improve both your critical thinking and analyzation skills as well. This stimulation is healthy for your mind and the sharpening your thought processes.
	Well, after several days of reading and looking up new words you don't understand, your vocabulary will begin to expand one word at a time. Words and phrases, if you read every day, fill your brain with a new vocabulary that you might never have learned without reading.
	Well, your brain immediately transports itself to a different world with different people. This change in pace can be a breath of fresh air for someone who is stressed out or suffers from extended periods of stress. By doing this, you can allow yourself to take a breath, relax, and be swept away to another world through the words written on the page.
	https://www.selfdevelopmentsecrets.com/benefits-importance-reading-books/

Research
1	**The inexorable advance of the Knowledge Society and Knowledge Economy - both fuelled by higher education, research and innovation (HERI) systems that have undergone profound changes in the past decade - have made 'research on research' increasingly important to all countries, whatever their level of development**. A new meta-dynamic that has emerged has been the observation and study of 'knowledge systems' in which higher education, research and innovation activities have converged and become strategically interlinked.
	In innovation, the dynamic comprises 'research for innovation' and 'research on innovation'. Exponential growth in partnerships between governments, the economic sector and higher education have linked new knowledge to development goals, and much innovation is also occurring outside academia. "Research system experts must understand the critical factors

	involved in order to advance this process." **Knowledge production systems today involve a vast range of entities including universities, public laboratories, research centres, think-tanks, the private sector and the military complex.** The *Research Report* shows that in the past decade these systems have transformed to emerge as the main motors of development, in a process that has also changed the landscape of higher education - especially the university sector. https://www.universityworldnews.com/post.php?story=20090622215201783
2	**Research is demanding and time consuming!** If you are heavily involved in extracurricular activities, or if you need a lot of time for study, research may be more of a burden to you than you would expect. For Biology research, the time demands are great Research can be frustrating **Do not do research if you think you need it to get into medical school.** A medical school applicant is evaluated as a total package, so if other areas of your application are weak (grades, MCAT scores, extracurricular involvement), the mere act of doing research will not help you get in to a school **Do not do research if you think you need it to get into a health professional school.** In the words of an alum: "Some health professional schools are more interested in your clinical experience than your lab experience". Study the requirements of your professional school (such as Veterinary Medicine or Physician's Assistant programs) before making a decision. **It adds stress, especially if you have deadlines to meet or out-of-town conferences to attend** https://www.scranton.edu/academics/cas/neuroscience/StudentResearch/Importance.shtml

Innovation	
1	**Thinking outside of the box generates excitement, passion and creativity.** Additionally, teamwork is oftentimes essential when coming up with outstanding ideas and solutions, as two heads are better that one. We perform better when we collaborate and when we look at the number one human need that activates the heart, it is connection. **Developing a creative culture takes time and it begins with management, being more open-minded and less judgmental to the suggestions of their team.** Patience is a virtue; you need to allow time for your team members to develop their creativity in the organization and to put their ideas together to find optimum solutions. **Most leaders are expected to think creatively and come up with innovative solutions to organizational problems.** However, by cultivating and utilizing the creative abilities of your team, it is likely to produce an even more prosperous selection of creative ideas and solutions to organizational problems. https://www.nibusinessinfo.co.uk/content/advantages-innovation

Chores	
1	**Research indicates that those children who do have a set of chores have higher self-esteem, are more responsible, and are better able to deal with frustration and delay gratification, all of which**

	contribute to greater success in school. Doing chores gives a child the opportunity **to give back** to their parents for all you do for them. Kids begin to see themselves as important contributors to the family. They feel a connection to the family. **Holding them accountable for their chores can increase a sense of themselves as responsible and actually make them more responsible.** Children will feel more capable for having met their obligations and completed their tasks. One of the most frequently sited causes of over-indulgence stems from parents doing too much for their children and not expecting enough of them. Not being taught the skills of everyday living can limit children's ability to function at age appropriate levels https://centerforparentingeducation.org/library-of-articles/responsibility-and-chores/part-i-benefits-of-chores/
2.	**It isn't hard to imagine reasons for this shift. Tightly packed schedules can leave kids little time for housework — which, unlike calculus assignments or soccer practice, probably won't influence college admissions decisions.** Some parents may want to spare their children the drudgery they endured. Others may find that nagging kids to do their chores is more of a burden than they bargained for." https://www.yourmodernfamily.com/should-kids-do-chores/

Uniforms	
1	**They take away social segregation.** The way you dress usually dictates what sort of click you belong to, such as the goths, jocks, nerds, and so on. If everyone is dressed the same, it can take away the need to put a label on each person and the tendency to just stick with your 'crowd.' **They encourage students to express themselves in other ways.** Because kids can't show their individuality through clothes, they will try to express themselves through other methods such as the arts, academics, sports, or extra-curricular school activities.
2	**They can hinder a child's decision making skills.** Since you do not allow students to choose what they can wear, you are taking away their right to make a choice for themselves. This can disrupt the development of their ability to form their own opinions or make choices, and interfere with their transition into adulthood. **They become a band aid solution to bigger problems.** Poor academic performance, school violence, and decreasing attendance are some of the major issues schools face today. Opposing proponents question if school uniforms are really the answer to solving these problems. https://connectusfund.org/20-disadvantages-and-advantages-of-school-uniforms

Homeschooling	
1	**Customized Education**. Homeschooling can work for any child, even kids diagnosed with ADD, dyslexia or other learning disability. Linda, a homeschool mom, advocate and author of a number of homeschooling books, says she has "seen homeschooling succeed in all different situations because the family's desire created the strength and determination to provide an alternative to the education system to their children." **Improved Learning Efficiency**. While a child sits in school for nearly eight hours, homeschooling may only take a few hours each day. This allows time for extracurricular activities, recess, co-ops and field trips. **Increased Flexibility**. Homeschooling does not have to occur during normal school hours or in a classroom. You can tweak the schedule to fit your child's learning style and your family's

	commitments.
2	**Eating Up Time.** Stay-at-home, work-from-home and even working parents can homeschool. However, it does take time to prepare lessons and schedule activities, in addition to teaching. **Losing a Second Income.** Having a stay-at-home parent works for many families, but it can be a tough transition if you're losing an income. A careful look at finances, including money saved by homeschooling versus attending private school, is part of evaluating the pros and cons of homeschooling. **You Are Always Parenting.** Every parent needs an occasional breather, even if only to use the bathroom without interruption. "Homeschooling is definitely demanding," Den says. "It takes a lot of time and research, planning and preparation to make sure the homeschool experience is going well." She emphasizes the importance for a family to find individual activities and spend some time apart. https://www.care.com/c/stories/3282/the-pros-and-cons-of-homeschooling/

Customer Complaints	
1	**Stay calm.** When a customer presents you with a complaint, keep in mind that the issue is not personal; he or she is not attacking you directly but rather the situation at hand. "Winning" the confrontation accomplishes nothing. A person who remains in control of his or her emotions deals from a position of strength. While it is perfectly natural to get defensive when attacked, choose to be the "professional" and keep your cool. **Listen well.** Let the irate customer blow off steam. Respond with phrases such as, "Hmm," "I see," and "Tell me more." Do not interrupt. As the customer vents and sees you are not reacting, he or she will begin to calm down. The customer needs to get into a calm frame of mind before he or she can hear your solution—or anything you say, for that matter. **Acknowledge the problem.** Let the customer know you hear what he or she is saying. If you or your company made a mistake, admit it. If you did not make a mistake and it is a misunderstanding, simply explain it to the customer: "I can see how that would be incredibly frustrating for you." You are not necessarily agreeing with what the customer is saying, but respecting how he or she perceives and feels about the situation. An excellent phrase for opening up this particular conversation would be, "So, if I understand you correctly…" After the customer responds, follow up with, "So, if I understand you correctly, we were to resolve the problem by noon today. I can see how that must be frustrating for you." Then be quiet. Usually, the customer will respond with "That's right" or "Exactly." By repeating to the customer what you think you heard, you lower his or her defenses, and win the right to be heard. https://trainingmag.com/content/how-handle-customer-complaints/

Music	
1	**Recent research shows that listening to music improves our mental well-being and boosts our physical health in surprising and astonishing ways.** If we take a music lesson or two, that musical training can help raise our IQs and even keep us sharp in old age. Here are 15 amazing scientifically-proven benefits of being hooked on music. **Research proves that when you listen to music you like, your brain releases dopamine, a "feel-good" neurotransmitter.** Valorie Salimpoor, a neuroscientist at McGill University, injected eight music-lovers with a radioactive substance that binds to dopamine receptors after they listened to their favorite music. A PET scan showed that large amounts of dopamine were released, which biologically caused the participants to feel emotions like happiness, excitement, and joy.

Listening to music you enjoy decreases levels of the stress hormone cortisol in your body, which counteracts the effects of chronic stress. This is an important finding since stress causes 60% of all our illnesses and disease. One study showed that if people actively participated in making music by playing various percussion instruments and singing, their immune system was boosted even more than if they passively listened

Researchers discovered that music can help you learn and recall information better, but it depends on how much you like the music and whether or not you're a musician. Subjects memorized Japanese characters while listening to music that either seemed positive or neutral to them.[13] The results showed that participants who were musicians learned better with neutral music but tested better when pleasurable music was playing. Non-musicians, on the other hand, learned better with positive music but tested better with neutral music.

https://www.lifehack.org/317747/scientists-find-15-amazing-benefits-listening-music

Climate and Weather	
1	**Global climate is a description of the climate of a planet as a whole, with all the regional differences averaged like the United States, different regions of the world have varying climates.** But, we can also describe the climate of an entire planet—referred to as the global climate. Global climate is a description of the climate of a planet as a whole, with all the regional differences averaged. Overall, global climate depends on the amount of energy received by the sun and the amount of energy that is trapped in the system. And, these amounts are different for different planets. Scientists who study Earth's climate look at the factors that affect our planet as a whole. **Today, climates are changing. Our Earth is warming more quickly than it has in the past** according to the research of scientists. Hot summer days may be quite typical of climates in many regions of the world, but warming is causing Earth's average global temperature to increase. The amount of solar radiation, the chemistry of the atmosphere, clouds, and the biosphere all affect Earth's climate. **As global climate changes, weather patterns are changing as well.** While it's impossible to say whether a particular day's weather was affected by climate change, it is possible to predict how patterns might change. For example, scientists predict more extreme weather events as Earth's climate warms. https://www.ncei.noaa.gov/news/weather-vs-climate

Pros and Cons of Owning a Home	
1	**Greater privacy.** Homes typically increase in value, build equity and provide a nest egg for the future. Your costs are predictable and more stable than renting because they're ideally based on a fixed-rate mortgage. The interest and property tax portion of your mortgage payment is a tax deduction. There's pride in homeownership, which also closely ties you to your community. Affordable options exist, like purchasing a lower cost manufactured home.
2	**Homeownership is a long-term financial commitment.** You're responsible for all maintenance on your home. This can include inexpensive repairs like fixing a broken toilet to complex and costly repairs like replacing a furnace. Owning a home ties you to your community, making it more difficult to suddenly pick up and leave a location.

	Although mortgage payments are usually fixed, they're generally higher than rent payments. Buying a home requires a down payment, closing costs and moving expenses. The value of your house may not increase – especially during the first few years. Borrowing against your home equity, to help you with a debt consolidation, for example, can leave you 'house poor'. https://www.incharge.org/housing/homebuyer-education/homeownership-guide/advantages-and-disadvantages-of-owning-a-home/

Pros and Cons of Owning a Business	
1	Advantage: Financial Rewards One big enticement for business ownership is reaping the bigger financial rewards. Successful business owners have the opportunity to make more money for the risks they take. A tax preparer who makes $15 per hour knows the firm charges several hundred dollars for the service he provides. When an employee feels his value is worth more than the pay scale, opening his own business begins to make a lot of sense. Advantage: Lifestyle Independence Business owners enjoy lifestyle flexibility, because they're creating their own schedule. This looks different for everyone, but it often includes the ability to attend kids' school and sports functions, take vacations when desired and adjust a work week to accommodate other personal needs.
2	Disadvantage: Financial Risk Losing money is one of the biggest risks of owning a business. There are start-up costs for materials and business establishment, as well as monthly obligations. Costs vary, depending on the type and size of the business. Many business owners take out a loan when starting a business, which means they are in debt from day one, while also trying to generate revenues. Disadvantage: Stress and Health Issues Business owners tend to experience high levels of stress as well as health issues. Not having a consistent paycheck means business owners always need to generate new sales and revenues. Owners often experience significant variations in monthly income and have potentially higher debt accumulation. Bigger businesses that have a higher monthly overhead and payroll mean the business owner is responsible for others' livelihood, which also adds to personal stress. https://smallbusiness.chron.com/advantages-disadvantages-owning-own-company-21125.html

Childhood	
1	Having a childhood is one of the most important areas of life a person can have. It can show kids how to act, what to do and what not to do and so much more. I remember, as a child, playing on the swings and running around with my friends. It was one of the greatest parts of being a kid. The ability to play and use my active imagination with other kids my age. And that's not all that was great about my childhood: it showed me how to act and taught me many things. https://www.theodysseyonline.com/reasons-childhood-important

Smoking bans	
1	**They reduce the risk of second-hand smoke.** Advocates for smoking bans claim that passing a law to prohibit smoking in public places can lessen the possibility of second-hand smoke being inhaled by non-smokers. Second-hand smoke, according to experts, can lead to increased risk to emphysema, cardiovascular disorders and respiratory problems. By restricting the places where smoking is allowed, this can be prevented. **They lessen air pollution.** Supporters also say that states and cities which have non-smoking policies and prohibited smoking in restaurants and public indoor spaces have better indoor air quality as opposed to cities which still allow smoking public.
2	**They take away freedom from people.** Some critics see smoking bans as a violation on one's personal liberty. They argue that people should have the autonomy to decide on what kind of lifestyle they will have. Although they are not totally against banning smoking, they say that it should be a personal choice. **They can affect businesses.** Business owners who are not in favor of smoking bans as well as smokers who are used to smoking in public places such as restaurants and coffee shops argue that restricting smoking in these places can drive customers away and this can be harmful to businesses. And as for establishments which are already smoke-free, competition will be higher. It will also be harder for them to leverage since there will be more businesses that are smoke-free. https://connectusfund.org/14-central-pros-and-cons-of-smoking-bans

Practice 7

Do you agree or disagree with the following statement? Leadership traits are inherited and cannot be learned.

Write your response here.

Student's response (5/5)

It is incontrovertible that there are certain traits that define a leader. After all, not everyone would consider himself or herself as being a competent leader and there is often something special about great leaders whether it is their intelligence or charisma. Yet, there could be a debate over the nature and origin of leadership traits; are they inherited or cultivated? Some might argue that leadership traits cannot be learned, and are only innately within certain individuals. However, I believe that leadership traits can be learned for two reasons.

To begin with, leadership is not necessarily an innate ability because certain skills are learned due to needing to survive or accomplish a task. In other words, there are some traits that are gained through nurture and not necessarily nature. From my personal experience, I never considered myself to be a leader of any kind. This was because I did not know what I needed to do in order to lead a group successfully. However, after reading, studying and examining the characteristics needed to be a leader, I decided to apply some of them. Soon I realized that with practice, I could learn to be one. This clearly depicts that not all traits are inherited, but some could be learned from our experiences and environment.

Another major consideration is that if it were only an inherited trait then leadership is reserved for the few. This means that in a group, it is plausible that each member does not have the innate abilities to lead, and if that is true, then there would be no one who would be able to lead them. To illustrate this, one should see no further than the number of leaders that change in almost any organization. There are so many people that have the capability of becoming a great leader. This is due to learned experiences; such as adapting to change, cultivating connections, optimizing opportunities, and trusting the team. Consequently, through practice and training a person could learn to gain these traits. Therefore, we can assume that not every leader is born with these traits; some people actually learn these traits.

In summary, there are numerous reasons to believe that many leaders learn how to cultivate their leadership qualities rather than being born as leaders. This view allows us to explain why some leadership skills are teachable and why anybody can become a leader depending on the circumstances.

Consider the following:

Decision makers often assume that a person who demonstrates competency and performs well in their job also is likely to have leadership and management potential. However, management and leadership require skillsets that are qualitatively very different to the tasks one performs in more content driven positions.

As a result, many new leaders and managers find themselves in roles for which they are entirely unprepared. If they believe, as many people do, that leadership is a quality one is born with and fear, as many new managers do, that they were not, they are likely to feel both uncomfortable and intimidated by the expectations thrust upon them.

Indeed, a recent study from the University of Illinois, Urbana-Champaign demonstrated that a fifteen week academic course was able to significantly improve the leadership skills of the participants by using the 'Ready, Willing and Able' model (which examines whether students are ready to lead, motivated to lead, and effective in their efforts).

The study identified the most important factor for successful students as being their 'Willingness'—how motivated they were to lead in the first place (or for new managers, how motivated they are to acquire and develop their own leadership skills).

---

https://www.psychologytoday.com/intl/blog/the-squeaky-wheel/201502/can-leadership-be-learned-or-are-you-born-it

Practice 8

When you have a problem, to whom would you go for advice between an old friend and a family member?

Write your response here.

Student's response (5/5)

It is incontrovertible that when we encounter a problem, we look to others for advice. After all, sometimes we need to gain other perspectives or listen to others who may have been in a similar situation. Yet, there could be a debate over from whom to seek advice: an old friend or family member. Some might argue that a family member is better since blood is thicker than water. However, I believe that seeking advice from a friend may be more helpful for two reasons.

To begin with, an old friend is someone who you have known for a long time, and have seen you through both thick and thin. In other words, you and your friend know each other on an intimate level, even more so than some of your family members. From my personal experience, whenever I had any issue in school and was in need of help, my parents didn't even know what I was going through. On the other hand, my old friend understood what I was talking about and was able to help me think through the situation, so I could make a sound decision that would be best for me. This was because my friend was my peer and was able to reflect on his own issues whenever he gave me his advice. Soon, I realized that old friends could provide great advice because they could see and understand my perspective and situation well. This clearly depicts that old friends could be better when it comes to seeking advice than family members.

Another major consideration is that your friends would be more respectful towards you as they share the same feelings or dilemmas you could be going through. This means that they could be less judgmental and understand the risks that you may want to take. To illustrate this, we should see no further than the typical advice we may get from our parents and friends. Although it may be useful, our parents may want us to make a decision that satisfies them rather than us. This is due to parents feeling more protective of their children rather than understanding their needs whereas our old friends would be more willing to understand the associated risks involved with a particular decision we are facing. Consequently, the advice from our parents may not be as satisfactory as the advice from our friends who take into account our desires and needs better.

In summary, there are numerous reasons to believe that going to our friends can be better than going to our family members for important advice. This will allow us to gain advice from somebody who knows us well and respect our feelings.

Consider the following:

It's complicated because, for one thing, we don't always know everything that's actually going on in another person's life, no matter how close we might be.

Most of us want from our friends is not advice, but someone to listen and support us as we grapple with issues.

To further complicate the situation, sometimes *not* saying something can damage a friendship, too.

https://www.psychologytoday.com/intl/blog/the-couch/201609/the-pros-and-cons-giving-friend-advice

---

Practice 9

Do you agree or disagree with the following statement?

Most advertisers lie about the quality of their product in order to make you buy it.

Write your response here.

Student's response (5/5)

It is incontrovertible that advertisers would do almost anything to entice consumers to buy their products. After all, their survival depends on the number of sales they attain. Yet, there could be a debate over whether or not advertisers lie about the quality of the product they are promoting. Some might argue that it is unethical for advertisers to lie about their product and should always be truthful because it could be detrimental to their business. However, I believe that most advertisers lie about product quality so that they can make a larger profit regardless of it being unethical.

To begin with, the main purpose of advertising is not to meet the ethical standards but to entice consumers to buy the product. In other words, their main goal is to increase their market share and profit margin through sales, and this naturally leads them to false claims and exaggerations. From my personal experience, I remembered that my mother had bought this one vacuum that was advertised on television. The advertiser said the vacuum is virtually indestructible and could pick up the smallest dust particle. Yet, it took only a week for the vacuum belt to break, and it didn't have as much suction power as mentioned. This was because the advertiser only wanted to appeal to its customer base so that they could buy the product. Soon I realized that you couldn't really trust advertisements because they only tell you what you want to hear. This clearly depicts that an advertiser is willing to lie about the quality in order to get buyers to purchase the product.

Another major consideration is that it is easy and customary for advertisers to embellish the truth about the product just a bit. This means that the product might be fairly decent but not quite the best as they claim to be. Even though it is technically a lie, advertisers don't get serious consequences in this case. To illustrate this one should look no further than certain products that do not last as long as one may perceive. In fact, it may last only as long as the limited warranty. This is due to having the product last long enough so that customers do not demand a refund or exchange. Consequently, the advertiser could earn their profits and then possibly cause consumers to buy the product again. Therefore, we can just assume that advertisers only care about the sales and nothing more.

In summary, it might seem that advertisers would want to be truthful. However, I believe that they would rather lie or embellish the truth a bit just to gain a much larger profit.

Consider the following:

I found that some companies with very low quality will say they're better than they are, and they couldn't stay in business if they didn't overstate their quality," Gardete says. For example, a company with products that would rate a 1 or 2 on a scale from 1 to 10 has every reason to claim in ads that their products are a 3 or 4, since that would attract customers who want decent quality without scaring away price-sensitive shoppers. "If people knew these sellers' true quality," he says, "they wouldn't even go into the store." Once customers do get lured into the store, many discover the poor quality and walk away—but enough settle for the shoddy product that it makes sense for the seller to stick with the formula.

Companies on the high end, in contrast, will simply tell the truth. "They have no incentive to say they're cheaper than they are," Gardete says, since doing so will turn away customers looking for the highest quality. Even companies offering middling quality and price tend to present themselves accurately, Gardete's model predicts. The problem is that customers can't tell whether they're dealing with a 4 or 1. "The middle-quality companies will say 'value

for money,' and the low-quality ones will also say 'value for money,'" Gardete explains. So, even when the majority of sellers are honest, the few bad apples spoil things for many of the rest. Consumers are always worse off when advertisers misrepresent themselves.
https://www.gsb.stanford.edu/insights/pedro-gardete-when-do-advertisers-tell-truth

Practice 10-12: Education

Practice 10

Some people think that high schools should start later in the day while other people believe that it should start earlier. Which one do you prefer?

Write your response here.

Student's response (5/5)

It is incontrovertible that teenagers need to go to school just as adults go to work. After all, the youth have to prepare for their future careers through education that motives them develop as successful individuals. Yet, there is a debate over when to start school since teenagers need enough rest and sleep. Some might argue that schools should start earlier so that teenagers can participate in more sports and work. However, I believe that it should start later for the following two reasons.

To begin with, adolescents need at least 8 hours of sleep to be able to function well in school, and teenagers also go through hormonal changes which affect their sleeping patterns in a negative manner. In other words, if teenagers don't get enough sleep and just go to school, they would not be able to focus during school hours and may rely on dangerous caffeinated drinks to stay alert and awake. From my personal experience, I remember having to start high school at 7a.m. I felt a lack of energy every morning. This was because I was sleep deprived and getting only 6 hours of sleep a night. Soon I realized that I needed more rest in order to completely concentrate on my school work. This clearly depicts the importance of a late start so that teenagers can get an adequate amount of sleep to perform better in school.

Another major consideration is the health issues that could accompany an early start. This means that there is a higher probability that adolescents may engage in dangerous activities, such as overindulgence on sugary and caffeinated drinks because they must wake up early for school. To illustrate this one should look no further than the number of teens who have died in traffic accidents. There are so many teens that may become tired, lose concentration, and rush to school, which might cause various health issues and even fatal accidents. This is due to waking up too early for school. Consequently, an early start time may not only affect high students academically but also their physical and mental health. Therefore, we can assume that a slightly later start time would be highly beneficial for an adolescent's well-being.

In summary, there are numerous reasons to believe that starting high school later in the day can be better than starting it earlier. This will allow rapidly growing teenagers to get enough sleep and avoid possible health risks.

Consider the following:

Researchers analyzed the harmful effects sleep deprivation—anything less than 8.5 to 9 hours of sleep on school nights—can have on young people.

They concluded that poor sleep is linked to increased reliance on caffeine, tobacco, and alcohol. They also discovered a link between sleep deprivation and poor academic performance. Sleep deprivation has also been linked to an increased risk of car accidents in teens.

Delaying junior high or high school start times would likely impact the schedule for all schools within a district.

Teens would get out of school later in the afternoons, which could pose problems for teens who provide childcare to younger siblings.

Students who participate in sports and extra-curricular activities would get home much later in the evenings.

Teens may stay up even later if they don't have to wake for school at an earlier time.

https://www.verywellfamily.com/the-pros-and-cons-of-starting-school-later-2609565

Practice 11

Do you agree or disagree with the following statement? Grades are important to measure a student's academic achievement.

Write your response here.

<table>
<tr><td></td></tr>
<tr><td></td></tr>
<tr><td></td></tr>
<tr><td></td></tr>
<tr><td></td></tr>
<tr><td></td></tr>
</table>

Student's response (5/5)

It is incontrovertible that students are measured for their academic achievement in schools. After all, parents and students alike would like to know how they are doing in school. Yet, there could be a debate on whether grades are an effective way to measure student achievement. Some might argue that grades are the best since they can easily classify student learning. However, I believe that grades do not consider all the facets that determine student's achievement for the following two reasons.

To begin with, grades are easily manipulated with other factors, such as extra credit or assignment re-dos. In other words, a student who did poorly on an assignment may have a chance to do a meaningless assignment for extra points. From my personal experience, I remember the amount of extra credit that was given enabled me to score 150 out of 100. This did not really convey my achievement as much as it showed how much work I was able to complete. This was because I was able to do extra work to boost my grade. Soon I realized that I didn't really learn more than my classmates based on my grade. This clearly depicts the faultiness of using grades as a measure of student achievement.

Another major consideration is that some teachers are discouraged from giving low grades as this might demotivate students. This means that even if a student is not really learning anything, the teacher may not be allowed to give him or her a failing grade. This is another way grades are inflated and do not necessarily show a correlation between state assessment tests and graded tests. To illustrate this one should look no further than the disparity that lies between grades and state tests. The test may show that the student is performing below grade level, but the grades may show that the student is above grade level. This is due to inflating grades and not adhering to true academic achievement. Consequently, grades would not be a clear and reliable indication of student achievement.

In summary, it may seem that there are some benefits to using grades as a way to evaluate student achievement. However, I believe that there are more disadvantages than advantages to using grades.

Consider the following:

After all, doing assignments, studying, and paying attention are the work students do when they're in school. But if "earning" grades gives people the idea that grades are students' pay for punching a clock, for showing up and being busy, and for following directions no matter what the outcome, then the image is harmful. The object of all this busy-ness isn't just the doing of it.

For grading to support learning, grades should reflect student achievement of intended learning outcomes. In schools today, these learning outcomes are usually stated as standards for achievement. Grades on both individual assessments and report cards should reflect students' achievement of performance standards on intended learning outcomes.

http://www.ascd.org/publications/books/117074/chapters/Grading-on-Standards-for-Achievement.aspx

Practice 12

Do you agree or disagree with the following statement? Children are less interested in learning today because of cell phones, online games and social media.

Write your response here.

_____

Student's response (5/5)

_____

It is incontrovertible that children are immersed in a variety of digital media in the 21ˢᵗ century. After all, everywhere they go, kids are exposed to media in all forms like cell phones, online games and social media today. So, there could be a debate over whether children are less interested in learning these days because of digital media or not. Some might argue that media plays a positive role in children's education and do not inhibit learning today. However, I believe that it does make children less interested in learning for two reasons.

To begin with, media can negatively influence how children feel, learn things, and behave. In other words, children may be more reluctant to learn about academic subjects because they become more fascinated with digital media. From my personal experience, I remember in school, I worked with another student on a project. The student was only interested in playing online games and did not really care about the project. This was because the student found the games more interesting than what was being taught in school. Soon I realized that some of my classmates were not interested in learning something new, but they were serious about winning the game and going to the next level. Predictably, they were also the students who received the lowest grades in my class. This clearly depicts that education took a back seat to digital media.

Another major consideration is that an overuse of online media can lead to addiction. This means that they may spend an excessive amount of time on digital media. To illustrate this one should look no further than the number of children who describe themselves as constantly connected. There are so many youths who are inundated with digital media that attracts their undivided attention. This is due to the command that the technology landscape has over the youth. Consequently, this could deter the desire for learning. Therefore, we can assume that digital media could consume children's minds and inhibit their education.

In summary, there are numerous reasons to believe that today's youngsters are less interested in learning because of cell phones, online games, and social media. Excessive amount of time children spend on multimedia may decrease their motivation to study in school and increase their chances of becoming addicted to media addiction, which impedes learning in general.

Consider the following:

Social media is a vital aspect of teenagers' and children's social and creative lives. They use social media to have fun, make and maintain friendships, share interests, explore identities and develop relationships with family. It's an extension of their offline and face-to-face interactions.

Digital media literacy: exploring and experimenting on social media can help your child build the knowledge and skills she needs to enjoy online activities and avoid online risks.

Collaborative learning: your child can use social media to share educational content, either informally or in formal school settings.

Creativity: your child can be creative with profile pages, photos and video, and modifications for games.

Mental health and wellbeing: connecting with extended family and friends and taking part in local and global online communities can give your child a sense of connection and belonging.

https://raisingchildren.net.au/teens/entertainment-technology/digital-life/social-media

Practice 13-15: Events

Practice 13

Do you prefer to travel with friends or with a tour group?

Write your response here.

Student's response (5/5)

It is incontrovertible that not only is traveling in a pack safer but it is also more fun to experience new places, cultures and cuisines with other people. After all, humans are social animals. Yet, there could be a debate over with whom we should travel: friends or a tour group. Some might argue that a tour group is better as it is organized by professional guides. However, I believe that traveling with friends may be more attractive for two reasons.

To begin with, traveling with your friends will deepen the friendship. In other words, as travel expands your mind to gain a new perspective, it will also allow you to test and strengthen your bond as you face difficulties and excitements on the road. From my personal experience, when I visited NYC with my best friend last year, I learned the true meaning of friendship. I got all pumped up and very excited in the beginning, and we were eager and set up the schedule months in advance. Unfortunately, when we arrived there, the weather condition was so bad that we couldn't even go out. All we did was staying at the hotel and watching movies. However, I felt really connected to my friend while talking with her about all the topics about our lives. When you've been friends with someone for years, you probably think you've heard all their stories, laughed at all their jokes, and witnessed all their shining moments. But no matter how well you think you know your squad, you can always dig a little deeper. To me, the otherwise disappointing trip to NYC was a great chance to develop my friendship and make unforgettable memories while getting to know more about my old friend. This was mainly because I went traveling with a true friend. This clearly depicts that going on a trip with friends can be a meaningful choice.

Another major consideration is that traveling with your friends would make you feel more comfortable doing what you really want to do. This means that with your friends, you have the same ideas on how things should be done and your perspectives are not distant. To illustrate this, one should see no further than the activities you can do together while on a trip. There are so many things you can do that are specifically meant for groups. Activities, such as camping, rafting, and trekking are best enjoyed with your friends, not with a bunch of strangers. This is due to the same interests you share with your friends. Consequently,

271

your trip will never get boring and you will fully enjoy everything a new place has to offer: the pictures you take, the experience and the destinations you uncover, and the insights you garner. Therefore, we can assume that traveling with friends is a wonderful way to make the most of a trip.

In summary, there are numerous reasons to believe that traveling with friends is better than traveling with a tour group. This will allow us to develop our friendship and enjoy the trip more.

Consider the following:

Figure out if you'll be happy doing the same activities, staying in the same type of accommodations, and generally moving at the same speed. Comparing travel styles also means considering transportation preferences; for instance, are you OK with taking a connecting flight to save some money, or do you only travel nonstop?

When planning a trip with friends, think about what you most want to get out of the trip. Are you longing for plenty of low-key beach time, or do you want to see every museum on your route?

There's a lot of leg work that goes into planning a trip with friends. If you don't have the time, patience, or organization to take charge of these details, don't volunteer to plan the whole trip.

https://www.smartertravel.com/tips-for-planning-a-trip-with-friends/

A tour group led by a guide that speaks your native language fluently might be the best way to see your dream destination. Your tour guide knows the local area and can give you tips for finding good restaurants and exploring during your free time. You will be able to ask your tour guide as many questions as you like so you can make the most of your vacation experience. There are times when driving in an unfamiliar place is not a good idea. You may be dealing with newly-diagnosed impaired vision, or you may just want to avoid driving on the other side of the road. If you have always wanted to travel to Cuba and are an American citizen, or you yearn to see penguins, a tour group might be your only option. Some travel opportunities are available only to tour groups.

https://www.tripsavvy.com/when-should-you-travel-with-tour-group-2972995

Practice 14

If you were the leader in your country, and the country is going through an economic crisis, how would you help people get a job? 1. Do not interfere with companies and large businesses. 2. Force companies to hire new people.

Write your response here.

Student's response (5/5)

It is incontrovertible that all leaders of countries want their nations to be prosperous and successful. After all, the state of the economy - especially what's happening with inflation, growth and employment – can have a huge impact on voters. Yet, there could be a debate over how leaders should cope with an economic crisis. Some might argue that they have to force companies to hire new people to lower the unemployment rate. However, I believe that political leaders should not interfere with companies and large businesses for two reasons.

To begin with, there will be negative consequences if political leaders interfere with the private sector and force companies to hire people while facing an economic downturn. In other words, recessions cannot be overcome by the use of political influence over employment. From my personal experience, I witnessed the president of my country trying to improve the economy by regulating the minimum number of regular workers during the economic crisis. This was mainly because of the assumption that it would have a positive impact on the national economy. However, I soon realized that many companies moved their headquarters to other countries where the labor regulation was more flexible. As a result, my country's economic depression got worse and the employment rate increased. This clearly depicts that governments and political leaders can only make things worse if they try to control the economy too much.

Another major consideration is that there are better measures to deal with economic problems than forcing businesses to hire unnecessary workers. To illustrate this, one should see no further than American history. There are so many things a political leader can learn from historical events during the Great Depression. The United States President Franklin D. Roosevelt, made a series of attempts to assess and recover from the enormous damage done on the American economy after the stock market crash in 1929. His economic policy, commonly known as the New Deal, redefined the role of the government, convincing the majority of ordinary Americans that the government not only could but should intervene in the economy as well as protect and provide direct support for American citizens facing an economic catastrophe. Under Franklin Roosevelt, and his New Deal; the government's role in America grew more than in any era before. During this time, there were numerous examples of growth of the government as new agencies, programs, and institutions were created to stimulate the dwindling economy. Consequently, the New Deal affected America in many positive ways. It was one of the reasons why America got out of the Great Depression. The New Deal provided jobs, hope, and a new future for many Americans. However, President Roosevelt never forced any private company to hire people because that will be against the principle of free market and capitalism which are the fabric of American culture and constitution. Instead, he used subsidies, loans, public programs, reliefs, and financial reforms. Therefore, we can assume that a country's leader has to come up with better methods than such a drastic measure as depriving freedom of companies to deal with economic issues.

In summary, there are numerous reasons to believe that a leader of a country should avoid any drastic interference with the country's economy even during the recession. This will allow the country to develop and recover from the economic crisis in a more sustainable manner without harming the constitutional values and freedom.

Consider the following:

Indeed, the private sector is the country's chief economic force, but it needs government regulation.

Government mandates that companies make financial information public, thereby protecting the rights of investors and facilitating further investment.

https://smallbusiness.chron.com/role-government-business-803.html

If a business is violating rights, then it is the purpose and responsibility of government to redress the violation, creating laws as necessary, and curtail or alter that business activity, and that's it.

If government would confine its activities regarding business to that, good business would flourish, bad business would diminish, and rights would be preserved.

The purpose of government is to safeguard rights, not regulate business. Capitalism works precisely because it allows markets to fail. Congress fails precisely because it attempts to regulate markets. The bad products, the poorly run businesses under Capitalism die a market death, and the better products, the well run businesses live a market life.
https://www.enotes.com/homework-help/should-government-regulate-businesses-392339

Practice 15

Do you agree or disagree with the following statement? In 20 years, we will all be using electric cars.

Write your response here.

| |
| |
| |
| |
| |
| |
| |
| |
| |
| |
| |
| |
| |
| |
| |
| |
| |
| |
| |
| |
| |
| |
| |
| |
| |
| |
| |
| |
| |
| |
| |
| |
| |

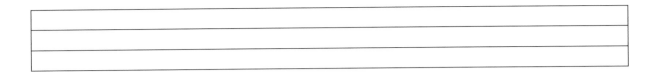

Student's response (5/5)

It is incontrovertible that people need transportation. After all, we need to get around and engage in a variety of activities, such as trade between people and deliver goods and services, which is essential for the development of civilizations. Yet, there could be a debate over what kind of vehicle will be most popular in the future. Some might argue that we will still drive gasoline cars as they have been around for a long time and it would be very difficult to replace all of them. However, I think we will be using more innovative electric cars in 20 years for two reasons.

To begin with, driving electric cars is an effective way to protect the environment. In other words, there will be no more fuel emissions, the air will be cleaner, and everyone can be healthier when you use electric cars. What's even more interesting is that it is really easy to switch to electric cars from gasoline cars in reality. From my personal experience, I used to live in a very dense city with many gasoline cars stuck in traffic at most times of the day. As a result, I often got sick and suffered from migraines and respiratory problems. In fact, the pollution issue was so severe that the majority of the citizens there were forced to stay inside just to avoid inhaling the dust. In order to counter this problem, one day the city started to introduce electric buses. This was because the pollution exceeded the limit and the government had to take action. Soon, everyone realized how much better the air became and were able to go out and enjoy the fresh air. Remarkably, the change happened within a couple of years, making the city livable and vibrant again. This clearly depicts that it is not only possible for us to opt for electric cars but also it can be done promptly. Of course, 20 years will be enough time to make this change globally.

Another major consideration is that electric cars are easier and cheaper to maintain. This means that this can help save households a lot of money. To illustrate this, one should look no further than the amount of times a car owner needs to get his car repaired or serviced. There are many cases in which people buy cheaper cars to save money or prolong the use of their current cars. This is because people want to save money, but they are often unaware of the fact that an electric car needs less maintenance since it doesn't use oil and there are fewer parts to repair. However, now more people consider the cost-effectiveness of electric cars and are switching to them. It is only logical to buy a car that will last longer and cost less in the long term, and we now know which option will be better for financial purposes. Consequently, this is becoming a trend around the world, and the sales of electric cars are soaring globally. Therefore, we can assume that the majority of us will have electric cars in 20 years because they will be even cheaper and easier to maintain.

In summary, there are many reasons to believe that people will be using electric cars in 20 years. By using electric cars, we can protect the environment and save money on maintenance. Most importantly, people are reasonable enough to make this change happen.

Consider the following:

New research from *BloombergNEF* says they could be cheaper than combustion-engine cars by 2022.
That's been driven by a steady reduction in the price and size of batteries, as well as a healthy kick up the backside from Tesla that jolted automotive incumbents into prioritizing electric vehicle development. Despite the progress, though, these cars still lag behind their gas-guzzling cousins on price, range, and refueling time.

The momentum in the market now seems unstoppable. Whether the crossover point when an electric vehicle becomes cheaper than a conventional one comes in three years or five, the transport sector looks set for a dramatic shift in the near future.

https://singularityhub.com/2019/04/29/electric-cars-are-estimated-to-be-cheaper-than-regular-cars-by-2022/

The number of electric vehicles on the world's roads is rising fast. Latest figures show there are more than three million and sales are growing at close to 75% a year.

Amnesty points to serious health risks to child and adult workers in cobalt mines in the Democratic Republic of Congo, documented in a report it issued. More than half the world's cobalt comes from southern DRC, much of it from artisanal mines that produce 20% of the country's output. Battery manufacture now accounts for 60% of the 125,000 tons of cobalt mined globally each year.

The pressure to go green is increasing as bans on the sale of new fossil-fuelled cars loom in Europe. Germany will stop the sale of all new petrol and diesel cars from 2030, Scotland from 2032, and France and the UK from 2040.

https://www.weforum.org/agenda/2019/03/the-dirty-secret-of-electric-vehicles/

PART 2

The Independent Task

20 Trending Questions & Sample Answers

Check What questions actually appeared on the test recently!

1. Some companies decide not to permit employees to reply to emails or text messages related to work during the holidays and on weekends. What do you think about this policy?

Write your response here.

Student's response (5/5)

It is incontrovertible that electronic communication is important to workplace collaboration in the 21st century. After all, we have become a world of interconnected people, carrying oversized cell phones in our pockets, toting oversized tablets in our backpacks, jumping from phone to watch to tablet to laptop to desktop to talking cylinders on our kitchen counters with ease. We start a thought on the subway, work on it at the office, add to it on the bus or in the car, and finish it in our home office. We are always connected. We are always wired in. We are always on. Yet, there could be a debate over whether it is good or not to expect employees to maintain contact during non-working hours. Some might argue that there are situations that may arise in which the employer, employees, or team members may need to continue working on the project after hours in order to meet deadlines. However, I generally believe that companies should not permit employees to reply to emails or text messages related to work at least during the holidays or weekends for two reasons.

To begin with, doing extra work at home can seriously harm your health. In other words, people can become highly stressed and develop cardiovascular diseases. From my personal experience, I struggled with ongoing illnesses that led to sinus infections because I had to constantly communicate with the company even during after work hours. This was because I was always on my phone, texting and emailing my co-workers and boss. Soon I realized that I was working every day for more than 13 hours a day, including on weekends. This clearly depicts that staying connected can be hazardous to one's health.

Another major consideration is that working long hours and being always connected can make a person less productive. This means that the employee may become more fatigue causing a loss of motivation and less job satisfaction. To illustrate this, one should look no further than the number of errors or accidents that can happen. There are so many cases of productivity being halted because of a mistake. This is due to not getting enough sleep or relaxation time away from work. Consequently, the employee becomes so exhausted that they cannot focus on completing their work properly. Hence, it is important to take a break from work activities, even simple ones, such as texting and email.

In summary, there are numerous reasons to believe that having to be constantly connected with work via email and text is detrimental to one's health and productivity. Therefore, by not permitting employees to answer texts or emails during holidays and weekends, the company will have healthier and more productive workers.

Consider the following:

Working abnormal or long hours has long been linked with depression, anxiety and even coronary heart disease. Crucially, the importance of weekend recovery has also been correlated with weekly job performance and personal initiative. While further research revealed psychological detachment during off-work time, reduced emotional exhaustion caused by high job demands and helped people stay engaged.

Some feel this shift is just a natural evolution of the workplace and a result our stubborn inability to unplug. Others find it more sinister.

Today, says Cooper, work emails are just a tap of a smartphone away. "You don't carry your laptop around when you're out to dinner, but you do carry your mobile phone," he says. "The smartphone changed everything."

"The higher the expectation for monitoring organizational email, the less people can detach, the more time they spend on work-related email after hours and the more they are emotionally exhausted," says Liuba Belkin,

https://www.bbc.com/worklife/article/20180830-what-would-happen-if-we-banned-work-emails-at-the-weekend

2. Do you agree or disagree with the following statement?

In order to be successful, businesses and companies must spend a lot of money on advertising.

Write your response here.

| |
| |
| |

Student's response (5/5)

It is incontrovertible that businesses and companies need to promote their products through advertising. After all, this is one method to reach out to consumers and expand their market share. Yet, there could be a debate on how much money should be spent on advertising costs. Some might argue that it is unnecessary to spend a lot of money on advertising. However, I believe that businesses and companies need to spend a lot of money on advertising in order to be successful for two reasons.

To begin with, it is important that companies can set themselves apart from the competition. In other words, they would need to do a lot of advertising to convince their potential consumers as to why they are different. Drawing from my experience, I once noticed that one of my company's products was not selling well. This was because there were other similar products on the market, so the competition was high. Soon I realized that my company would need to spend more on advertising so that the product could be differentiated. Luckily, after using a more aggressive and expensive advertising campaign, the product sales went up drastically. This clearly depicts the importance of spending money for advertising.

Another major consideration is that some advertising mediums can be quite costly. This means that it could become a heavy expense easily, and if the company would like to strengthen their campaign in order to gain a better market reach, it would need to spend more money. To illustrate this, one should see no further than the companies that market during a major sports event that millions of people may watch. Usually this type of commercial or promotion can cost a lot of money because of the huge amount of attention the sports broadcasts will garner. There are so many situations in which companies' sales increased dramatically. This is due to paying more for a premium advertising spot or even using a more expensive medium, such as a television commercial. Consequently, the more expensive the advertising space is, the more attention it may garner. Hence, it is important to spend a lot of money on advertising to be successful.

In summary, there are numerous reasons to believe that increasing advertising costs is correlated with a company or business' success. Even though the expense is higher, this will allow for the company to increase sales and eventually gain a substantial profit.

Consider the following:

One-third of small businesses (37%) spend less than $10,000 on advertising, which shows that businesses don't have to spend a lot of money to have a successful advertising strategy.

Nearly all small businesses (91%) plan to increase their advertising spending in 2019, indicating that small businesses prioritize advertising and see it as a beneficial marketing strategy.

The right advertising budget varies by business needs and market. However, experts agree that businesses of all sizes should spend some of their overall budgets on advertising.

"Millennials understand that they have to really invest in marketing and advertising to be successful," Smith said. "Older people tend to look at advertising as an expense and an obligation. Younger people tend to look at it as an investment and an opportunity."

"Advertising not only increases sales but [also] helps us build our brand for the long haul by increasing brand recognition and solidifying ourselves as the leader in our product category."

https://themanifest.com/advertising/small-business-advertising-spending-2019

Spending more money on advertising does not necessarily mean more business! More often than not, it just means you've spent more money, and you now have less money in the bank account. Spending more on advertising may or may not be the key to bringing in more business. As you'll learn, effective advertising requires you to deliver the right message to the right people at the right time in the right way. Simply having more website ads, or a bigger Pay Per Click budget is often not the way to bring in more business.

https://www.visualscope.com/marketing102.html

3. Which one of the following options is better for a company to increase its profitability?

- **Improve the employees' skills in technology**
- **Redesign the working environment to help the employees to feel comfortable**

Write your response here.

Student's response (5/5)

It is incontrovertible that companies are always trying to think of ways to increase profitability. After all, the company cannot have a long life and become successful without revenues. Yet, there could be debate over where to spend the money internally in order to increase their profits. Some might argue that businesses have to improve the employees' skills in technology for that. However, I believe that redesigning the working environment to help the employees to feel comfortable is more beneficial for the company's earnings for two reasons.

To begin with, it is important that employees feel that their company cares for their mental and physical health to be motivated to work harder. In other words, providing a comfortable office space would provide benefits to their well-being, and employees would become more productive. Drawing from my experience, I once worked at a company that provided employees with a decent size desks and ergonomic chairs. The company also had a separate room with a recliner for employees to de-stress or have a moment to themselves. This was because the company cared about the employees' needs to take a moment to refocus on their work so they can be more productive. Soon I realized that I felt very comfortable going to work and was able to be more efficient and productive at work because of the environment. This clearly depicts the importance of the employees' healthy physical and mental states in regards to productivity, which in turn would result in higher profits for the company.

Another major consideration is office space that is conducive to collaboration would foster synthesis and innovation, which is very important to a company's profitability. This means that the office's layout could affect teamwork and communication. To illustrate this, one should see no further than companies like Google, which has a climbing wall, a bowling alley and a beach volleyball court. There are many other companies that offer these extra perks for their employees, and these activities at Google help employees to build teams and bond so that they may collaborate better together. Also, the activities could help the employee relax enough so that they can be more innovative. This is due to having a clear mind and being less stressed at work.   Consequently, a mentally healthy employee is more valuable to the company. Hence, the office layout is important.

In summary, there are numerous reasons to believe that redesigning a workspace would help employees work better, which would ultimately lead to higher profits for the company. This will allow the employees to look forward to working every day, and happy employees are generally the most innovative and productive, thus, leading to greater profits for the company.

Consider the following:

Technology allows businesses to speed up production processes. You can analyse how your staff are spending their time and introduce processes to make your systems more efficient.

Task management tools allow you to stay on top of daily responsibilities so you don't miss anything.

Interactive websites, online chat support services and 24/7 customer service via social media can set you apart from the competition and help increase your profits.

https://www.localmarketlaunch.com/business/5-ways-technology-can-improve-your-business/

Higher employee wellbeing is associated with higher productivity and firm performance

We find employee satisfaction to have a substantial positive correlation with customer loyalty and a substantial negative correlation with staff turnover. The correlation with productivity is positive and strong. Importantly, higher customer loyalty and employee productivity, as well as lower staff turnover, are also reflected in higher profitability of business units, as evidenced by a moderately positive correlation between employee satisfaction and profitability.

https://www.weforum.org/agenda/2019/07/happy-employees-and-their-impact-on-firm-performance/

4. Do you agree or disagree with the following statement?

Primary school students (aged 5-10) should not do more than 30 minutes of homework every day because they already get enough instruction in regular classes in school.

Write your response here.

Student's response (5/5)

It is incontrovertible that primary students have homework to do on most nights. After all, this is one of the most common ways to reinforce what was learned in school. Yet, there could be a debate on exactly how much homework a student should receive. Some might argue that young students should get as much as two hours' worth of homework every night. However, I believe that primary school students should not receive more than 30 minutes of homework every day for two reasons.

To begin with, too much homework can limit the amount of time young students spend playing with friends. In other words, too much homework can impede children's social development. Drawing from my experience, in the third grade, I didn't have many friends and felt awkward around people. This was because I spent more than 3 hours a night doing homework. Soon I realized that I was always alone and felt dejected. In fact, I could not really socialize with the other children until I moved to another school where teachers were more progressive and flexible about homework assignments. This clearly depicts how too much homework can be detrimental to a young child's well-being.

Another major consideration is that an abundance of homework could become not only tedious but also meaningless. This means that children would possibly lose their interests in their studies, and choose not to complete their assignments. To illustrate this, one should see not further the number of students who actually complete their homework assignments. There are many cases in which, students would risk getting a lower grade and don't even try to complete the homework assignments. This is due to students feeling that homework is unnecessary to their learning. Furthermore, the research on homework shows beneficial effects on learning only when appropriate assignments are given and completed, and the benefits increase with grade level. The truth is that there is little to no learning benefit in the early grades. Hence, excessive homework would be pointless.

In summary, there are numerous reasons for primary grade students to receive only 30 minutes of homework daily. This will allow them to develop socially and increase the beneficial effects on learning through homework without pressuring the young students too much.

Consider the following:

Studies show that homework improves student achievement in terms of improved grades, test results, and the likelihood to attend college.

Research published in the High School Journal indicates that students who spent between 31 and 90 minutes each day on homework "scored about 40 points higher on the SAT-

A poll of high school students in California found that 59% thought they had too much homework. 43% of respondents said that homework was their greatest source of stress, and 82% agreed that they were "often or always stressed by schoolwork.

The American Educational Research Association says that "whenever homework crowds out social experience, outdoor recreation, and creative activities, and whenever it usurps time that should be devoted to sleep, it is not meeting the basic needs of children and adolescents."

https://www.procon.org/headline.php?headlineID=005411

5. **Do you agree or disagree with the following statement?**

A school decided to make it mandatory for all students to complete a public speaking course in order to graduate.

Write your response here.

| |
| |
| |
| |
| |
| |
| |
| |

Student's response (5/5)

It is incontrovertible that one's communication skills are essential to his or her success. After all, humans are social animals and we have to persuade, listen to, and interact with various people through our lives. So, there could be a debate over whether universities have to make it mandatory for the students to take a public speaking course to graduate or not. Some might argue that a public speaking course can be useless and does not offer any value to a student's education or future career. However, I believe that a public speaking course may actually be beneficial to the student for two reasons.

To begin with, it is important to understand that one might have to speak frequently in front of an audience in his or her career. So, acquiring this ability could prepare the student for success in his or her field. Drawing from my experience, I remember having to take a public speaking course, and I was not looking forward to it. This was because I was afraid to speak in front of people and always had issues when it comes to communication. Luckily, I soon realized that the course actually helped me overcome my fear when I had to speak in front of a large number of people professionally. My presentations for work became actually more successful, and my boss offered me a promotion. This clearly depicts how a public speaking course helped my professional life.

Another major consideration is that it can help some students break out of their comfort zone. This means that it can offer them the practice they need to become more confident. To illustrate this, one should look no further than professionals at a work function. There are so many different reasons why one would need to speak to other people in similar fields. This is due to the need to socialize and network with others, whether it is for a better position or a business deal. Consequently, they would need to confidently talk to many different people in their field. Hence, a public speaking course enables students to gain the confidence needed in a public work setting.

In summary, there are so many reasons to require students to take a public speaking course. This course would be more advantageous in the long run.

Consider the following:
Nearly all performers or politicians have experienced stage fright at some point in their lives, even if public speaking is what they do for a living. The best way to get over the fear and to learn to manage your nerves is to practice, practice, practice.
Some students argue that they do not want to be actors or politicians, so learning public speaking has no purpose. However, public speaking is extremely useful in everyday life. All students will have college and job interviews at some point, and the ability to clearly articulate a point gives us the best chance of impressing a potential admissions representative or employer, and possibly giving us an advantage over the next person.
https://theschreibertimes.com/2015/05/19/public-speaking-courses-should-be-mandatory/

It can be stress-inducing to give a presentation or speech, and time-consuming as there are hours of planning, writing and practicing involved with any public speaking engagement. There is also the risk of embarrassment and failure, which can deplete self-esteem, although the audience typically notices far less errors than the speaker imagines.

For some, anxiety surrounding public speaking may be more than a simple fear reaction; it may be a social phobia with more extreme physical manifestations such as dread, a fight-flight response or even an anxiety attack. Negative experiences during public speaking may serve to support these fearful feelings and unpleasant reactions.
https://penandthepad.com/list-7677144-disadvantages-public-speaking.html

---

6. Which do you prefer between eating at restaurants or cooking and eating at home?

Write your response here.

Student's response (5/5)

It is incontrovertible that people look forward to eating delicious meals every day. After all, eating is not only the source of nutrition for our survival but also a pleasurable activity for our happiness. Yet, there could be a debate over the choice between eating at restaurants and eating at home. Some might argue that eating at restaurants is more convenient and the food is more delicious than eating at home. However, I believe that cooking and eating at home is actually better for two reasons.

To begin with, it is important to understand that habitually eating at restaurants is rather unhealthy. In other words, you cannot control the ingredients that are used at restaurants and the number of calories you might intake. Drawing from my experience, I remember that I was so busy that I ate at restaurants often. The food was delicious, but it also ended up making me sick. This was because restaurant food is not guaranteed to be healthy and it often contains artificial ingredients that can be harmful. Soon I realized that I needed to change my eating habits and cook more at home so that I can feel better. This clearly depicts that restaurant food can be detrimental to my body.

Another major consideration is that cooking at home could give you a sense of pride and satisfaction. This means that after cooking something delicious, you may feel a sense of accomplishment, especially if it is a dish you have never cooked before. To illustrate this one should look no further than people who come together to share their food and eat. There are so many reasons why people enjoy cooking. This is due to wanting to try something new and even sharing it with others. Consequently, people enjoy cooking and eating at home, particularly when they can share their achievements with others. Therefore, we can assume that having a meal at home is much more rewarding and delicious.

In summary, there are so many reasons why a home cooked meal is much healthier and tastier than eating at a restaurant. This will even allow people to enjoy an activity that doesn't concern work.

Consider the following:

One of the biggest 'pros' cited by most people is the convenience of eating out. You just order a burger or a soup and in few minutes or half an hour you're being fed. On the other hand though, cooking at home (and from scratch, not heating some processed meals) doesn't have to take such a long time either.

Some would claim buying the groceries and cooking at home might get more expensive, but overall eating out is pricey.

Unless you found out a really good restaurant with a lot of care about the customers' health, many of them provide oversized portions

Cooking at home can be fun and is certainly cheaper.

If you are dining out as a family with young children, this can (and I speak from experience) sometimes be a little stressful.

https://www.surveycompare.net/blog/eating-out-versus-cooking-home

7. Some students prefer to choose smaller classes with fewer students while others prefer to take bigger classes with lots of students. Which do you prefer?

Write your response here.

Student's response (5/5)

It is incontrovertible that students will take a number of big and small classes in college. After all, many of these classes are required to be taken in order to graduate, and it is hard to standardize the size of the class. Yet, there could be a debate over the choice between smaller classes with fewer students or bigger classes with lots of students. Some might argue that bigger classes will give students more opportunities to socialize. However, I prefer smaller classes with fewer students for two reasons.

To begin with, it is important that I feel a part of a learning community, and smaller classes are more likely to offer that kind of ambience to students than bigger classes. So, in smaller classes, I feel as though I would learn more by interacting with my professors and colleagues who are very close to me. Drawing from my experience, I took both large and small classes in college. Looking back, in the larger classes, I didn't feel as though I was truly learning as in my smaller classes. This was because in the auditorium lecture classes, I only needed to memorize information and there were not many interactions between the students and professors. Soon I realized that after taking an exam, I did not even retain the information I gained in the class, unlike my smaller classes, which allowed me to discuss with others about the subject matter. This clearly depicts why small classes are more beneficial.

Another major consideration is that some topics are more difficult than others, and it would be a great benefit to get more personal attention. This means that in a smaller class, I would be able to reach out to the professor easily if I have a question about the material. To illustrate this, one should look no further than the student to professor ratio. There are so many students that are able to succeed and learn more when the ratio is smaller. This is due to the personal attention that students would be able to get. Consequently, they would be able to learn more and even enjoy learning. Therefore, we can assume that smaller classes are better.

In summary, there are numerous reasons to believe that smaller classes provide better learning opportunities for students than bigger classes. This will allow students to be a part of a learning community and also get the attention they need.

Consider the following:
In a small class teachers have more of an opportunity to get to know students on a personal level, helping them to tailor their teaching strategies to meet individual learning needs. This also helps teachers build stronger relationships with students which in turn, creates a happier class environment.

As noted above, teachers of a small group are able to better tailor their lessons to incorporate all learning abilities in the class. Fewer pupils in class also means that teachers have more time to review work, give detailed feedback and identify where pupils need extra support which can result in higher test scores.
A smaller class is less likely to represent a varied cross-section of society. Students benefit from diversity because it gives them the opportunity to be exposed to viewpoints that contrast greatly from their own.

If 1 or 2 students are absent from a large class, it is not noticeable. From a small class however, it can make a huge difference. Planned lessons can be difficult to carry out if a few students are absent as they account for a larger percentage of the class population.
https://www.getadministrate.com/blog/which-class-size-works-best-for-student/

8. Many schools require young children (aged 5-11) to study together in small groups instead of studying alone. Do you agree or disagree with that?

Write your response here.

Student's response (5/5)

It is incontrovertible that young children participate in many learning activities. After all, adolescence is formative years and building a strong foundation through social interaction is crucial. Yet, there could be a debate over whether or not they should study in small groups. Some might argue that studying alone is better for children to gain some independence. However, I believe that young children should study in small groups rather than alone for two reasons.

To begin with, it is important that young children learn to cooperate with one another. In other words, in the future, we must work as a team with various people, and it is a good idea that children learn this at a young age. Drawing from my experience, I didn't know how to cooperate with others to accomplish any task although I could successfully complete the same tasks individually. This was because every member of my group had different ideas about how to get the work done. Soon I realized that learning to work together is essential because it is important to listen to other ideas and not just your own. Thanks to this experience, I was able to develop effective communication skills and began to utilize different perspectives whenever I had to work in groups. This clearly depicts the importance of getting young children to work in small groups.

Another major consideration is that elementary school children are still developing their social skills. This means that working as a team could facilitate socialization, as they must work with others that are not their friends. To illustrate this, one should look no further than a group of young children working together on a project in the classroom. Through this they learn to socialize in the group. This is due to having a common goal and in order to accomplish it, they must talk to each other. Consequently, they learn how to get along and communicate effectively. Therefore, we can assume that socialization skills are developed through group work.

In summary, there are numerous benefits to working in a group rather than individually. This will allow students to cooperate and develop social skills.

Consider the following:

Teamwork helps in increasing collaboration and has a scope for brainstorming, which results in getting more ideas. Therefore you can see a growth in productivity

While working in a team, conflicts might occur in case when one person works less than the other.

You need not depend on others and also can decide things independently.

No interference from others and extra meeting so you can focus on your work and complete it faster.

You will be the one who is responsible for the work done, and you don't have to share the credit with others.

While working in a team, conflicts might occur in case when one person works less than the other.

https://content.wisestep.com/top-advantages-and-disadvantages-of-working-in-a-group/

9. **Some people think that younger children should be taken care of by other children in a family while others think that younger children should be taken care of by their parents or other adults. What's your opinion?**

Write your response here.

Student's response (5/5)

It is incontrovertible that family dynamics have changed in recent years, and mothers are no longer the only caregivers of children. After all, many households need two working parents in order to support the family. Yet, there could be a debate over who should take care of younger children. Some might argue that the parents or other adults should still take care of the young children. However, I believe that older children should take care of their siblings for two reasons.

To begin with, sometimes parents need the assistance of older children. In other words, there are some situations in which the older child can help rather than relying on another adult, especially if it is an unfamiliar person. Drawing from my experience, I remember having to take care of my younger siblings. This was because my mom had to get a job to help support the family. Soon I realized that my mom needed my help, and it was better for me to take care of my siblings rather than relying on a complete stranger. This clearly depicts the importance of older children in taking care of the younger children.

Another major consideration is that older children can bond with their younger siblings by taking care of them. This means that younger children will look up to the older children, and they may do various activities with them. To illustrate this, one should look no further than the strong relationship that siblings develop just by being a part of each other's lives. There are so many memories brothers and sisters share with each other by being a part of each other's life and helping each other through care and love. Consequently, these moments create a bond between the children, and they become not only family but also friends. Therefore, we can assume that having older children take care of younger ones can help build special bond and connection that can last a lifetime.

In summary, older children should help out with caring for younger children. This will allow the family to become stronger and closer throughout the lifetime.

Consider the following:
Health care experts have begun focusing on the impact of giving a child too much responsibility or assigning responsibility before a child is mature enough to handle it. Some children do not function well under pressure while others may not be mature enough to temper the inclination to boss around a younger sibling.

Adding to the fray is the potential for resentment for the need to act like an adult or miss out on what their friends are doing. While many older children do demonstrate varying levels of resentment, most do not exhibit any more resentment for caring for a sibling than they do for taking out the trash or performing other routine chores.

https://www.sheknows.com/parenting/articles/7318/children-raising-children-should-siblings-babysit/

10. Do you agree or disagree with the following statement?
The most important goal of education is to teach people how to educate themselves.

The purpose of education?

Write your response here.

Student's response (5/5)

It is incontrovertible that throughout history education has been playing a vital role in human life. After all, we cannot survive without education, and historically all civilizations started to develop as we began sharing our knowledge. Yet, there could be a debate over the ultimate goal of education as multiple paradigms of our society and our education are going through a major and irreversible transformation. Some might simply say that the overall goal of education is to provide students with useful knowledge in school and prepare them for their future careers. However, I believe that there is more to education than just the input process. In fact, the most fundamental goal of education might be to teach people how to educate themselves in order to lead their lives intelligently and creatively.

To begin with, it is important to understand that we have to be constantly learning to become more successful, understand ourselves better, and adapt to the evolving world more proactively. In other words, education's main goal should be to create lifelong and self-motivated learners. Drawing from my own experience, I became interested in linguistics because of my bilingual background. Although my teachers instilled the basic linguistic knowledge in me throughout my high school and college years, the real motivation for me to continuously study about language to this day lies in the problems and questions that everyday has to offer as I interact with people from different countries. Because of my natural curiosity about the subject and my unique situation, I go further and research about many topics in linguistics even though there is nobody asking me to do so now. When life asks us strange questions, we cannot avoid them. Hence, I realized that essentially education is for problem solving, and since every individual has different problems every day, we have to learn how to teach ourselves the best methods to address those issues more than anything else.

Another major consideration is that teachers cannot always spoon-feed us with their expertise and experiences. Once the formal education is over, individuals cannot easily go back to teachers to get quick help and advice. As a result, they have to independently learn to deal with their issues, and the skills to efficiently achieve that goal are what education should offer. To illustrate this one should look no further than a medical laboratory scientist. Most of the medical breakthroughs he makes will come from his own experiments and research rather than his professors and text books. But he learned how to conduct the experiment and analyze research results from the medical school. This means that the school taught the scientist how to teach himself how to successfully resolve medical issues. Indeed, all of us have to face the reality where nothing can be 100 percent certain and no one can offer the unequivocal solutions to problems. Therefore, it is clear that education is to help one develop the ability to teach himself or herself in real life situations.

In summary, there are many reasons to believe that education is to teach people how to educate themselves. This view allows us to understand the real motivations of learning and the function of foundational knowledge in life.

Consider the following:

But I also want her to be the kind of person who will keep building on what she got in my school, who will keep developing skills, keep learning, and keep growing. Each of us, if we live to be just 70 years old, spends only 9 percent of our lives in school. Considering that the other 91 percent is spent "out there," then the only really substantial thing education can do is help us to become continuous, lifelong learners.

I want students to be able to find the information they need, to be able to go through the process of finding learning. And the key is that they are motivated to do it.

http://www.ascd.org/publications/books/104438/chapters/The-Real-Goals-of-Education.aspx

---

11. Do you agree or disagree with the following statement?

Students don't respect their teachers as much as they did in the past.

Write your response here.

| |
| |
| |
| |
| |
| |
| |
| |
| |

Student's response (5/5)

It is incontrovertible that students' attitudes toward their teachers can change over time. After all, social values and beliefs constantly evolve through generations as they reshape their cultural norms and ethical standards with new perspectives and desires. So, there might be a debate over whether today's students respect their teachers as much as they did in the past or not. Some might argue that students still hold their teachers in high esteem since they are the ultimate mentors. However, I believe that students do not respect their teachers now as much as they did before for two reasons.

To begin with, it is important that we consider that teachers are more scrutinized today than before. In other words, teachers could easily be punished for the smallest infraction, which gives students the upper hand in the classroom. Drawing from my experience, I remember seeing a student curse at his teacher because he was not allowed to play games on his cell phone. While the teacher tried to take the cell phone away, the phone dropped. The student got highly upset and told the administration. In the end, the teacher had to pay for the cell phone damage. This was because the teacher was at fault for trying to take the cell phone away even though the student was not following classroom rules. Soon I realized that the teacher was not respected in the classroom since the teacher's rules were not followed, and rather than punishing the student, the teacher got punished. This clearly depicts the lack of respect a teacher has these days.

Another major consideration is that a teacher is often blamed for a student's failure. This means that even if the student didn't study, his or her teacher still faces the label as being an ineffective instructor. To illustrate this, one should look no further than the high turnover for teaching jobs. It is true that there are so many cases of ineffective teachers, but also there are some effective ones that are blamed for a student's failure. Thus, regardless of the teacher, there is a lack of respect. This is due to not really understanding or being aware of the failure itself but placing blame on the whole group of teachers. Consequently, it isn't just the few that are disrespected; instead, all teachers end up being blamed and lose respect. Therefore, we can assume that based on this pattern, students are not as respectful of teachers today as in the past.

In summary, there are numerous reasons to believe that a teacher does not get as much respect today as in the past. This is mainly because of the shift in one's perception of a teacher's role.

Consider the following:

A new Harris Poll out Thursday finds that fewer adults believe teachers respect parents or students — and that fewer believe parents and students respect teachers. In other words, just about every relationship in a school has soured a bit.

We have gone from a time when parents believed what the teacher said in regards to their child's behavior and reacted accordingly to the present, where parents stare in disbelief and think of a million excuses as to why their child misbehaves.

The level of respect in school hasn't necessarily gotten worse. "I was a sideshow attraction at our school because I was 6-foot-2-inches in middle school," she says. "I was constantly teased and ridiculed, and teachers and counselors knew it. They did nothing." Most mornings, she recalls, "I was throwing up in the car, but I made myself go."

https://www.usatoday.com/story/news/nation/2014/01/23/respect-schools-teachers-parents-students/4789283/

---

12. A university will spend money on dormitories to improve the students' quality of life. Which of the following options do you think is the best way?

- **Study room**
- **Exercise room**
- **Entertainment room to watch movies**

Write your response here.

Student's response (5/5)

It is incontrovertible that dormitories are a major part of college students' life. After all, they will spend a great amount of time there. Yet, there could be a debate over what could improve the quality of life in the dormitories. Some might argue that a study room or entertainment room would be a good addition to the dorms. However, I believe that an exercise room would be a great way to improve students' quality of life for two reasons.

To begin with, an exercise room would allow students to relieve stress by working out. In other words, assignments could become so stressful and tedious that students may need an outlet to de-stress. Drawing from my experience, I remember feeling more exhausted and stressed. This was due to the amount of reading and writing I had to do in college. Later on, I decided to take walks and even joined a gym. I felt better and more energized. Soon I realized the benefits exercising had on my studies and quality of life. This clearly depicts that having an exercise room could actually be advantageous for the students' quality of life.

Another major consideration is that being physically healthy also helps the brain. This means that the brain can stay sharp because exercise helps bring oxygen to the brain and grow new blood vessels. To illustrate this, one should look no further than the scientific findings that have demonstrated the positive benefits that exercise has on not just the body but also the brain. There are many cases of people getting sick, weak and lose the ability to think clearly with lack of exercise. This is due to not allowing the blood to circulate and getting the nutrients to the brain. Consequently, our brain can die without blood, vitamins and other nutrients that we derive from food sources. Therefore, we can assume that exercising is a vital part of brain health and our health.

In summary, there are numerous reasons to support having an exercise room in the dorm. This is mainly because it can help support a healthy lifestyle for the student and help with his or her own college success.

Consider the following:

Kitchens, private bathrooms, study lounges and social spaces are considered basic necessities in student housing. The study-bedroom is an essential component that must be provided in all students housing. The study-bedroom is a multi-purpose room that combines study, living and sleeping facilities. This room can serve multiple purposes, such as a location to surf the Internet or a place to study.

A television room is a place for socialization; students rate it highly as a place to make friends

http://citeseerx.ist.psu.edu/viewdoc/download?doi=10.1.1.1016.5291&rep=rep1&type=pdf

---

13. Is it good to take a lot of time to make an important decision?

Write your response here.

Student's response (5/5)

It is incontrovertible that there are some types of decisions that are hard to make like buying a house or studying abroad. After all, these decisions could affect our lives profoundly. Yet, there could be a debate over whether or not it is a good idea to take a lot of time to make an important decision. Some might argue that we could lose opportunities if we take too long to decide. However, I believe that we should take some time to make an important decision for two reasons.

To begin with, it is important that some decisions should be made carefully because it can impact our lives. In other words, hasty decisions can be detrimental and could change our lives for the worst. Drawing from my experience, I remember having to make an important career decision for myself. I had two job opportunities, and instead of looking at both opportunities carefully, I thoughtlessly chose one as I wanted to change my job and move into a new position quickly. Soon I realized that the choice I made was not the best one for me. I ended up hating and quitting the new job in one month. This clearly depicts the importance of taking some time to make a decision.

Another major consideration is that some decisions require a bit of research. This means that it may take some time to get the necessary facts and information needed. To illustrate this, one should look no further than public relations decisions. If a company is facing some bad publicity, the public relations team would need to research the reasons that caused the problem because making a decision without looking further into it could exacerbate the situation. There are many cases in which a company ends up losing a tremendous amount of profits because of hurried decisions. This is due to not fully looking into the root of the problem and finding a variety of solutions. Consequently, it could end up even causing the demise of the company and losing trust with its consumer base. Therefore, we can assume that everyone, even companies, should look at and research all viable possibilities before making a decision.

In summary, it is beneficial to take some time before making important decisions. This is mainly because no one wants to make a decision that could ultimately result in negative consequences.

Consider the following:

Harness the power of your mind, which involves your thinking brain; the source of slower, thoughtful responses.

Gut reactions can be important because they cut to the chase and reveal how you really feel about each option. But sometimes thinking seems to get you nowhere. Even after days of analyzing your options, you may be unable to effectively weigh the pros and cons, determine what you really want, or settle on what you think is best.

Mindfulness means you're able to pause, reflect, and listen to your inner wisdom. Mindfulness means that you can focus on the relevant information, know when to cut your losses, stay aware of your biases, and check your ego.

https://www.psychologytoday.com/intl/blog/laugh-cry-live/201706/how-mindfully-make-important-life-decisions

14. Do you agree or disagree with the following statement?

Schools should increase young children's (aged 5-11) time spent on science education and decrease the time spent on music and art.

Write your response here.

<table>
<tr><td></td></tr>
</table>

Student's response (5/5)

It is incontrovertible that young children should study a variety of different subjects. After all, the different subjects help broaden young children's mind and curiosity. Yet, there could be a debate about the amount of time spent on certain subjects. Some might argue that there should be more time spent on science education and less time on music and art. However, I believe that the amount of time spent on music and art should not decrease for two reasons.

To begin with, it is important to recognize that art is an integral part of cognitive development. In other words, it helps develop creativity, critical thinking and confidence. Drawing from my experience, I remember how I changed the workflow process at work to make it more efficient. This was because both music and art made me think about things that were not within certain constructs. Soon I realized the benefits music and art had on my creative thinking skills. This clearly depicts the importance of the arts.

Another major consideration is that the skills learned in art could be beneficial to the sciences. This means that being able to critically and creatively think would foster new experiments and hypothesis. To illustrate this, one should look no further than the number of artists and scientists that have collaborated to find new discoveries. There are also so many artists who have become scientists. This is due to the desire to understand and describe the world around us. Consequently, new innovations are made through this creative process. Therefore, we can assume that both science and art can be closely related and mutually benefit one another.

In summary, there are numerous reasons why the amount of time spent on art and music education should not be reduced. This is mainly because these subjects can mutually benefit one another.

Consider the following:

Educator-scientists are meeting some of these challenges by infusing creativity—by means of the arts—into the education and training of future scientists. Many are superficially aware of these efforts through familiarity with the STEAM acronym, a modification of the STEM acronym to include the Arts (Science, Technology, Engineering, Arts, and Mathematics). When we think of integrating arts and science, the most obvious art form that comes to mind is the visual arts. After all, most scientists have had to generate diagrams to communicate their science effectively.

Art can reinterpret scientific themes, providing us with new ways to look at our understanding of the natural universe—from finding new ways to visualize oceanic data that reveal the impact of climate change on marine life to new points of view on the microscopic from artists shadowing scientists at the lab bench.

While the relationship between performing arts and STEM is less obvious than that of STEM and visual communication, we easily recognize the importance of performance skills in teaching, presenting, collaborating, and even learning itself, all key components of a scientific career.

https://www.ncbi.nlm.nih.gov/pmc/articles/PMC5969448/

15. A university recognized that first year students have poor study skills. The best way to address this is to make it mandatory for them to take a course on study skills. Do you agree or disagree with it?

Write your response here.

Student's response (5/5)

It is incontrovertible that students should know how to study to be successful at university. After all, university is a place where young minds get challenged and develop to master academic and career skills for their future. Yet, there could be a debate over the method to achieve this goal. Some might even argue that, especially for the first year students who often struggle with their academics, universities should make it mandatory for them to take a course on study skills. However, I believe that this idea is not necessarily conducive to better learning experiences for two reasons.

To begin with, it is important to acknowledge that university students are always busy working on different tasks; including writing, reading, and researching while taking various core academic courses, and they might not have enough time for an additional mandatory course on study skills. In other words, universities should not burden students whose hands are already full by making them take an unnecessary course about study skills. Drawing from my experiences, the major issue I had regarding my schoolwork was the lack of time when I was in university. This was because I had to juggle between my part-time job and education on a daily basis. Even when I was studying, I was often too tired to focus on complicated concepts professors talked about. Soon, I realized that my GPA was falling down due to my lack of sleep and overwhelming workload. In the end, I had to give up on my job to improve my academics in the second semester. This clearly depicts that what university students need is not an extra course but a balanced lifestyle.

Another major consideration is that the skills we can learn to study better might not be applicable to all subjects. This means that even when the first year university students take a course to be better equipped with effective learning skills, it might not be translated into their scores. To illustrate this, one should see no further than the strategies students use for math. There are so many reliable formulas for various questions in math that you might think you will be good at anything once you master them. However, the results are often the opposite. Are great mathematicians always good at art or literature? It is not clearly the case in reality. This is due to the disparities among academic subjects that require different skill sets. Consequently, one size fits all style of education methodology to improve learning abilities cannot really help students who have to face diverse courses in school. Therefore, we can assume that the study skills course might be a waste of time for many students although it is well intended.

In summary, there are many reasons why a study skills course is not needed for university students. This is mainly because there isn't enough time to take another course, and study skills can vary from one discipline to the next.

Consider the following:

Extra-curricular skills courses are often not attended by the students who need them most, but by higher achieving students who want to enhance their performance further (Durkin & Main, 2002). In view of the above claims that all students need support for effective learning, the bolt-on approach is of limited use.

The provision of advice on study skills in the format of instructional texts contradicts experiential learning theories which emphasize that effective learning takes place when learners experience a problem and take action, reflect on the action, form concepts on the basis of their reflection and apply these concepts in new situations.

The labels of most study skills describe academic tasks, for instance 'essay writing', 'presentation' and 'note-taking'. Study skills training should enable students to carry out these tasks.

https://ipark.hud.ac.uk/sites/embeddingskills.hud.ac.uk/files/Wingate.pdf

16. To evaluate your presentation, which is better between watching the recording of yourself and getting feedback from the audience?

Write your response here.

___

Student's response (5/5)

___

It is incontrovertible that we have to objectively reflect on our performance in order to improve and evaluate our presentation skills. After all, speakers can be easily biased about themselves and may ignore their problems if they don't see themselves as a third person. Yet, there could be a debate over the best method to achieve that goal. Some might prefer watching their own performances by recording themselves giving a presentation while others opt for getting feedback from the audience. Personally, I believe that recording yourself giving a presentation is better than getting feedback from the audience for two reasons.

To begin with, it is important that you have to see your own mistakes clearly and objectively, which might be difficult if you rely on the audience's feedback alone. In other words, your audience's feedback can be elusive as they might want to avoid hurting your feelings or just don't care about your issues whereas video footages or audio files can show the whole presentation in detail so that you can easily gain more insight into your performance.

Drawing from my experiences, I used to be on a debate team in high school so that I may improve my presentation skills. Every time I gave a speech or debated, I would ask around and seek some advice from the audience. However, they would casually tell me it was good and there was no specific feedback that taught me about my problems as a speaker. This was because my audience was busy and didn't really pay attention to my personal concerns. Soon, I realized that I needed to see my own performance and began filming myself talking in front of a live audience. As a result, I was able to see there were many problems in my nonverbal communication skills as well as stylistic choices in language. This actually helped me greatly improve my presentation skills and I gained more confidence quickly. This clearly depicts the competitive advantage of recording yourself over getting feedback from the audience.

Another major consideration is that recording your presentation allows you to observe and analyze what you care most about regarding your presentation skills as closely as possible. This means that you can focus on the most urgent issues you have as a speaker to effectively address them. To illustrate this, one should see no further than football matches on TV. You will see so many slow motion video analysis segments to show the highlights of games and performances of great importance. This is due to the efficacy of replays of those visuals in terms of understanding how things actually happened during the matches. Consequently, audience and experts will learn what went well and what went wrong in the game through the factual and visual analysis specifically focused on certain aspects or moments of the game. Likewise, we can assume that speaker can also scientifically analyze their mistakes at specific moments by reviewing the video footages of their performances. This will certainly provide them with valuable insights into their own weakness.

In summary, watching a video-taped performance of one's presentation is more beneficial than just asking for feedback. This is mainly because of possibly biased and a great way to analyze oneself.

Consider the following:

Both verbal and nonverbal communication captured by the camera lens allows speakers an opportunity to assess their speechmaking as the audience did during the speech.

Evaluating one's speech by way of video provides the potential as a tool to minimize and/or eliminate discrepancies between self and audience perceptions of behavior.

https://ecommons.udayton.edu/cgi/viewcontent.cgi?referer=https://www.google.com/&httpsredir=1&article=1504&context=bcca

17. Do you agree or disagree with the following statement?

It's better to travel when you are young than when you are older.

Travel when you are old?

Write your response here.

Student's response (5/5)

It is incontrovertible that leisure travel is enjoyable for both the young and old. After all, anybody would love to take a vacation from everyday life, stay in nice hotels or resorts, relax on beaches or in a room, go on guided tours, and experience local tourist attractions. Yet, there could be a debate over which group of people can enjoy traveling more between the youth and the elderly. Some might argue that there is no significant difference between them. However, I believe that traveling when you are young is better than traveling when you old for two reasons.

To begin with, it is important that you are physically capable of getting around and doing the activities while you are traveling in order to truly enjoy the experience. Otherwise, you might end up being confined in a hotel room and watching TV, which is not essentially different from staying home. Drawing from my experiences, I had a time of my life when I visited Cebu, the Philippines, as a young college student years ago. This was because I was healthy and eager to do anything in the foreign country that had lots of things to offer. I took strolls on white sand beaches, swam with shark whales in the blue ocean, and visited exotic waterfalls hidden in gorgeous mountains. Soon, I realized that it would have been physically demanding to do all the things I had done there if I were old. In fact, I didn't see many tourists with white hair and wrinkly faces in any adventurous places while exploring the country and this didn't surprise me at all; even young and vigorous tourists like me found the journey quite challenging. This clearly depicts that people can enjoy traveling more when they are young and healthy than when they are too old and sedentary.

Another major consideration is that young travelers are more likely to make exciting social and meaningful connections than elderly travelers. This means that they will meet and interact with interesting people and get the most out of their trips whereas their older counterparts will try to stay in their comfort zone as recipients of services from caregivers and service individuals. To illustrate this, one should see no further than popular tourist attractions among young and old travelers. While older people prefer to stay at resorts and massage parlors, young people go to markets and clubs to meet locals and other travelers. This is due to young people's enthusiasm and open-mindedness and older people's lack of it. Consequently, the active and gregarious youth are often more satisfied with their trips than older travelers.

In summary, traveling while young can offer a lot more memorable experiences. This is mainly because of youthful stamina and social connections that are available to younger people.

Consider the following:

Like many senior travelers, they were flawlessly informed, patient and curious, and the very best sort of adventurers. Those advancing in years, unfettered by youthful debt and the need to work, are showing younger wanderers how to explore the world. They're the ones who don't care about a bumpy overnight bus ride through some gnarly part of Panama – they just want to be there. Yes, you might say the older traveler is more thorough and considered in their approach to travel, while the younger folk are going off like firecrackers in all directions but that's because they can. They can spring out of bed, rather than click into place in stages.

https://www.lonelyplanet.com/blog/2011/04/13/travel-debate-who-travels-better-the-young-or-the-old/

18. Do you agree or disagree with the following statement?

All scientific discoveries should be shared by the whole world. Governments and businesses should not keep scientific discoveries and secrets.

Write your response here.

Student's response (5/5)

It is incontrovertible that great scientific discoveries can offer people around the world major benefits. After all, human civilizations have all begun with technologies and inventions. Yet, there could be a debate over the extent to which we have to share scientific knowledge with the whole world. Some might argue that governments and businesses should never keep scientific discoveries and secrets. However, I believe that there are many occasions when we cannot expect complete transparency from governments and companies regarding important scientific discoveries for two reasons.

To begin with, it is important to acknowledge that there are certain confidential technologies for governments to protect for security and defense purposes. In other words, not all information is supposed to be shared by everyone around the world as some secret knowledge can bring about international disasters. Drawing from American history, the American government had to race against the Soviet Union from WWII to the end of the Cold War Era regarding space programs and nuclear capabilities. This was because both countries were international superpowers and wanted to maintain their global influences by displaying their technological superiorities. If any of the American government officials shared the country's technological breakthroughs with the Soviet Union back then, it would have been considered treason and the USA might have lost the competition or war against its communist rival. This clearly depicts that sometimes governments cannot share their technological innovations with other countries.

Another major consideration is that individual companies create and develop new technologies in order to generate profits. This means that the rightful owners of innovated technologies have to protect them from industrial thieves and spies. To illustrate this, one should see no further than legal battles among big phone companies such as Apple and Samsung. There are so many court trials where the two competing companies try to persuade the judges that the rights to use certain technologies and designs lawfully belong to them, accusing each other of stealing the valuable ideas worth millions of dollars if not billions. This is due to the huge amount of money the companies have invested over the years into the high-tech industry. Consequently, they want to recoup the investment with a large amount of interests or profits. Although it may sound unfair and even selfish, this is the only way capitalism motivates people and companies to create better products and become sustainable. If companies always had to share their technological secrets with others, they wouldn't invest more money into research and development for the better products. Therefore, we can assume that developers of technologies have to be guaranteed to be the only beneficiaries of them.

In summary, it is necessary for government and businesses to keep some of the new scientific discoveries and secrets. This is mainly due to preventing international disasters and maintaining a company success and profits.

Consider the following:
The trend toward secrecy in science means that it is harder for scientists to check each other's experiments for mistakes and ensure the integrity of published research.
Secrecy also is interfering with education of graduate students and hindering those seeking to launch their research careers, a related Harvard survey of scientists at 233 medical schools shows.
https://www.latimes.com/archives/la-xpm-2002-feb-11-sci-secret11-story.html

---

19. Do you agree or disagree with the following statement? Nowadays, it is not important for families to have a meal together every day.

Write your response here.

| |
| |
| |
| |
| |
| |
| |
| |
| |
| |
| |

Student's response (5/5)

It is incontrovertible that people have hectic lifestyles in the 21st century. After all, we keep moving, working, learning, and gong after so many dreams and aspirations in our lives in this highly mobile era. So, there could be a debate over whether our traditional value of having a meal with our families every day is still intact or not. Some might argue that it is something we can't ignore as family is the backbone of our society. However, I believe that this notion is no longer valid now for two reasons.

To begin with, it is important to acknowledge that people are busier than ever before in the 21st century and we have less time to spend with our family. In other words, it is simply not realistic to expect that we can still have at least one meal with our family a day. Drawing from my experiences, I remember my father trying to take care of his parents and spend as much time as possible with them. However, he was rarely able to see them and even during the holidays, he didn't have enough time to have meals with his parents. This was because he was a company owner with lots of tasks to accomplish. Growing up in that kind of environment, I realized that, whether one likes it or not, it's not easy to spend quality time with one's family in this world and age. This clearly depicts that having a meal with your family can be too idealistic and hard to achieve in reality.

Another major consideration is that thanks to today's advanced communication technology, there are many other feasible ways to stay close to your family now without having to rely on the family meal time. This means that we can embrace the new world of technologies and high mobility and improve our family relationships as well. To illustrate this, one should see no further than smartphones. There are so many applications available for smartphone users to have video chat with their loving families. By talking to your family on a daily basis or anytime you want to through this technology, you will be able to learn how your parents live and show them how much you care for them without the burden of traveling far to meet them physically. Consequently, we can actually get closer to our family even though we may not be able to make it to the family dinner every evening.

In summary, sometimes it is not feasible to have a nightly dinner with the family because of everyone's schedule. However, there are other ways to keep the family unit intact without having to find the time to have dinner together, such as using smartphone applications.

Consider the following:
For many families, school, work schedules and extracurricular activities can make it difficult to find time to eat together and some go days or weeks without sitting down as a family to share a meal. However, family meals are important and should be considered part of our daily requirements.

Family meals are more nutritious. A Harvard study found that families who eat together are twice as likely to eat their five servings of fruits and vegetables as families who don't eat together.

Research shows that kids who eat family meals have a lower chance of engaging in high risk behaviors such as substance use and violence, and fewer psychological problems.

https://www.fcconline.org/the-importance-of-family-mealtime/

20. Which one of the following do you think is the most important factor for a student to be successful in university?

- **Tutors in university**
- **The encouragement from family and friends**
- **High quality education from high school**

Write your response here.

Student's response (5/5)

It is incontrovertible that there are many factors for a student's successful academic career in university. After all, university students have to study multiple specialized and advanced subjects meticulously to stand out among a body of excellent students. Yet, there could be a debate over the most important factor for a student to be successful in university. Some might argue that great faculty and teacher's assistants will be enough for their success. However, I believe that tutors in university can also be a huge factor for students to achieve their academic goals for two reasons.

To begin with, it is important that university education is significantly different from high school education, and students need additional help from tutors to adjust to the new level of academic rigor. In other words, the learning experience in high school cannot completely prepare students for university level courses. Drawing from my experiences, I thought I was ready for college education when I was about to graduate from high school and was very confident about my academic skills. However, once I got into college, things changed drastically. From the way I wrote my essays to communication styles, just about everything university students were expected to do differed from what I had been used to in high school. This was because university education is usually for professional preparation and requires proactive creativity rather than just a passive way of learning. For example, as an art major student, I not only needed to follow artistic styles the professors taught but also had to analyze artistic trend and market to produce more compelling body works. Soon, I realized that I needed better informed input from experienced tutors in order to meet my objectives, which was something I never thought about in high school. This clearly depicts that there is the clear need for tutors in universities.

Another major consideration is that often professors and even teacher's assistants are not available as they have many other things to do when new students want to learn more. This means that university students are generally on their own despite the huge amount of tuition they have to pay. To illustrate this, one should see no further than "term papers" or "research papers". There are so many students who don't know where to start and how to write those things. Yet, there is no special help for that from the faculty or teacher's assistants. This is due to the limited amount of office hours and other duties the teachers have to assume, such as grading and encoding information. Of course, some schools offer a writing center where students can learn the basics of academic writing. Nevertheless, knowing the basics of writing and writing about a specific subject in-depth are two distinguishable things. Consequently, college students rely on study groups and online resources, but they surely cannot be as good as having well educated and seasoned tutors around them.

In summary, tutors are valuable resources for students' success. This is mainly because of the rigor of university educator and the faculty is not always readily available

Consider the following:
The new analysis found that "mind-set"—a student's sense of social belonging or grit, for example—is a stronger predictor of whether a student is likely to graduate than previously believed.
Income and whether or not your parents went to college can't be changed. But how someone engages with their work and institutions can.

https://blogs.wsj.com/experts/2015/09/16/the-most-important-factor-in-a-college-students-success/

Education hasn't changed much in the last 300 years. Many people in education are passionate about improvement and innovation, but unfortunately the system is set up to be risk averse.

https://www.forbes.com/sites/groupthink/2013/05/06/top-quality-education-for-everyone-but-whats-top-quality/#191fd0de6ca2